SIBLINGS IN ADOLESCENCE

How do brothers and sisters shape one another? *Siblings in Adolescence* provides a comprehensive overview of the most up-to-date, international empirical research on the sibling bond during the critical adolescent years. The authors examine how the relationship impacts on adolescent development, as well as the effect on and within the family, using evidence from behaviour genetics, cross-cultural studies, and research utilizing both quantitative and qualitative methods.

The book presents a multi-faceted dynamic view of the adolescent sibling relationship, drawing on perspectives from sociological, psychological, and ecological and systems science. It introduces a novel theoretical perspective which covers sibling dynamics across various key environments such as their families, communities, and cultures. Parents and siblings will also find useful coverage of the following issues:

- school and life transitions
- parental separation
- health, illness, and disability
- diverse family experiences.

Siblings in Adolescence will be indispensable for advanced undergraduate and postgraduate students studying human development, and will supplement postgraduate courses for teachers, counsellors, and social, youth, and health workers. It will also be required reading for all those who work and do research with families and young people.

Aiden Sisler is a doctoral student at the Institute of Education at the Technische Universität Berlin (TUB), Germany, where she investigates the intersection of culture, gender, education, and politics. With 15 years of experience working with children, and 28 years of being one, Aiden lends her expertise to projects dedicated to youths' well-being.

Angela Ittel is Professor of Educational Psychology at the Institute of Education at the Technische Universität Berlin (TUB), Germany. Dr Ittel's research focuses on gender and cultural factors in education as well as familial and school-based contexts for development.

Additional contributor

Markus Hess is a research associate at the Division of Developmental Science and Applied Developmental Psychology at Freie Universität Berlin, Germany. His research interests focus on violence prevention, social development, and the structure and interaction processes within families and peer groups during childhood and adolescence.

Studies in Adolescent Development

Series Editors: Professors Leo B. Hendry, Marion Kloep,
Inge Seiffge-Krenke

The *Studies in Adolescent Development* series is published in conjunction with the European Association for Research on Adolescence and is committed to publishing and promoting the highest quality of writing in the field of adolescent development.

The series aims to respond to the recent shifts in the social and ecological environments of adolescents and in the new theoretical perspectives within the social science by providing a range of books, each of which deals in depth with an aspect of current interest within the field of adolescent development.

Each book focuses on a specific aspect of adolescence and provides either a clear picture of the research endeavours which are currently serving to extend the boundaries of our knowledge and understanding of the field, or an insightful theoretical perspective of adolescent development. The editors encourage publications which represent original contributions to the field.

Also available in this series:

Adolescence Affect and Health
Donna Spruijt-Metz

**The Transition to Adulthood
and Family Relations**
An intergenerational approach
*Eugenia Scabini, Elena Marta and
Margherita Lanz*

Deception
A young person's life skill?
Rachel Taylor and Lynsey Gozna

**A Dynamic Systems Approach to
Adolescent Development**
Edited by Saskia Elske Kunnen

Siblings in Adolescence
Emerging individuals, lasting bonds
Aiden Sisler and Angela Ittel

SIBLINGS IN ADOLESCENCE

Emerging individuals, lasting bonds

Aiden Sisler and Angela Ittel

Psychology Press
Taylor & Francis Group

LONDON AND NEW YORK

First published 2015
by Psychology Press
27 Church Road, Hove, East Sussex BN3 2FA

and by Psychology Press
711 Third Avenue, New York, NY 10017

Psychology Press is an imprint of the Taylor & Francis Group, an informa business

British Library Cataloguing in Publication Data
A catalogue record for this book is available from the British Library

Library of Congress Cataloging in Publication Data
Ittel, Angela.
Siblings in adolescence : emerging individuals, lasting bonds / Angela Ittel and Aiden Sisler.
pages cm
(Studies in adolescent development)Includes bibliographical references and index.
1. Brothers and sisters—Psychological aspects. 2. Adolescence. 3. Adolescent psychology. I. Sisler, Aiden. II. Title. BF723.S43I88 2015
155.5'1924—dc23
2014025121

ISBN: 978-1-84169-703-1 (hbk)
ISBN: 978-1-138-81841-5 (pbk)
ISBN: 978-1-315-73749-2 (ebk)

Typeset in Bembo
by Swales & Willis Ltd, Exeter, Devon, UK

Printed and bound in Great Britain by
TJ International Ltd, Padstow, Cornwall

Aiden Sisler: To Warne and Kieran, Deanna and John. How far we've come since initial remarks to the tune of, 'they're cute but do we have to keep them?'. Thanks be to Laurence. Looking forward to our continued growth.

CONTENTS

FIGURES

SERIES PREFACE

In the eyes of the mass media and in the minds of many adults, adolescents are often portrayed in largely negative terms, focusing on features such as their noisy and exuberant social behaviour; teenage gangs and their often violent, anti-social activities; teenage pregnancy; drinking; smoking; drug-taking; anti-school attitudes; and disagreements with parents.

Such portrayals are painted as if they were typical of what most, if not all, adolescents do, and, accordingly, regarded as a justification for adult society to consider the teenage years as a problem period in human development and adolescents as a problem for society.

For much of the twentieth century, this popular, stereotypic picture was supported by what was written by social scientists in books and other publications, which presented adolescence as a period of 'storm and stress'. Adolescence was seen as a period of turbulence, inner turmoil and confusion, characterized by conflicts with parents, teachers, and other authority figures.

Over the last three decades of the twentieth century, important theoretical changes began to emerge. Psychologists began to question the 'storm and stress' perspective and to provide evidence that this developmental pattern was neither a typical nor a necessary part of adolescence. In parallel with this, a less problem-centred approach to thinking about adolescence began to emerge: an approach that emphasized processes of change and adjustment which young people undergo in responding to the varied tasks and transitions they face. An increasing number of books and articles on adolescence began to appear which differed markedly from earlier publications in emphasis and orientation. In contrast to the clinical perspective, this new work was based on a more empirical approach and focused upon a variety of different aspects of adolescent development. Further, longitudinal assessments over large time spans basically support the idea of a more gradual change leading to an overall positive outcome. Such publications stimulated further interest in adolescence as an area of study and in doing so started a process which led on to the emergence of research on adolescence as one of the most active fields in developmental psychological research. As a result, discussion of many aspects of adolescence has become a prominent feature of developmental conferences and scientific journals in Europe and elsewhere.

However, times change. The early years of the new millennium have seen technological innovations, global risks from terrorism, and demographic shifts occurring in most countries of the world. For example, there are now as many people over the age of 65 years as there are teenagers in most of the world's societies. Macrosocial changes such as growing up in a context of ethnic diversity and living in single-parent families are increasingly experienced by adolescents in Western industrialized countries.

Further, as the new millennium advances, psychology now takes a more positive view of human development, seeing changes and transitions as challenges within the developmental progress of young people, in society generally, *vis-à-vis* cultural and technological innovations and in relation to other generations.

The European Association for Research on Adolescence (EARA) is an organization which aims to promote and conduct high-quality fundamental and applied research on all aspects of adolescent development. Its founder and then President, the late Sandy Jackson, devoted much of his professional life to advancing these aims. Before his death in 2003, he initiated a co-operation with Psychology Press to start this series, *Studies in Adolescent Development*, and commissioned and published two books during his editorship. We, the current editors, are grateful for Sandy's vision and trust that we can progress the academic and practitioner interest in adolescence as an area of scholarly study which he initiated.

This series aims to respond to the recent shifts in the social and ecological environments of adolescents and in the new theoretical perspectives within the social sciences, by providing a range of books, each of which deals in depth with an aspect of current interest within the field of adolescent development.

The co-editors delineate a number of broad topics that require significant attention and invite academics, researchers, and practitioners to submit book proposals. Each proposal is carefully evaluated by the co-editors for selection in the series. Hence, each book is written by a chosen expert (or experts) in a specific aspect of adolescence and sets out to provide either a clear picture of the research endeavours which are currently serving to extend the boundaries of our knowledge and understanding of the field, or an insightful theoretical perspective of adolescent development.

Each book in the series represents a step towards the fulfilment of this aim. The EARA is grateful to Psychology Press for all that it has done in developing and promoting the series and for assisting EARA in extending knowledge and understanding of the many aspects of adolescent development in a rapidly changing and challenging world.

Professors Leo B. Hendry,
Marion Kloep, and Inge Seiffge-Krenke
Series Editors

INTRODUCTION

Contents

Siblings in adolescence

A review of research on the social networks of adolescents calls attention to the pronounced lack of empirical analysis into the role of siblings in contrast to the influence of parents, peers, friends, and romantic partners. While a body of literature on the sibling relationship in childhood exists, inquiry into adolescent siblings is especially scarce. Sibling relationships in the main outlive those of parents and even friends, making the omission of correspondent research all the more stark. We, therefore, believe there is a pressing need for a systematic compilation of the scattered findings from this particular family subsystem and its role in adolescent development. While several sub-disciplines within psychology and the wider social sciences, such as behavioural genetics or sociology of the family, provide an initial base for the study of adolescent siblings, these isolated investigations take on a compartmentalized focus in both their thematic and methodological approach. Consequently, there is no comprehensive model of the adolescent sibling relationship and its significance currently available that unites these various strands of research into a coherent whole.

Siblings in Adolescence attempts to address this gap in several important ways. We aim to make a contribution to the systematic study of the sibling relationship throughout adolescence by presenting a comprehensive overview of studies from different sub-disciplines of developmental research, summarizing and establishing links among the past and present findings through the generation of a synthesizing model. To situate the particular developmental course of adolescence, we at times depict life course scholarship, bridging childhood and adulthood for the reader's benefit. This book further covers theoretical issues within various relevant topics such as behavioural genetics and cross-cultural study as well as empirical evidence based on results from diverse data sets from across the globe. We believe this book will be of benefit to academics and students of developmental studies and social work, in addition to health and social care professionals.

Introducing siblings: An overview

From Cain and Abel to Bart and Lisa, the importance of the sibling bond, rooted in love and animosity, embodied in fiction and manifested in reality, has resounded across cultures since time immemorial. Indeed, Cain and Abel excluded, the ubiquitous sibling relationship tends to outlive that of any other bond, generally enduring over the entirety of an individual's life (Cicirelli, 1982). What is more, upwards of 8 in 10 people have a sibling, and growing up with a father figure is less common (McHale, Updegraff, & Whiteman, 2012; Milevsky & Heerwagen, 2013).

Understanding siblings in adolescence, a time marked by radical change (Arnett, 2010; Kuhn, 2006), helps us understand individuals and families as a whole. Adolescence is characterized by a number of physical, emotional, cognitive, and socio-attitudinal developments, all of which positively or negatively impact upon the burgeoning individual (Yurgelun-Todd, 2007). Brody (1998) suggests that these changes are further propelled by the sibling relationship, 'comprised of a balance of both prosocial and conflicted interactions' that ultimately contributes to the adolescent's subsequent psychosocial, social, and cognitive development. Provided this importance, one would surmise that the corpus of adolescent sibling study would be vast and varied, yet there remains an extensive gap in knowledge and, in fact, the very conceptualization of sibling relations in adolescence. Our volume seeks to fill that gap by uniting the various strands of literature to ultimately put forth a coherent framework for future avenues of inquiry. We aim to cogently fulfil this objective by elucidating theoretical groundings with a selection of current developments in the field.

We start by exploring the nature and the influences on individual and group differences within and across siblings and sibling groups with the conceptual tools of a variety of social and behavioural sciences. Although a review of all possible perspectives is beyond the scope of our aims here, we maintain that the psychoanalytic, social learning, and social psychological approaches; the social constructionist and feminist sociological lenses; ecological and systems views; and the evolutionary and genetic biological perspectives help form a conceptual foundation from which a coherent model can be created. We review these topical categories in Chapter 1.

Using this theoretical overview as a springboard, the remainder of the book presents empirical work and issues we hope will stimulate future research in the field. Chapter 2 discusses, through the lens of a within family approach, aspects of how siblings and their dynamic interrelationships develop during the teenage years. Several key issues regarding within family variation are touched upon, including how family structure and climate, parenting practices, and the socialization processes shape both the nature of the whole family unit and its various subsystems, concentrating on the sibling relationship.

In Chapter 3, we discuss the developmental correlates of siblings and their direct and indirect associations, such as health and risk behaviour, sexual behaviour, and wider social and gender development. We source this broad survey from a well-balanced variety of empirical studies drawn from diverse international samples. From there, Chapter 4 guides readers into the cutting-edge science of behavioural genetics, where genetic and environmental influences on adolescent development intersect. Some of the data drawn from large-scale systematic studies of adolescent siblings enlist these methods that help to disentangle genetic and environmental influences. In particular, we examine the importance of the non-shared environmental influence of within family variation on the sibling relationship.

In Chapter 5, we paint with broad strokes a historical portrait of cross-cultural sibling study and, in the accompanying Appendix, highlight contemporary projects on adolescent sibling relationships from an international perspective. As the study of siblings presents researchers with a number of logistical issues as well as specific methodological challenges, we look in-depth into strategies to tackle these challenges, including the application of methodological procedures to family study in Chapter 6. In the final chapter, we synthesize the theoretical and empirical foundation laid down by the preceding entries, and draft out our suggestions for engaging in meaningful research on the sibling relationship across adolescence.

We hope that the research presented here assists in throwing light on the importance of considering adolescent sibling relationships not only within the family context but also beyond, whether at school, in the workplace, or in local communities. Brothers and sisters themselves offer a place for dynamic development where adolescents negotiate their identity and social claims. Siblings afford a variety of experiences and impart direct and indirect effects, such as pressing younger siblings to spend time with older peers or to take their first hit of a joint, to the trickle-down influence of a quarrel with a schoolteacher. Furthermore, the unique sibling tie, as it consists of both hierarchical and reciprocal qualities, informs other close relationships (Dunn, 2007; East, 2009; McHale, Kim, & Whiteman, 2006; Whiteman, McHale, & Soli, 2011). Siblings can shift how they relate to each other and can alter scripts of interaction through their mutual influence, though these scripts may be relatively embedded and resistant to change as in the case of lasting sibling conflict effects from adolescence and their impact on later romantic bonds

(Shalash, Wood, & Parker, 2013). We learn then of the nature of close relation-ships from this unique arrangement, whereby each member of the sibling dyad influences the other and changes the dynamics of the relationship.

If you, the reader, find yourself applying the concepts within these pages to your own experiences and relationships, we will have fulfilled our objectives in part. Beyond that, our hope is to instil the value of regarding brothers and sisters as meaningful 'objects of inquiry' within empirical and theoretical scholarship, a notion already embraced by literature and, for the lucky among us, the phenom-enology of lived experience.

Who and what is a sibling?

A sibling, according to the Merriam-Webster dictionary entry, is 'one of two or more individuals having one common parent; a brother or sister'. If one adheres to this technical, and arguably reductionistic, terminology, siblings are biologi-cally related through at least one parent (Edwards, Hadfield, Lucey, & Mauthner, 2006). However, how particular societies, cultures, groups, families, and children themselves understand and use the label of sibling is varied and complex. In fact, considering all possible sibling pair constellations, including step-, adopted-, and twin siblings, there exist no less than 26 distinct arrangements (Treffers, Goedhart, Waltz, & Koudijs, 1990). If one accounts for kinship bonds and ties, the myriad constellations can boggle the mind, including dominant extended family relation-ships in diverse cultures (e.g. Fleischer, 2007; Rogoff, 2003) and concepts of 'milk' siblings within some Islamic communities, where biologically unrelated children nursed from the same breast are regarded as siblings. Frequently, these definitions are equally, if not more, binding than standard Western conceptualizations.

The above-mentioned relationships are meaningful and central in their own right, yet we constrict our definition here, unless otherwise noted, to the biologi-cal and social conceptualizations of siblinghood most at use within the available empirical research. At the same time, we do recognize the call for greater attention to the intersection and divergences between the typical sibling, kinship-derived formulations, and meaningful socially constructed bonds (Edwards *et al.*, 2006) over and above strictly biologically privileged notions of sibling relatedness, in order to inform the socially constructed and emotional nature of relationships in general (Whiteman *et al.*, 2011). For further reading on the socially constructed understandings of siblinghood from children and youth themselves, we refer the reader to the cited work of Edwards and colleagues' (2006) that offers direct insight into the emotional quality of lateral relationships and dynamic identifications and differentiations between sisters and brothers.

Why siblings matter

The majority of individuals grow up with at least one sibling (Milevsky, 2011; World Family Map, 2013), and this bond is often the longest lasting over one's life course (Cicirelli, 1995; Noller, 2005). More time is spent playing, negotiating, quarrelling, loving, caring, and sharing with siblings than any other individual in a child's and young person's life (Sanders, 2004). Siblings can serve as companions, role models, play mates, intimates, competitors, and confidants in their families (Dunn, 2007). They hold significant sway over wider social networks and systems, like that of the family and peer group (Cox & Paley, 1997). Siblings bring their own personal attributes to the sibling dynamic, reciprocally influencing – directly and indirectly – one another's development.

Furthermore, the sibling relationship, imbued with emotion and conflict, is a fount for formative experiences and drives socio-cognitive and emotional development through a unique mixture of complementary and reciprocal elements (Dunn, 2007). The sheer frequency and accessibility of interaction, the longevity of the bond, volume of shared experience, and availability of meaningful culturally ascribed roles and scripts foster a context ripe for the development of socio-emotional skill sets (Cicirelli, 1992). The basic tools of social life, blueprints of relationality, and understanding of the very nature of the social world and intimacy are forged, for most children and youth, in the sibling bond (Parke, 2004).

The potential advantages of sharing a close connection with one or more siblings are well documented (e.g. Bryant & Crockenberg, 1980; Downey & Condron, 2004; Dunn, Brown, Slomkowski, Telsa, & Youngblade, 1991; Howe & Ross, 1990; Milevsky, 2005; 2011). Positive sibling ties bolster multiple dimensions of well-being and adjustment, and impact upon outcomes extending from childhood to adulthood and beyond (Bryant & Crockenberg, 1980; Cicirelli, 1995; Dunn *et al.*, 1991; Howe & Ross, 1990). However, in addition to supportive effects, siblings may also hold wide-ranging negative consequences dependent upon specific features of the relationship and less understood convergent and divergent influence processes (Caffaro, 2013; Whiteman, Jensen, & Maggs, 2014). More concretely, siblings exert both proximal and distal influence on one another's development and are closely implicated in diverse outcomes including intelligence, personality type, educational attainment and motivation, career and vocational success, and a range of risky and adaptive behaviours (e.g. Carr Steelman, Powell, Werum, & Carter, 2002; Fagan & Najman, 2003; McHale *et al.*, 2012). Moreover, many of these effects remain after consideration of parental and peer forces, and may, in some cases, arise as among the most potent influences (Brook, Whiteman, Gordon, & Brook, 1990). Empirically speaking, brothers and sisters are clearly of great significance – although this surely comes as redundant for those who have first-hand knowledge of the weight of a sibling bond.

Despite the universality and centrality of siblinghood, the limited sibling research is dominated by individual psychological accounts and tends to be driven by a 'problem'-focused agenda (Edwards *et al.*, 2006; Noller, 2005; Whiteman *et al.*, 2011). Adoption studies, foster family placements, and family interventions housed in clinical and therapeutic practice prevail, shaping the majority of research by way, and result of, frequently policy-driven mediation efforts (Edwards & Gillies, 2004). By acknowledging the literature's historical antecedents, we can reveal assumptions about the nature of the typical family, of individuals within the familial system, and human development more generally. This is vital in order to address where future study ought to focus and where to direct intervention efforts that will promote positive relationships and development. We cover the landscape of these theoretical forbearers more directly within Chapter 1.

As our gaze shifts from standard views of the nuclear family and its accompanying hegemonic assumptions of 'normalcy' in the realm of family life, we require new and more flexible models of what it means to be a family and, accordingly, what it means to be a brother or sister. Changing social sites, localities, increasing geographic and, arguably, social mobility all contribute to re-formulations of family and personhood (Arnett, 2010; McGuire & Shanahan, 2010; Ribbens McCarthy, Edwards, & Gillies, 2004; Weeks, Heaphy, & Donovan, 2001). Other contributing factors include longer life spans (Matthews, 1987), turns from the obligations of traditional life to novel, and negotiated rather than prescribed forms of association and relatedness (e.g. Giddens, 1992; Greenfield, 2009); and an increasing awareness of the complex interplay between economic, social, and cultural capital (Savage & Bennett, 2005). If identity and relationships are mutually constitutive, then, in our view, which echoes that of Whiteman *et al.* (2011), sibling investigations offer an ideal point at which to investigate identification and relatedness processes and their developmental progress. Certainly, in rapidly shifting socio-environmental worlds, the understanding of individual development and intimate relationships, of which siblings are often the most durable, is aided and necessitated by sibling study.

Siblings and adolescent development across time and place

While the sibling relationship serves as an empirical tool for exploring social and individual development, it is a worthy point of inquiry in its own right. The everyday interactions and experiences of children and youth are largely neglected inside top-down academic approaches, and much of this can be attributed, when we accurately analyse science's historical embeddedness, to scientific dictates of the past (Edwards, Hadfield, & Mauthner, 2005; Ittel & Kretschmer, 2007). Even anthropology, where Margaret Mead's (1928/1978) pioneering work on adolescent Pacific Islanders shot a bullet across multiple disciplines in the social sciences, has tended to shy from engaging children and adolescents, and rarely addresses developmental continuities, processes, and mechanisms of action directly (Hirschfeld, 2002).

Perhaps the availability and proliferation of youth and emerging adulthood research has taken time to gain steam due to a past lack of satisfactory definitions for childhood, adolescence, and youth in general. The Ancient Greeks imagined childhood in three stages: *infantia*, or infancy, spanning from birth to 7, where parents ought to nurture and train; *pueritia*, lasting until 14 for boys but only 12 for girls, which marked the onset of puberty and the ability to procreate; and finally, *adolescentia*, lasting until adulthood, in which boys should find vocation, and girls, marriage (Levi & Schmitt, 1997). A corresponding dark age for children was experienced during the

Middle Ages, partly due to high mortality rates, which might have reduced parental attachment by necessity. During the industrial revolution, children were but small adults, soon-to-be or, in many cases, premature workers. This trend continued into the beginning of the twentieth century, when the rise of compulsory schooling redefined childhood as a period of learning, and when schooling was extended into late adolescence in the second half of the twentieth century, school became one of the main marking features of childhood and adolescence. Adolescence is now a protracted life stage; age of onset continues to fall due to improved health, and full adult status is conferred at later ages (Gluckman & Hayne, 2011).

Basic overviews of human development demarcate middle childhood as spanning from 5 to approximately 12 years of age (or the onset of puberty) and adolescence reaching from pubertal onset until roughly 20 years of age. These definitions vary according to whether developmental researchers categorize the end of adolescence and beginning of adulthood upon an individual's entry into the work force and exercises relative independence from their parents (see Shaffer & Kipp, 2014). As we shall see, developmental continuities and courses within individuals, across cultures, over time, and even between siblings, are variable and complex.

Both children and adolescents are currently seen to be multifaceted beings constructed by and actively participating in their physiological and psychosocial changes (Maughan, 2011). A number of additional frameworks expound how adolescents assert their own identities and form their social selves inside and outside of the familial context; a topic we touch on in the second chapter. Although adolescent portraits are still taking shape, we continue to gather knowledge of the interplay among sibling structure characteristics, relationship processes, and family and socio-cultural contextual conditions (McHale et al., 2012). Moreover, we are mindful of cultural variations in adolescence and the diverse experiences teens encounter, and so broadly use the term to refer to the stage of life between childhood and adulthood, its accompanying physiological changes, and, often, its socio-cultural expectations.

Understanding how adolescents acquire, shape, and transform cultural meanings as they negotiate developmental tasks and spheres during the transition to adulthood provides insight into the role they play and inhabit in larger socio-cultural evolution (Manago, 2010). While sociologists and anthropologists have, at times, targeted the depth of the sibling relationship and its cultural meanings and practices by enlisting qualitative methodology and person-centred research approaches, much of the existing research in psychological and behavioural sciences we draw on is biased towards the quantitative and directly measureable (Noller, 2005). Here, a socio-cultural approach, for example, that integrates cognitive, social, perceptual, motivational, physical, emotional, and other processes in human development as aspects of socio-cultural activity moves us past standard views of static and normative stage theories of development (Rogoff, 2003). We seek to blend and complement various perspectives to accommodate for their relative weaknesses and strengths. Nevertheless, it should be noted that no one paradigm is seen as sufficient for describing concepts as complex as identity formation, social relationships, the sibling relationship, and their meanings during the varied stage of adolescence.

Adolescence is considered a prime sensitive period in psychosocial development, as developing individuals carve out their sense of personhood and social identifications in the social world through socialization and identity formation processes (Erikson, 1968; Kroger, 2004; Marcia, 1980). Socialization agents exert influence on and assist in socializing individuals into different socio-cultural ways (Davis, 2007; Parsons & Bales, 1955), and social interactions and relationships act as contexts in themselves that likewise drive psychosocial development (Bukowski & Lisboa, 2007; Lewin, 1939). The sway of similar age-peers, siblings included, grows as relations with parents decrease, and adolescents shape and are increasingly shaped by their own experiences (Degirmencioglu, Urber, Tolson, & Richard, 1998; Savin-Williams & Berndt, 1990).

Yet families as whole units and individual family members continue to exert strong socializing influences over the course of adolescence, as observed in processes of value transmission or construction of ideology (e.g. ethnicity, Vollebergh, Iedema, & Raaijmakers, 2001; politics, Acock & Bengtson, 1978; religion, Myers, 1996; and gender, Moen, Erickson, & Dempster-McClain, 1997; Thornton, Alwin, & Camburn, 1983). Reciprocal impact models of socialization that acknowledge the dynamic interplay between adolescents, socialization agents, and their environs (e.g. Scarr & McCartney, 1983) help us to refine the complex manner in which socialization occurs. All the same, research to-date has vacillated on the relative impact of prime socialization figures such as family members and peers, presumably due to the distinct fluctuating nature of adolescents' attitudes, beliefs, and behaviours, as well as their exposure to progressively diverse contexts (Cunningham, Beutel, Barber, & Thornton, 2005; Vespa, 2009). We, therefore, consider it imperative to keep in mind, while studying groupings of adolescent siblings, that individual adolescents vary as a function of their interplay with contextual factors like education, employment, and family arrangements.

Emerging individuals and lasting bonds

While these budding social agents progress through adolescence, a time largely marked by complex socio-emotional and cognitive change, siblings shift from their 'function' of playmate to that of supporter and intimate other (Yenes Conde, Olabarrieta, Arranz, & Artamendi, 2000). Prior work suggests that when siblings move from childhood to puberty, the tendency toward matching, joining, and imitating of earlier years decreases (Bank & Kahn, 1982). Sibling teens engage in more detailed and complex processes of social comparison, projection, identification, and differentiation (Edwards et al., 2006; Feinberg, McHale, Crouter, & Cumsille, 2003). The precise nature of the sibling relationship and individual development largely remains hazy, however, as the limited existing literature equivocates on sibling relational dynamics and implications for future outcomes (Oliva & Arranz, 2005).

Conflict purportedly rises during the early teen years (Brody, Stoneman, & McCoy, 1994), although some researchers contend that these findings are tied to the 'problem-focused' research agenda that pervades sibling study (Edwards *et al.*, 2006). Others still cite extensive accounts of sibling-inflicted abuse at the extreme (e.g. Caffaro & Conn-Caffaro, 2005). Sub-pathological levels of envy, aggression, and rivalry are all natural, if not unpleasant components of the sibling experience – particularly according to Western parents and the many self-help books geared towards them (e.g. Borden, 2003; Faber & Mazlish, 1988; Hart, 2001; McEwan, 1996; Wolf, 2003). Other researchers contend that conflict between siblings, while somewhat commonplace, is not the most prevalent interaction pattern (Newman, 1994), and siblings are important figures in negotiation relational dimensions such as intimacy and companionship (Buhrmester & Furman, 1990). Indeed, in some non-Western cultures, adolescent conflict and sibling rivalry are not held as a universal imperative (Nuckolls, 1993; Weisner, 1993), a concept we delve into further in Chapter 7 and exemplify with international data.

Following this initial pre-teenage intensification in antagonism in Western contexts, conflict levels supposedly decrease, while levels of intimacy increase or plateau during early to late adolescence (Buhrmester, 1992; Updegraff, McHale, & Crouter, 2002). That notwithstanding, the paucity of well-rounded research from cross-cultural and within culture analyses of under-represented groups on the significance of sibling relationships speaks to the timely need for integrated research programmes; study must account for familial and cultural dynamics outside the standard (Western) attachment looking glass and its parent–child link (Coles, 2003; Dunn, 1983, 1993; Oliva & Arranz, 2005). With prior empirical work implicating sibling network impacts on varied correlates and outcomes like health and risk behaviour, academics, and long-term resiliency (e.g. Bouchey, Shoulberg, Jodl, & Eccles, 2010; Campbell, Connidis, & Davies, 1999; Carr Steelman *et al.*, 2002; Cawson, Walters, Booker, & Kelly, 2000), exactly how this pivotal relationship develops in different contexts necessitates serious further inquiry.

Taken altogether, the limited existing studies illustrate that the sibling relationship is one of the most important predictors of future relationships and outcomes in adolescents' lives, having implications into young adulthood and beyond. Extending past the empirics, direct sibling accounts tell us siblings always matter, and a lot at that (Chamberlain, 1999; Coles, 2003; Mauthner, 2002; Weisner, 1989). Bearing in mind the identified gaps in theorization and empirical work alike, we proffer a modus for which to study siblings over the critical period of adolescence. With wider application and subsequent fine-tuning, the research programme proposed could inform study of close relational ties surpassing the sibling bond, family system, to wider social relations. At least, this is our sincere hope and belief.

References

Acock, A. C., & Bengtson, V. L. (1978). On the relative influence of mothers and fathers: A covariance analysis of political and religious socialization. *Journal of Marriage and the Family, 40*, 519–530.

Arnett, J. J. (2010). *Adolescence and emerging adulthood* (4th ed.). Englewood Cliffs, NJ: Prentice Hall.

Bank, S., & Kahn, M. D. (1982). *The sibling bond*. New York: Basic Books.

Borden, M. (2003). *Baffled parent's guide to sibling rivalry*. Chicago, IL: McGraw-Hill/Contemporary Books.

Bouchey, H. A., Shoulberg, E. K., Jodl, K. M., & Eccles, J. S. (2010). Longitudinal links between older sibling features and younger siblings' academic adjustment during early adolescence. *Journal of Educational Psychology, 102*, 197–211.

Brody, G. (1998). Sibling relationship quality: Its causes and consequences. *Annual Review of Psychology, 49*, 1–24.

Brody, G. H., Stoneman, Z., & McCoy, J. K. (1994). Forecasting sibling relationships in early adolescence from child temperaments and family processes in middle childhood. *Child Development, 65*(3), 771–784.

Brook, J. S., Whiteman, M., Gordon, A. S., & Brook, D. W. (1990). The role of older brothers in younger brothers' drug use viewed in the context of parent and peer influences. *Journal of Genetic Psychology, 151*, 59–75.

Bryant, N., & Crockenberg, S. (1980). Correlates and dimensions of prosocial behavior: A study of female siblings with their mothers. *Child Development, 51*, 529–544.

Buhrmester, D. (1992). The developmental courses of sibling and peer relationships. In F. Boer & Dunn, J. (Eds.), *Children's sibling relationships: Developmental and clinical issues* (pp. 19–40). Hillsdale, NJ: Lawrence Erlbaum Associates.

Buhrmester, D., & Furman, W. (1990). Perceptions of sibling relationships during middle childhood and adolescence. *Child Development, 61*(5), 1387–1398.

Bukowski, W., & Lisboa, C. (2007). Understanding the place of place in developmental psychology. In C. Rutger, E. Engels, & M. Kerr (Eds.), *Friends, lovers and groups: Key relationships in adolescence* (pp. 167–173). West Sussex: John Wiley & Sons.

Caffaro, J. V. (2013). *Sibling abuse trauma: Assessment and intervention strategies for children, families, and adults* (2nd ed.). Oxon: Routledge.

Caffaro, J. V., & Conn-Caffaro, A. (2005). Treating sibling abuse families. *Aggression and Violent Behavior, 10*(5), 604–623.

Campbell, L. D., Connidis, I. A., & Davies, L. (1999). Sibling ties in later life: A social network analysis. *Journal of Family Issues, 20*(1), 114–148.

Carr Steelman, L., Powell, B., Werum, R., & Carter, S. (2002). Reconsidering the effects of sibling configuration: Recent advances and challenges. *Annual Review of Sociology, 28*, 243–269.

Cawson, P., Walters, C., Booker, S., & Kelly, G. (2000). *Child maltreatment in the United Kingdom: A study of the prevalence of child abuse and neglect*. London: National Society for the Prevention of Cruelty to Children.

Chamberlain, M. (1999). Brothers and sisters, uncles and aunts: A lateral perspective on Caribbean families. In E. Silva & C. Smart (Eds.), *The new family?* (pp. 129–142). London: Sage.

Cicirelli, V. G. (1982). Sibling influence throughout the lifespan. In M. E. Lamb & B. Sutton-Smith (Eds.), *Sibling relationships: Their nature and significance across the lifespan* (pp. 267–284). Hillsdale, NJ: Lawrence Erlbaum Associates.

Cicirelli, V. G. (1992). *Family caregiving: Autonomous and paternalistic decision-making*. Newbury Park, CA: Sage.

Cicirelli, V. G. (1995). *Sibling relationships across the life span*. New York: Plenum.

Coles, P. (2003). *The importance of sibling relationships in psychoanalysis*. London: Karnac Books.

Cox, M. J., & Paley, B. (1997). Families as systems. *Annual Review of Psychology, 48*, 243–267.

Cunningham, M., Beutel, A., Barber, J., & Thornton, A. (2005). Reciprocal relationships between attitudes about gender and social contexts during young adulthood. *Social Science Research, 34*, 862–892.

Davis, S. (2007). Gender ideology construction from adolescence to young adulthood. *Social Science Research, 36*(3), 1021–1041.

Degirmencioglu, S. M., Urber, K. A., Tolson, J. M., & Richard, P. (1998). Adolescent friendship networks: Continuity and change over the school years. *Merrill-Palmer Quarterly, 44*, 313–337.

Downey, D. B., & Condron, D. J. (2004). Playing well with others in kindergarten: The benefits of siblings at home. *Journal of Marriage and Family, 66*, 333–350.

Dunn, J. (1983). Sibling relationships in early childhood. *Child Development, 54*, 787–811.

Dunn, J. (1993). *Young children's close relationships: Beyond attachment*. London: Sage.

Dunn, J. (2007). Siblings and socialization. In J. Grusec & P. Hastings (Eds.), *Handbook of socialization: Theory and research* (pp. 309–329). New York: Guilford Press.

Dunn, J., Brown, J. R., Slomkowski, C., Telsa, C., & Youngblade, L. M. (1991). Young children's understanding of other people's feelings and beliefs: Individual differences and their antecedents. *Child Development, 62*, 1352–1366.

East, P. (2009). Adolescents' relationships with siblings. In R. Lerner & L. Steinberg (Eds.), *Handbook of adolescent psychology: Contextual influences on adolescent development* (3rd ed., pp. 43–73). Hoboken, NJ: Wiley.

Edwards, R., & Gillies, V. (2004). Support in parenting: Values and consensus concerning who to turn to. *Journal of Social Policy, 33*(4), 627–647.

Edwards, R., Hadfield, L., Lucey, H., & Mauthner, M. (2006). *Sibling identity and relationships: Sisters and brothers*. Oxon: Routledge.

Edwards, R., Hadfield, L., & Mauthner, M. (2005). *Children's understandings of their sibling relationships*. London: National Children's Bureau/Joseph Rowntree Foundation.

Erikson, E. H. (1968). *Identity: Youth and crisis*. New York: W. W. Norton.

Faber, A., & Mazlish, E. (1988). *Siblings without rivalry: How to help your children live together so you can live too*. London: Sidgwick & Jackson.

Fagan, A. A., & Najman, J. M. (2003). Sibling influences on adolescent delinquent behaviour: An Australian longitudinal study. *Journal of Adolescence, 26*, 546–558.

Feinberg, M. E., McHale, S. M., Crouter, A. C., & Cumsille, P. (2003). Sibling differentiation: Sibling and parent relationship trajectories in adolescence. *Child Development, 74*(5), 1261–1274.

Fleischer, A. (2007). Family, obligations, and migration: The role of kinship in Cameroon. *Demographic Research, 16*(13), 413–440.

Giddens, A. (1992). *The transformation of intimacy: Sexuality, love and eroticism in modern societies*. Cambridge: Polity Press.

Gluckman, P. D., & Hayne, H. (2011). *Improving the transition: Reducing social and psychological morbidity during adolescence*. New Zealand: Office of the Prime Minister's Science Advisory Committee.

Greenfield, P. M. (2009). Linking social change and developmental change: Shifting pathways of human development. *Developmental Psychology, 45*(2), 401–418.

Hart, S. (2001). *Preventing sibling rivalry: Six strategies to build a jealousy-free home*. New York: Free Press.

Hirschfeld, L. A. (2002). Why don't anthropologists like children? *American Anthropologist, 104*(2), 611–627.

Howe, N., & Ross, H. S. (1990). Socialization, perspective-taking, and the sibling relationship. *Developmental Psychology, 26*, 160–165.

Ittel, A., & Kretschmer, T. (2007). Historical roots of developmental science. *European Journal of Developmental Science, 1*(1), 23–32.

Kroger, J. (2004). *Identity in adolescence*. New York: Routledge.

Kuhn, D. (2006). Do cognitive changes accompany developments in the adolescent brain? *Perspectives on Psychological Science, 1*(1), 59–67.

Levi, G., & Schmitt, J.-C. (1997). *A history of young people in the West: Ancient and medieval rites of passage* (C. Nash, Trans.). Cambridge, MA: Harvard University Press.

Lewin, K. (1939). The field theory approach to adolescence. *American Journal of Sociology, 44,* 868–897.

Manago, A. M. (2010). Studying Maya adolescents in a new high school in Zinacantan, Mexico. *CSW Update Newsletter, UCLA Center for the Study of Women,* 6–10.

Marcia, J. E. (1980). Identity in adolescence. In J. Adelson (Ed.), *Handbook of adolescent psychology* (pp. 159–187). New York: Wiley.

Matthews, S. H. (1987). Provision of care to old parents: Division of responsibility among adult children. *Research on Aging, 9*(1), 45–60.

Maughan, B. (2011). Family and systemic influences. In D. Skuse, H. Bruce, L. Dowdney, & D. Mrazek (Eds.), *Child psychology and psychiatry: Frameworks for practice* (2nd ed., pp. 3–7). West Sussex: John Wiley & Sons.

Mauthner, M. (2002). *Sistering: Power and change in female relationships.* Basingstoke: Palgrave.

McEwan, E. K. (1996). *Mom, he hit me! What to do about sibling rivalry.* Colorado Springs, CO: Waterbrook Press.

McGuire, S., & Shanahan, L. (2010). Sibling experiences in diverse family contexts. *Child Development Perspectives, 4*(2), 72–79.

McHale, S. M., Kim, J., & Whiteman, S. D. (2006). Sibling relationships in childhood and adolescence. In P. Noller & J. A. Feeney (Eds.), *Close relationships: Functions, forms, and processes* (pp. 128–149). New York: Psychology Press.

McHale, S. M., Updegraff, K. A., & Whiteman, S. D. (2012). Sibling relationships and influences in childhood and adolescence. *Journal of Marriage and Family, 74*(5), 913–930.

Mead, M. (1928/1978). *Culture and commitment: The new relationships between the generations in the 1970s* (Rev. ed.). New York: Anchor Press/Doubleday.

Milevsky, A. (2005). Compensatory patterns of sibling support in emerging adult-hood: Variations in loneliness, self-esteem, depression and life satisfaction. *Journal of Social and Personal Relationships, 22,* 743–755.

Milevsky, A. (2011). *Sibling relationships in childhood and adolescence: Predictors and outcomes.* New York: Columbia University Press.

Milevsky, A., & Heerwagen, M. (2013). A phenomenological examination of sibling relationships in emerging adulthood. *Marriage & Family Review, 49*(3), 251–263.

Moen, P., Erickson, M. A., & Dempster-McClain, D. (1997). Their mother's daughters? The intergenerational transmission of gender attitudes in a world of changing roles. *Journal of Marriage and the Family, 59*(2), 281–293.

Myers, S. M. (1996). An interactive model of religiosity inheritance: The importance of family context. *American Sociological Review, 61*(5), 858–866.

Newman, J. (1994). Conflict and friendship in sibling relationships: A review. *Child Study Journal, 24,* 119–152.

Noller, P. (2005). Sibling relationships in adolescence: Learning and growing together. *Personal Relationships, 12,* 1–22.

Nuckolls, C. W. (1993). *Siblings in South Asia: Brothers and sisters in cultural context.* New York: Guilford Press.

Oliva, A., & Arranz, E. (2005). Sibling relationships during adolescence. *European Journal of Developmental Psychology, 2*(3), 253–270.

Parke, R. D. (2004). Development in the family. *Annual Review of Psychology, 55,* 365–399.

Parsons, T., & Bales, R. (1955). *Family, socialization, and interaction process.* Glencoe, IL: Free Press.

Ribbens McCarthy, J., Edwards, R., & Gillies, V. (2004). *Making families: Moral tales of parenting and step-parenting.* Durham, NC: Sociology Press.

Rogoff, B. (2003). *The cultural nature of human development*. Oxford: Oxford University Press.

Sanders, R. (2004). *Sibling relationships: Theory and issues for practice*. New York: Palgrave Macmillan.

Savage, M., & Bennett, T. (2005). Editors' introduction: Cultural capital and social inequality. *The British Journal of Sociology, 56*(1), 1–12.

Savin-Williams, R. C., & Berndt, T. J. (1990). Friendship and peer relations. In S. S. Feldman & G. R. Elliott (Eds.), *At the threshold: The developing adolescent* (pp. 277–307). Cambridge, MA: Harvard University Press.

Scarr, S., & McCartney, K. (1983). How people make their own environments: A theory of genotype-environment effects. *Child Development, 54*(2), 424–435.

Shaffer, D., & Kipp, K. (2014). *Developmental psychology: Childhood and adolescence* (9th ed.). Belmont, CA: Cengage Learning.

Shalash, F. M., Wood, N. D., & Parker, T. S. (2013). Our problems are your sibling's fault: Exploring the connections between conflict styles of siblings during adolescence and later adult committed relationships. *American Journal of Family Therapy, 41*, 288–298.

Thornton, A., Alwin, D. F., & Camburn, D. (1983). Causes and consequences of sex-role attitudes and attitude change. *American Sociological Review, 48*(2), 211–227.

Treffers, P. D., Goedhart, A. W., Waltz, J. W., & Koudijs, E. (1990). The systematic collection of patient data in a centre for child and adolescent psychiatry. *The British Journal of Psychiatry, 157*(5), 744–748.

Updegraff, K. A., McHale, S. M., & Crouter, A. C. (2002). Adolescents' sibling relationship and friendship experiences: Developmental patterns and relationship linkages. *Social Development, 11*(2), 182–204.

Vespa, J. (2009). Gender ideology construction: A life course and intersectional approach. *Gender & Society, 23*, 363–387.

Vollebergh, W. A., Iedema, J., & Raaijmakers, Q. A. (2001). Intergenerational transmission and the formation of cultural orientations in adolescence and young adulthood. *Journal of Marriage and Family, 63*(4), 1185–1198.

Weeks, J., Heaphy, B., & Donovan, C. (2001). *Same sex intimacies: Families of choice and other life experiments*. London: Routledge.

Weisner, T. S. (1989). Comparing sibling relationships across cultures. In P. G. Zukow (Ed.), *Sibling interaction across cultures: Theoretical and methodological issues* (pp. 11–22). New York: Springer-Verlag.

Weisner, T. S. (1993). Overview: Sibling similarity and difference in different cultures. In C. Nuckolls (Ed.), *Siblings in South Asia: Brothers and sisters in cultural context* (pp. 1–17). New York: Guilford Press.

Whiteman, S. D., Jensen, A. C., & Maggs, J. L. (2014). Similarities and differences in adolescent siblings' alcohol-related attitudes, use, and delinquency: Evidence for convergent and divergent influence processes. *Journal of Youth and Adolescence, 43*(5), 687–697.

Whiteman, S. D., McHale, S. M., & Soli, A. (2011). Theoretical perspectives on sibling relationships. *Journal of Family Theory & Review, 3*(2), 124–139.

Wolf, A. (2003). *Mom, Jason's breathing on me! The solution to sibling bickering*. New York: Ballantine Books.

World Family Map. (2013). *Mapping family change and child well-being outcomes*. Child Trends. Retrieved from http://worldfamilymap.org/2013/wp-content/uploads/2013/01/WFM-2013-Final-lores-11513.pdf

Yenes Conde, F., Olabarrieta, F., Arranz, E., & Artamendi, J. A. (2000). Fiabilidad entre jueces de un sistema de categorías sobre las representaciones infantiles de las relaciones fraternas. *Psicothema, 12*, 563–566.

Yurgelun-Todd, D. (2007). Emotional and cognitive changes during adolescence. *Current Opinion in Neurobiology, 17*(2), 251–257.

1

THEORETICAL AND THEMATIC PLURALITY IN SIBLING RESEARCH

Sibling study in summary: Is thematic plurality a boon or a burden?

We start out our brief, but wide-ranging theoretical review by considering a variety of different perspectives. We will explore psychoanalytic, social learning, and social psychological approaches, and social constructionist, ecological and systems science, feminist sociological paradigms, and evolutionary and (genetic) biological perspectives. Each framework will be positioned historically and accompanied by contextualized examples of typical empirical research *vis-à-vis* the sibling bond. We will then attempt, in turn, to synthesize and evaluate their respective research programmes. In so doing, we lay the base for a more considered research and practice-driven approach that will be addressed in the book's remainder.

In performing an initial attempt to gather the seemingly disjointed strands of sibling-related work, both theoretical and applied, one is struck by the plurality of the field. Academics have entertained multiple research foci, ranging from the instinct-driven psychoanalytic writings of Freud and Klein, with their classical leanings toward deep-seated sibling rivalry, anxiety, and conflict, to less-studied social constructivist and feminist family sociological takes on the dynamic intersubjectivities involved in development that often embrace positive and community psychology precepts (e.g. McHale, Crouter, & Whiteman, 2003; Rodríguez & Moro, 2008). Cultural studies go on to suggest that what it means to be brother or sister varies vastly from one group to the next. This multiplicity across theoretical time and space is understandable, given the complexities in tracing human development – a most 'ultra-social' of species – and our consequent ever-evolving conceptualizations (Zlatev, 2008).

As we bid to unite these fragmented, yet thematically interrelated, sub-disciplines, we necessarily limit our central concentration to the sibling relationship over adolescence, particularly due to the twofold reasons of the importance of adolescence in development and the shortfall of accompanying sibling research. This is, of course, not to say that valuable scholarship and inroads have not been produced in this vein: McHale, Crouter, and Family Relationships Project colleagues at Penn State; Conger and researchers at UC Davis' Human Development and Family Studies consort; and Pike and associates at the University of Sussex are but a few examples of academics doing serious work on brothers and sisters across the lifespan. Nevertheless, as McHale, Updegraff, and Whiteman (2012) show, the relative shortage of focus placed on siblings is glaring both in and among family and developmental studies. For further readings on childhood-specific, young adulthood–specific, and adult-specific sibling inquiry, we refer the reader to the infancy (e.g. Volling, 1997, 2001; Volling & Belsky, 1992), young adulthood (e.g. Conger & Little, 2010; Milevsky, 2004, 2005; Milevsky & Heerwagen, 2013), and life course work by the likes of Elder (1996), White (2001), and Cicirelli (1992, 1995).

Setting the theoretical stage

Since Freud's post-Victorian psychoanalytic cogitations, psychological theorizing and research efforts have privileged sibling and familial effects in the conceptualization of development. Corresponding individual-level differences born largely of intrapsychic and familial processes that influence personality and temperament factors assumed leading importance (Pike & Kretschmer, 2009). From the intrapersonal level, social psychology and sociology imparted insight into dyadic and group-level processes, and family systems and feminist perspectives such as feminist family sociology likewise drew attention to individuals embedded in dynamic socio-environmental contexts and their divergent experiences (Ferree, 1990; McHale *et al.*, 2003). Other socio-cultural approaches taken up by developmentalists – Greenfield's (2009) theory of human development and socio-cultural change, for instance – contributed to our understanding of the extensive forces prevalent in maturation, drawing much needed attention to the interface between individuals, their interrelationships, and how they form and are formed by the environments they live in.

Dynamic interdisciplinary developmental work started relatively late, yet the multipartite theoretical movement (e.g. developmental systems perspectives (Scheithauer, Niebank, & Ittel, 2009)) has recently ignited interest for those concerned with a more holistic research programme, and continues to hold promise, cropping up in the latest research pursuits and publications (Ittel & Kretschmer, 2007). However, an overwhelming minority of publications takes an interdisciplinary approach to the developmental study of siblings in adolescence (McHale *et al.*, 2012). Researchers must contend with theoretical and logistical complexity, and are in want of a methodological beacon.

While no one line of inquiry, inter- and trans-disciplinary methodologies included, can account for the rich intricacies of a living being's development, new conceptualizations like developmental systems perspectives stimulate the research landscape. This grouping seeks to overcome gaps and blind spots by complementing various research approaches. For example, Edwards and colleagues quest to offer a portrait of the meaning of siblings from the perspective of young people themselves modelled this timely tactic through their augmentation of combined psychoanalytic (inner psyche/psychological) and social constructivist (intrapersonal) tenets (Edwards, Hadfield, Lucey, & Mauthner, 2006). We assert that such considered perspectives provide a bountiful breeding ground for best-practice exploration. This is, however, tricky to achieve, as no one 'sibling theory' or model currently exists, and even causal explanations within the family are scarce (Caspi, 2011).

Individual and dyadic psychological processes and siblings

Psychoanalytic and evolutionary psychology

We start with an abridged depiction of Bowlby's theory of attachment and Adler's theory of individual psychology, two focal theories of the psychoanalytic tradition that can help elucidate the intrapsychic processes involved in sibling relationships (Whiteman, McHale, & Soli, 2011). These notions of social relations draw extensively on post–World War I theories of human nature and development, of which Freud's theory of human desire and consciousness was the most influential (Fromm, 1956). Biological laws from Tinbergen's (1951) ethological theory to classic Darwinism (Darwin, 1859) directly understood (human) development in terms of survival of the fittest; species-typical instinctual social patterns of behaviour were seen to bestow certain adaptive survival mechanisms. The principle of divergence, for instance, maintains that sibling diversification processes operate through ordinal rank and so direct children's opportunities to engage in particular activities (Sulloway, 2007, 2010). Following the spike in interest of socio-biological accounts of human evolution and sociality, the sibling relationship has been once more positioned as a worthy point of focus for developmentalists (Whiteman *et al.*, 2011).

Importantly, psychodynamic theory, in its seeking to understand the root functions of close intimate relationships, draws attention to the function of familial relationships over and above exhibited behaviours. It seeks to understand the root functions of close intimate relationships. According to Freud (1953–1974), the dynamic unconscious and the Oedipal complex are central in the development of individual personality; parent–child interactions set the stage for all subsequent psychological developments. Kleinian and object relations theorists equally house the locus of emotional growth and health in the parent–child relationship (Klein, 1952). This notion relegates siblings to a secondary role in individual maturation. Here, dysfunctional, inadequate parenting is seen to motivate a survival response behind significant sibling attachment and meaning (Coles, 2003; Mitchell, 2003).

Otherwise, lending from unconscious drives and impulses, siblings from the Freudian perspective are mostly objects of suspicion and figures of rivalrous desires. The firstborn is accorded blanket importance such that status effects and individual sibling's perspectives are largely neglected (Coles, 2003). Primogeniture, the granting of status or material claims to the family's firstborn (male) by right, by law or by practice further exemplifies this status hierarchy and often widespread means of succession. Here, one can conjecture that the influence of psychodynamic and historical assumptions which pervades early works on social relationships focused research on problems rather than solutions.

Attachment relations

Individual differences also occupy a critical role with respect to social bonds in attachment theory. Bowlby (1969/1982) and other attachment theorists (e.g. Ainsworth, Blehar, Waters, & Wall, 1978; Baumrind, 1967; Maccoby & Martin, 1983; Shaver & Mikulincer, 2002) have endeavoured to explain developmental maturation, although whereas Bowlby held attachment to be an all-or-nothing mother–child process, subsequent views embrace variation evident in recent attachment research. Attachment figures, or primary caregivers, are crucial for the young infant's survival from the first moments of life and provide different degrees of security based on their own sensitivity and responsiveness. The infant attempts to influence parental warmth and responsiveness through the use of proximity-seeking behaviours like crying. All other social relationships are seen to stem from relational blueprints laid down by the attachment figure–infant bond. Individual expectancies, understandings, emotions, and behaviours are fundamentally shaped in a series of intimate dyadic interactions between parent and offspring. It follows that the caregiver–child bond holds long-lasting implications for social relationships, with secure attachment affording close and trusting intimate relations with others such as sisters and brothers. Conversely, insecure attachment relations are believed to result in relationships less satisfying at best, and dysfunctional and damaging at worst.

So where does this leave siblings? In consideration of the parent–child union and its assumed greater repercussions, healthy parental attachment relationships bolster and scaffold adaptive and secure attachment to others, particularly siblings. Moreover, brothers and sisters can serve as attachment objects themselves, acting as important sources of security and support from which their siblings can venture into the environment (e.g. Samuels, 1980). Furthermore, older siblings can actively encourage exploration (Samuels, 1980) or provide comfort during times of distress in the face of a primary caregiver's absence (Stewart, 1983; Teti & Ablard, 1989).

Those individuals who have a sibling as primary attachment figure are seen as seeking an attachment object in response to a dysfunctional, negligent parent, who should, in keeping with psychodynamic and Bowlby-based theory, be the mother. Current empirical work, albeit not of a decided psychodynamic thrust, runs contrary to this proposition and reveals that siblings can indeed form important attachment bonds with one another and offer vital emotional support (e.g. Jenkins, 1992; Kim, McHale, Wayne Osgood, & Crouter, 2006; Voorpostel & Blieszner, 2008). Compatible evidence tells of increased affinity for support on the part of older siblings, especially in mixed-dyads (e.g. Oliva & Arranz, 2005; Ryherd, 2011; Stewart, 1983), which implicates both the potential for rivalry and conflict in same-gender dyads (Whiteman *et al.*, 2011) and the gendered role prescriptions of care and intimacy (e.g. Cole & Kerns, 2001). However, this strand of inquiry awaits further elaboration as other studies tell a perpendicular story of an absence of mixed-dyad effects or more positive close relations between sisters (e.g. Brody, Stoneman, & McCoy, 1994; Feinberg, McHale, Crouter, & Cumsille, 2003; Furman & Buhrmester, 1992).

Again, the drought of literature on adolescent-specific sibling attachment relations makes for difficult depiction. In a sample drawn from the Netherlands, adolescents at approximately age 12 displayed a significant increase in attachment bonds to their sibling, partly attributed to new, shared environments, and experiences as the younger joined the older sibling in high school (Buist, Deković, Meeus, & van Aken, 2002). During the transitional period from childhood to adolescence and adolescence to young adulthood, attachment relationships with siblings may become progressively voluntary and peer-like. Constructs like empathy and shared experiences may underpin sibling attachment relationship development, partially due to its characteristic and unique dual reciprocal and hierarchical qualities (e.g. Dunn, 2007; East, 2009; McHale, Kim, & Whiteman, 2006). Like Whiteman *et al.* (2011) state, not all relationships possess requisite attachment relation qualities; therefore, future care should be taken in delineating their difference among siblings. Examining lasting intimate sibling ties can assist in understanding these relational disparities and development, particularly during the intense socio-emotional development in adolescence; for testing of this proposition, longitudinal assessments are needed.

Individual psychology theories of development

Stability and change in personality are held as principally the results of intrinsic and prescribed processes as per the five-factor theory (FFT) of individual differences (McCrae & Costa, 1999). Twin and adoption studies offer some support showing that individual differences are influenced by genetic factors (Loehlin, 1992). The personality of monozygotic and dizygotic twins studied over 10 years showed 80 per cent of the variance between individuals was attributable to genetic influences (McGue, Bacon, & Lykken, 1993). McCrae *et al.* (2000) also showed remarkably similar age trends in personality development across nations with vastly different cultural backgrounds. Nonetheless, the issue of stability and change in personality and the proportion of their variance traceable to genetic versus environmental influence remain at the forefront of individual psychology debates (Sturaro, Denissen, van Aken, & Asendorpf, 2008). (For more on the genetic and biological influences of sibling differences, see Chapter 4.)

Of these disparate individual-level accounts, Alfred Adler, a preeminent psychoanalytic theorist, proposed that family systems are paramount in the development of individual motivations and personality differentiation (Adler, 1928; Ansbacher & Ansbacher, 1956; Watts, 2003). External social influences and, above all, the family as a whole and its composite sibling interactions mould an individual's sense of self. Social comparisons and power dynamics are believed to impart strong effects on the development of self-esteem and life practices; inferiority complexes were predicted from maladaptive family social comparison processes. In fact, Adler and others (Dreikurs & Stolz, 1964) championed egalitarian sibling treatment based on such dynamics (Whiteman *et al.*, 2011).

In the context of familial interactions, personality development owes in large part to sibling dynamics, according to the Adlerian view. Siblings make competing claims on parents' time and attention, and access to resources such as afterschool activity demands (Downey, 2001). While brothers and sisters contend for positive parental treatment, differentiation or individuation processes allow for each child to establish a unique 'niche' in order to reduce competition; the more individual personal qualities and characteristics are salient, the more likely siblings are to receive focus and care (Sulloway, 1996). Differentiation also makes sense from the evolutionary perspective in that the more unique the traits offspring possess, the more likely that at least one child will survive adverse circumstances (Belsky, 2005). What is more, in families of greater sibship size, the strain on presumably limited parental resources further drives differentiation among siblings (Downey, 2001). These socio-biological accounts have found some empirical evidence, for instance, accounting for family structure characteristics such as birth order and personality findings (covered in Chapter 2) (Salmon & Daly, 1998; Sulloway, 2007). Prime examples include the universal claim of lowered academic achievement by sibship size accounting for socio-economic background (e.g. Sulloway, 2000) as well as conscientious, high-achieving firstborns (e.g. Healey & Ellis, 2007).

At the family system and sibling subsystem level, harmonious interactions and decreased conflict are seen as likely consequences of these differentiation processes. On the other hand, differential favourable parental treatment has been postulated to stoke the fires of rivalry and conflict and lead to greater sibling discord in early childhood and adolescence (Brody, Stoneman, & Burke, 1987; Shanahan, McHale, Crouter, & Osgood, 2008; Stocker, Dunn, & Plomin, 1989). Still, the specifics of the developmental route of sibling rivalry as it relates to differentiation and important convergence processes (see Wong *et al.*, 2010) remain to be seen, and compelling findings of sibling rivalry present across nations, but with variable effect sizes, add to the mystery (Wolter, 2003). At any rate, some empirical findings can attest to the veracity of portions of Adler's claims; the influence of siblings on individual outcomes depends upon variables such as the family's socio-economic status and gender make-up of the sibling dyad. We cover sibling rivalry and relational dynamics more fully in the next chapter.

One reason cited for differential treatment on the part of parents themselves is the different personal qualities and characteristics of their children (McHale & Crouter, 2003). However, siblings' perceptions of their parents' groundings for distinct treatment (Kowal & Kramer, 1997) and parental fairness (McHale, Updegraff, Jackson-Newsom, Tucker, & Crouter, 2000) may be more central than actual differences in behaviour. Familial and cultural norms also likely play a critical role in the impact of differential treatment and differentiation processes between siblings. Societal scripts and normative rules may be more explicit among members of collectivistic cultures (i.e. specific gender and age expectations as opposed to favouritism), raising perceptions of fairness, and feasibly lowering or even completely removing the negative impact of differential treatment of brothers and sisters (McHale, Updegraff, Shanahan, Crouter, & Killoren, 2005; Nuckolls, 1993; Weisner, 1993). How exactly the treatment of siblings within a family and their concomitant personality development relate to one another is unclear, whether viewed through psychoanalytic, Adlerian, or evolutionary lenses. Systems theory can contribute to the dialogue here, which we cover in the forthcoming sections, and touch on again when we explore differential treatment in the second chapter.

Theories on social processes

We now switch our focus to a rich line of exploration: the perception of siblings themselves. Distinct meanings, attitudes, beliefs, and behaviours of individual agents are particularly important in social interactions. We have seen that siblings' perceptions of their parents' behaviour can have tangible effects on family systems and their quality of functioning (Kowal & Kramer, 1997; McHale *et al.*, 2000). Theories of social psychology and social processes can additionally assist in clarifying the adolescent sibling relationship and related dynamics. These perspectives attempt to explain the influence of others on an individual – how socializing agents motivate attitudes, behaviour, and cognitions. Important to note are the attributions a child makes to their relationship partner's behaviours or life events as per attribution theory (Weiner, 1979). Group processes are part and parcel of this perspective that hones in on social norms, role prescriptions, and the dynamics of social interactions. That being said, social psychology is rarely applied to sibling studies (Whiteman *et al.*, 2011).

Festinger's (1954) theory of social comparison speaks to the popular topic of sibling rivalry and the valence of sibling interactions. Like Adler's psychoanalytic bent on the differentiation processes believed to influence sibling personality development, social comparison theory involves the way in which siblings compare themselves to each other. Upward comparison bolsters self-esteem when commonalities between high-level status individuals are perceived, while downward comparison operates when individuals believe themselves to be more positively positioned than others; both offer ego protection effects (Suls, Martin, & Wheeler, 2002). As siblings are both closely related and similar, and yet diverge into unique individuals by way of relevant differentiation and individuation processes, this relationship is thought abound with social comparison influences.

Few empirical studies have taken social comparison theory directly to task by testing specific processes and mechanisms, instead opting to investigate sibling relationship outcomes (McHale *et al.*, 2012). Nonetheless, intriguing and promising findings are still to be uncovered like those of Noller, Conway, and Blakeley-Smith (2008) who detected the importance of the nature and history of the sibling relationship as well as age spacing and the level of domain importance for the individual. Moreover, the effects of sibling birth order reiterate psychoanalytic focus on the disparate comparative and evaluative manner in which younger versus older siblings are more or less likely to engage in upward comparison processes (in the case of the former) or downward (for the latter) (Feinberg, Neiderhiser, Simmens, Reiss, & Hetherington, 2000). Whiteman and colleagues' (2011) contribution reviews other social comparison processes implicated in the adult sibling relationship such as equity theory (Adams, 1965; Walster, Walster, & Berscheid, 1978) and social exchange theory (Thibaut & Kelley, 1959), which both assist in explaining the nature of voluntary relationships. We do not cover these frameworks here as they typically hold more relevance for adults with their focus on individual more than developmental differences, and greater consideration of voluntary interaction in adulthood.

Social learning and socialization in the sibling relationship

Social learning theories applied to the sibling relationship in particular come into their own during the teenage years. As developing individuals gather sets of behaviours and cognitive frameworks like social attitudes and beliefs, other socialization agents' reinforcement, observation, and imitation shape these newfound social ways of operating (Bandura, 1977). The family is seen as a prime setting for social learning processes, and individual family members and the family system as a whole wield strong influence. Parents can reinforce harmonious sibling interactions with overt verbal feedback or indirectly model conflict resolution skills in the context of their partnership (e.g. Parke & Buriel, 1998). Importantly, siblings are active co-constructors of their relationships, reciprocally reinforcing positive or negative behaviours, and learning through mutual observation.

Social learning tenets hold that high status, similar, nurturant others, such as parents or older siblings, have greater relative sway in observational learning (Bandura, 1977). Not all observational learning is inherently positive – negative ways of relating are equally likely to be conveyed. For instance, siblings may reinforce one another through coercive cycles of escalating hostility and aggression during conflict. These cycles are thought to contribute to the notion of sibling relationships as training grounds for aggression (Patterson, 1986). Other instances of influential sibling effects on individual social behaviour and development can be found in the vast number of studies on sibling correlates, for example, health and risk behaviours and practices (Brook & Brook, 1990). The manner in which modelling and reinforcement occur in social learning processes is understandably complex, as potential moderators like attachment style, relationship dynamics, and power and status are all implicated, yet rarely explicitly studied (Whiteman, Becerra, & Killoren, 2009). This area of work is promising, and we review individual- and family-level correlates of sibling ties in the third chapter.

Structural theories of socialization state that children and adolescents internalize cultural ideologies through their families, whereby parents operate as their offspring's primary model and source for learning social norms (Parsons & Bales, 1955). The family, a social system itself, socializes the developing child through the reflection and communication of broader cultural values and norms. Parents are assumed to both model behaviours and expose their children to experiences concordant with certain ways of being and specific ideological sets (Kulik, 2002; McHale et al., 2003). Less understood are the ways in which siblings socialize one another and various familial subsystems, and their relative importance. We attempt to integrate empirical data utilizing within-family system approaches to elucidate socialization processes and their role in sibling relationship development in Chapter 2.

One must not forget that siblings are social agents in their own right who play a central role in the shaping of their relationships (Brady & Stoneman, 1988; Sameroff & MacKenzie, 2003). The difficulty in picking apart the relative influence and mechanisms through which siblings model and socialize one another resides in past work's tendency to study interactions in isolation without taking the entire family context into account. It is plain to see that siblings can act as models, although again we are left to deduce modelling effects from correlations between siblings like associations in delinquency and aggression rates (Slomkowski, Rende, Conger, Simons, & Conger, 2001), and self-esteem and well-being (Oliva & Arranz, 2005). In order to unpack modes of influence in the sibling relationship, within-family research designs, which consider the family unit as a whole and broader social environments are compulsory (Pike & Kretschmer, 2009).

Anthropological takes, sociological turns

Sociological and anthropological views examine the development, structure, and functioning of a particular human society and offer a comparative take on societies, culture, and their development. Our review does not aim to explicitly address the variety of sociological and anthropological work in this regard. However, we now offer a cursory glance as these fields undergird and cross-fertilize later interdisciplinary research programmes like the feminist transactional approach. For further cultural differences in sibling research, we believe our seventh chapter on international differences and developments will interest the reader.

Systems theories

The departure from what was once thought to be mutually exclusive, quantitative or qualitative approaches has owed considerably to the advancement of the interdisciplinary study of dynamic systems (Kampis, 1991). Corresponding trans- and interdisciplinary work and the demands inherent within such efforts further support the value of comprehensive integration of individual, group, and socio-environmental levels of analysis. Indeed, this theoretical grouping, which arose from Von Bertalanffy's general systems theory (GST) (Von Bertalanffy, 1950; Von Bertalanffy, Hempel, Bass, & Jonas, 1951) and includes developmental systems theory (Ford & Lerner, 1992), the ecological systems theory (Bronfenbrenner, 1979), the transactional perspective (Sameroff, 1975a, 1975b; Sameroff & MacKenzie, 2003), and the epigenetic view (Gottlieb, 1991), is multiperspectival in nature. These developmental systems theories attempt to account for the organism's open systems nature and self-regulatory behaviours that operate through complex interdependent reciprocal feedback systems (Scheithauer et al., 2009).

This systemic approach is useful in conceptualizing and explaining the sibling relationship, the development of individual family members, particular familial subsystems, the whole family, and can even extend to provide a comprehensive portrait of socio-environmental influence and growth, like the school context or macrocultural milieus (Kitayama, 2002). Above all, meta-analytic systemic views of development emphasize the dynamic *active* nature of the individual, the environment, and their transactions, in contrast to the static entity theories so often (*mis-*) applied in sibling study. We believe systems theories' wider conceptualization of individual development is crucial to its understanding. In the subsequent sections, we appraise a few particular systems science approaches, namely, ecological systems theory, family systems theory, and feminist revisions on systems theory and feminist sociology.

Ecological family approaches

Bronfenbrenner's (1979) pioneering work, *The Ecology of Human Development*, expounded his ecological theory that privileges the notion of multiple interacting levels or systems in an individuals' development. Here, the developing child or adolescent is nested within surrounding structures, influencing and being influenced by them. Within the most proximal microsystem – meaning here an individual's daily life setting of which the family is of chief importance to the growing child – roles, relationships, and daily activities are deemed to be critical elements in psychosocial and biological development. The mesosystem comprises interconnected microsystem contexts and encompasses factors such as norms surrounding gender and age. Exosystemic effects at the next level include once-removed yet still influential variables, for instance, parental workplace arrangements that indirectly impact the child through the microsystem (e.g. Hess, Ittel, & Sisler, 2014). In the outermost component of Bronfenbrenner's depiction, macrosystemic forces impart influence in the form of political, economic, social, and cultural dynamisms that mould individual development. The importance of these macrocultural powers is further laid out in the third and seventh chapters.

Ecological systems theory helps us understand sibling studies by breaking down particular family arrangements into dyadic (e.g. sibling–sibling, parent–child), triadic (sibling pair–father), and so on, relationships, extending into distant relative relations. In doing so, the influence of particular relationships can be modelled across time and space, in place of isolated static investigations. As the sibling relationship has been relatively neglected in the analysis of individual development and family functioning in tandem, ecological theory allows us to grant the deserved value to this particular bond by emphasizing its meaning and significance to each family member considered together and apart.

Family system theory

The family viewed as a dynamic arrangement, open to external influence, brings broader forces implicated in individual development and relationships into the fray (Becvar & Becvar, 2000; Guttman, 1991; Nichols & Schwartz, 2005). Although typically not directly enlisted in sibling study, the family system approach acknowledges the sibling subsystem (Minuchin, 1985). Several assumptions are at play in family systems theory, including the belief that individual family members are intricately linked to one another, and that experiences in one particular portion of the system affect all other members. Family theorists stress the role of reciprocal interactions in family functioning and place importance on the notion of circular causality: individual effects are the result of multiple causes, and effects in turn influence the causal pathways themselves (Murray, 2006). For instance, when an adolescent transitions from elementary to high school, they likely begin to spend more and more time with peers than with their family. Everyone else in the family has to adapt, and their adaptations impact other family members. Perhaps the mother copes by acquiring a new family dog or even produces another family member. The adolescent, their siblings, parents, and potential new family member are all intertwined in the functioning of the family system.

Akin to social constructivist approaches and the acknowledgement of intersubjectivities in experience, meanings and realities are negotiated and shared between family members, for better or worse (Berger & Luckmann, 1967; Gergen, 2001; Zlatev, Racine, Sinha, & Itkonen, 2008). Bowen's family system theory recruits system theory to describe such complex interactions in a family and to give individuals within the emotional unit of the family a voice (Bowen, 1966; Kerr & Bowen, 1988; Papero, 1990). Indeed, siblings do not exist in a vacuum: at any one point, brothers and sisters and their individual developmental trajectories reciprocally impact family dynamics. Families are intensely emotionally connected as their members solicit each other's attention, approval, and support, and react to each other's needs, expectations, and feelings. This interdependent reactivity and connectedness that flows in give-and-take exchanges between individuals presumably stems from the over-arching ability of a family to provide protection, shelter, and other basic necessities. However, as outlined in family systems therapy, this connectedness often leads to escalating tensions in the family, differentially effecting individual members. These discrepant impacts and bi-directional influences are helpful for comprehending relationship dynamics between siblings, rooted within family arrangements (Cox, 2010; Conger & Little, 2010). We speculate that as most family research borrows from these core tenets particular in examining problem-behaviours as opposed to optimal functioning, this is a further reason why a problem-centred approach primarily drives sibling studies.

Feminist revisions and transactional family systems theory

The post-structural and feminist revisions in psychology, including family systems theory, came in the wake of the second wave of feminism and related social movements that challenged social institutions and stressed the need to address issues of gender, race, and power (Brown & Gilligan, 1992; Knudson-Martin, 1994; Lerner, 1985, 1989; McGoldrick, 1998; Miller, 1986). Individual empowerment further revised family system's initial conceptualization (Lerner, 1985, 1989; Murray, 2006). Likewise, post-structural visions of social constructionism sounded the need to think of individuals as competent social agents who construct the social world through their everyday communications and create social meaning though interaction, while being subject to the influence of broad social forces (Foucault, 1981).

Traditional takes on family studies (like family systems theory) came under harsh critique from feminist scholars due to how they conceptualized particular familial power dynamics (Murray, 2006). For instance, if a family member is abused within the family systems perspective, should this damaging behaviour on the part of the abusive individual be understood not as 'bad' but rather, 'functional' in the family context (if one takes the functional emphasis to its most extreme)? At what expense should families be held together, and should individuals be encouraged or even coerced to 'adapt' to improve 'optimal functioning'? Questions of this nature are critically addressed through feminist lenses and are increasingly relevant considering the new flexibilities in formulations, definitions, and arrangements of families, and changes to the nuclear family (McGuire & Shanahan, 2010). Feminist and sociological accounts raise awareness of the issues of the placement of siblings in foster care, adoption, assisted reproductive technologies, families and family members with diverse needs, and 'blended' families. In our chapter on within-family dynamics involved in sibling research, we place value on these post-structural and feminist traditions in fleshing out concepts such as family dynamics and expectations, gender, social development, and value transmission.

The inclusion of transpersonal aspects into research on siblings also offers the opportunity to move beyond the problem-focused research agendas that disputably plague the field (Edwards *et al.*, 2006). Transactional approaches merge various transpersonal elements; they are holistic and encourage integration of the mind, body, spirit, emotions, creative expression, family, and community (Lazarus, 2010; Sameroff, 2009). Because it is this 'transcendental' nature that allows for study over and above personal ego levels of development, it attends to both 'problematic' or the so-called dysfunctional patterns of being as well as healthy and empowering practices and patterns. Moreover, it recognizes that what may be considered maladaptive for one individual or family member may not necessarily be so for the other. Individuals and their own meanings are seen as worthy and central in the study of their family experiences.

Edwards *et al.* (2006), Mauthner (2002), Coles (2003), and Chamberlain (1999), among others, have either directly or unintentionally adopted this approach in their work on siblings, with some of these researchers drawing on the sociological and anthropological principles that privilege individual narratives and the meaning and significance of social exchange. We believe in the adoption of a narrative and/ or person-centred approach implicated in feminist and sociological perspectives in conjunction with study of specific social processes and mechanisms involved in sibling interactions. In this way, sibling research holds the promise of adding to our knowledge base of lifelong bonds, and the processes and contexts behind them (Whiteman *et al.*, 2011).

Spectrum of sibling study

Sibling interactions are diverse and multifaceted; they span from day-to-day conflicts to complex communication to subtle social learning processes. It is therefore important to incorporate issues and concepts from disparate theoretical traditions into a comprehensive study of the sibling relationship. Several research traditions can advise the little-understood, multidimensional sibling relationship and thus future inquiry into intimate relationship development. As we have argued, psychoanalytic theories and their emphasis on relationship dynamics and personality development; social psychological processes and their role in the construction of attitudes and behaviours, plus their impact on social relationships and their perceptions; systems theories and their role in comprehensive modelling of individual development and reciprocal relations; and the thus far vastly neglected multiperspectival accounts of relationships and growth all have something to offer to sibling research. Among these frameworks, psychoanalytic and quantitative measuring of sibling outcomes and behaviours have dominated the field, keeping in mind the overall lack of knowledge on this relationship.

No one approach is without limitations. Most of these tactics do not readily lend themselves to multidimensional developmental study, at least not without careful application and thorough conceptualization and planning. In this regard, McHale *et al.*'s (2012) summative presentation of sibling research in childhood and adolescence can act as a guide for the challenge they pose to researchers: how to enhance the integration of concepts and methods toward an interdisciplinary scheme for studying sibling relationships. Additionally, almost all investigations that use these different lines of research have not enlisted within-family designs, and even fewer in tandem with longitudinal repeated measures, resulting in many unanswered questions and therefore wide-open avenues for fruitful future inquiry. We hope that through our brief highlighting of these distinct paradigms, and our upcoming presentation of past empirical work, we set the stage for advanced comprehensive study of adolescent sibling relationships.

References

Adams, J. S. (1965). Inequity in social exchange. *Advances in Experimental Social Psychology, 2*, 267–299.

Adler, A. (1928). Characteristics of the first, second, and third child. *Children, 3*, 14–52.

Ainsworth, M. D. S., Blehar, M. C., Waters, E., & Wall, S. (1978). *Patterns of attachment: A psychological study of the strange situation*. Oxford: Lawrence Erlbaum Associates.

Ansbacher, M. L., & Ansbacher, R. (1956). *The individual psychology of Alfred Adler*. New York: Basic Books.

Bandura, A. (1977). *Social learning theory*. Englewood Cliffs, NJ: Prentice Hall.

Baumrind, D. (1967). Child care practices anteceding three patterns of preschool behavior. *Genetic Psychology Monographs, 75*, 43–88.

Becvar, D. S., & Becvar, R. J. (2000). *Family therapy: A systemic integration* (4th ed.). Boston: Allyn & Bacon.

Belsky, J. (2005). Differential susceptibility to rearing influences: An evolutionary hypothesis and some evidence. In B. Ellis & D. Bjorklund (Eds.), *Origins of the social mind: Evolutionary psychology and child development* (pp. 139–163). New York: Guilford Press.

Berger, P., & Luckmann, T. (1967). *The social construction of reality: A treatise in the sociology of knowledge*. Garden City, NY: Anchor Books.

Bowen, M. (1966). The use of family theory in clinical practice. *Comprehensive Psychiatry, 7*(5), 345–374.

Bowlby, J. (1969/1982). *Attachment and loss: Attachment* (Vol. I). New York: Basic Books.

Brady, G. H., & Stoneman, Z. (1988). Sibling conflict: Contributions of the siblings themselves, the parent-sibling relationship, and the broader family system. *Journal of Children in Contemporary Society, 19*(3–4), 39–53.

Brody, G. H., Stoneman, Z., & Burke, M. (1987). Child temperaments, maternal differential behavior, and sibling relationships. *Developmental Psychology, 23*(3), 354–362.

Brody, G. H., Stoneman, Z., & McCoy, J. K. (1994). Forecasting sibling relationships in early adolescence from child temperaments and family processes in middle childhood. *Child Development, 65*(3), 771–784.

Bronfenbrenner, U. (1979). Contexts of child rearing: Problems and prospects. *American Psychologist, 34*(10), 844–850.

Brook, D., & Brook, J. (1990). The etiology and consequences of adolescent drug use. In R. Watson (Ed.), *Drug and alcohol abuse prevention* (pp. 339–362). Clifton, NJ: Humana Press.

Brown, L., & Gilligan, C. (1992). *Meeting at the crossroads: Women's psychology and girls' development*. Cambridge, MA: Harvard University Press.

Buist, K. L., Deković, M., Meeus, W., & van Aken, M. A. (2002). Developmental patterns in adolescent attachment to mother, father and sibling. *Journal of Youth and Adolescence, 31*(3), 167–176.

Caspi, J. (2011). Future directions for sibling research, practice, and theory. In J. Caspi (Ed.), *Sibling development: Implications for mental health practitioners* (pp. 377–390). New York: Springer.

Chamberlain, M. (1999). Brothers and sisters, uncles and aunts: A lateral perspective on Caribbean families. In E. Silva & C. Smart (Eds.), *The new family?* (pp. 129–143). London: Sage.

Cicirelli, V. G. (1992). *Family caregiving: Autonomous and paternalistic decision making*. Newbury Park, CA: Sage.

Cicirelli, V. G. (1995). *Sibling relationships across the life span*. New York: Plenum Press.

Cole, A., & Kerns, K. A. (2001). Perceptions of sibling qualities and activities of early adolescents. *Journal of Early Adolescence, 21*, 204–227.

Coles, P. (2003). *The importance of sibling relationships in psychoanalysis*. London: Karnac Books.

Conger, K. J., & Little, W. M. (2010). Sibling relationships during the transition to adulthood. *Child Development Perspectives, 4*(2), 87–94.

Cox, M. J. (2010). Family systems and sibling relationships. *Child Development Perspectives, 4*(2), 95–96.

Darwin, C. (1859). *On the origin of species by means of natural selection*. London: Murray.

Downey, D. B. (2001). Number of siblings and intellectual development: The resource dilution explanation. *American Psychologist, 56*(6–7), 497–504.

Dreikurs, R., & Stolz, V. (1964). *Children: The challenge*. New York: Hawthorn Books.

Dunn, J. (2007). Siblings and socialization. In J. Grusec & P. Hastings (Eds.), *Handbook of socialization: Theory and research* (pp. 309–329). New York: Guilford Press.

East, P. (2009). Adolescents' relationships with siblings. In R. Lerner & L. Steinberg (Eds.), *Handbook of adolescent psychology: Contextual influences on adolescent development* (3rd ed., pp. 43–73). Hoboken, NJ: Wiley.

Edwards, R., Hadfield, L., Lucey, H., & Mauthner, M. (2006). *Sibling identity and relationships: Sisters and brothers*. Oxon: Routledge.

Elder, G. H., Jr. (1996). Human lives in changing societies: Life course and developmental insights. In R. B. Cairns, G. H. Elder, Jr., & E. J. Costello (Eds.), *Developmental Science* (pp. 31–62). New York: Cambridge University Press.

Feinberg, M. E., McHale, S. M., Crouter, A. C., & Cumsille, P. (2003). Sibling differentiation: Sibling and parent relationship trajectories in adolescence. *Child Development, 74*(5), 1261–1274.

Feinberg, M. E., Neiderhiser, J. M., Simmens, S., Reiss, D., & Hetherington, E. M. (2000). Sibling comparison of differential parental treatment in adolescence: Gender, self-esteem, and emotionality as mediators of the parenting-adjustment association. *Child Development, 71*(6), 1611–1628.

Ferree, M. M. (1990). Beyond separate spheres: Feminism and family research. *Journal of Marriage and the Family, 52*(4), 866–884.

Festinger, L. (1954). A theory of social comparison processes. *Human Relations, 7*(2), 117–140.

Ford, D. H., & Lerner, R. M. (1992). *Developmental systems theory: An integrative approach*. Thousand Oaks, CA: Sage.

Foucault, M. (1981). *The history of sexuality* (Vol. 1). London: Allen Lane.

Freud, S. (1953–1974). *The standard edition of the complete psychological works of Sigmund Freud* (J. Strachey, Ed., 24 Vols). London: Hogarth Press and The Institute of Psychoanalysis.

Fromm, E. (1956). *The art of loving*. New York: Perennial Library.

Furman, W., & Buhrmester, D. (1992). Age and sex differences in perceptions of networks of personal relationships. *Child Development, 63*(1), 103–115.

Gergen, K. J. (2001). *Social construction in context*. Thousand Oaks, CA: Sage.

Gottlieb, G. (1991). Epigenetic systems view of human development. *Developmental Psychology, 27*(1), 33–34.

Greenfield, P. M. (2009). Linking social change and developmental change: Shifting pathways of human development. *Developmental Psychology, 45*(2), 401–418.

Guttman, H. A. (1991). Systems theory, cybernetics, and epistemology. In A. S. Gurman & D. P. Kniskern (Eds.), *Handbook of family therapy* (Vol. 2, pp. 41–61). New York: Brunner/Mazel.

Healey, M. D., & Ellis, B. J. (2007). Birth order, conscientiousness, and openness to experience: Tests of the family-niche model of personality using a within-family methodology. *Evolution and Human Behavior, 28*, 55–59.

Hess, M., Ittel, A., & Sisler, A. (2014). Gender-specific macro- and micro-level processes in the transmission of gender role orientation in adolescence: The role of fathers. *European Journal of Developmental Psychology, 11*, 211–226.

Ittel, A., & Kretschmer, T. (2007). Historical roots of developmental science. *International Journal of Developmental Science, 1*(1), 23–32.

Jenkins, J. (1992). Sibling relationships in disharmonious homes: Potential difficulties and protective effects. In F. Boer & J. Dunn (Eds.), *Children's sibling relationships: Developmental and clinical issues* (pp. 125–138). Hillsdale, NJ: Lawrence Erlbaum Associates.

Kampis, G. (1991). *Self-modifying systems in biology and cognitive science*. Oxford: Pergamon Press.

Kerr, M. E., & Bowen, M. (1988). *Family evaluation: An approach based on Bowen theory*. New York: W. W. Norton.

Kim, J. Y., McHale, S. M., Wayne Osgood, D., & Crouter, A. C. (2006). Longitudinal course and family correlates of sibling relationships from childhood through adolescence. *Child Development, 77*(6), 1746–1761.

Kitayama, S. (2002). Culture and basic psychological processes – Toward a system view of culture: Comment on Oyserman et al. (2002). *Psychological Bulletin, 128*, 89–96.

Klein, M. (1952). *Developments in psychoanalysis*. London: Hogarth Press and The Institute of Psychoanalysis.

Knudson-Martin, C. (1994). The female voice: Applications to Bowen's family systems theory. *Journal of Marital and Family Therapy, 20*(1), 35–46.

Kowal, A., & Kramer, L. (1997). Children's understanding of parental differential treatment. *Child Development, 68*(1), 113–126.

Kulik, L. (2002). The impact of social background on gender-role ideology parents' versus children's attitudes. *Journal of Family Issues, 23*(1), 53–73.

Lazarus, I. (2010). A transpersonal feminist approach to family systems. *International Journal of Transpersonal Studies, 29*(2), 121–136.

Lerner, H. (1985). *The dance of anger: A woman's guide to changing the patterns of intimate relationships*. New York: Harper & Row.

Lerner, H. (1989). *The dance of intimacy: A woman's guide to courageous acts of change in key relationships*. New York: Harper & Row.

Loehlin, J. C. (1992). *Genes and environment in personality development*. Thousand Oaks, CA: Sage.

Maccoby, E., & Martin, J. (1983). Socialization in the context of the family: Parent–child interaction. In P. H. Mussen & E. M. Hetherington (Eds.), *Handbook of child psychology: Socialization, personality, and social development* (4th ed., Vol. 4, pp. 1–101). New York: Wiley.

Mauthner, M. (2002). *Sistering: Power and change in female relationships*. Basingstoke: Palgrave.

McCrae, R. R., & Costa, P. T., Jr. (1999). A five-factor theory of personality. *Handbook of Personality: Theory and Research, 2*, 139–153.

McCrae, R. R., Costa, P. T., Jr., Ostendorf, F., Angleitner, A., Hřebíčková, M., Avia, M. D., & Smith, P. B. (2000). Nature over nurture: Temperament, personality, and life span development. *Journal of Personality and Social Psychology, 78*(1), 173–186.

McGoldrick, M. (1998). *Re-visioning family therapy: Race, culture and gender in clinical practice.* New York: Guilford Press.

McGue, M., Bacon, S., & Lykken, D. T. (1993). Personality stability and change in early adulthood: A behavioral genetic analysis. *Developmental Psychology, 29*(1), 96–109.

McGuire, S., & Shanahan, L. (2010). Sibling experiences in diverse family contexts. *Child Development Perspectives, 4*(2), 72–79.

McHale, S. M., & Crouter, A. C. (2003). How do children exert an impact on family life? In A. C. Crouter & A. Booth (Eds.), *Children's influence on family dynamics: The neglected side of family relationships* (pp. 207–220). Mahwah, NJ: Lawrence Erlbaum Associates.

McHale, S. M., Crouter, A. C., & Whiteman, S. D. (2003). The family contexts of gender development in childhood and adolescence. *Social Development, 12*, 125–148.

McHale, S. M., Kim, J., & Whiteman, S. D. (2006). Sibling relationships in childhood and adolescence. In P. Noller & J. A. Feeney (Eds.), *Close relationships: Functions, forms, and processes* (pp. 128–149). New York: Psychology Press.

McHale, S. M., Updegraff, K. A., Jackson-Newsom, J., Tucker, C. J., & Crouter, A. C. (2000). When does parents' differential treatment have negative implications for siblings? *Social Development, 9*(2), 149–172.

McHale, S. M., Updegraff, K. A., Shanahan, L., Crouter, A. C., & Killoren, S. E. (2005). Siblings' differential treatment in Mexican American families. *Journal of Marriage and Family, 67*(5), 1259–1274.

McHale, S. M., Updegraff, K. A., & Whiteman, S. D. (2012). Sibling relationships and influences in childhood and adolescence. *Journal of Marriage and Family, 74*(5), 913–930.

Milevsky, A. (2004). Perceived parental marital satisfaction and divorce: Effects on sibling relations in emerging adults. *Journal of Divorce & Remarriage, 41*(1–2), 115–128.

Milevsky, A. (2005). Compensatory patterns of sibling support in emerging adulthood: Variations in loneliness, self-esteem, depression and life satisfaction. *Journal of Social and Personal Relationships, 22*, 743–755.

Milevsky, A., & Heerwagen, M. (2013). A phenomenological examination of sibling relationships in emerging adulthood. *Marriage & Family Review, 49*(3), 251–263.

Miller, J. (1986). *Toward a new psychology of women* (2nd ed.). Boston, MA: Beacon Press.

Minuchin, P. (1985). Families and individual development: Provocations from the field of family therapy. *Child Development, 56*, 289–302.

Mitchell, J. (2003). *Siblings, sex and violence.* Cambridge: Polity Press.

Murray, C. E. (2006). Controversy, constraints, and context: Understanding family violence through family systems theory. *The Family Journal: Counseling and Therapy for Couples and Families, 14*(3), 234–239.

Nichols, M. P., & Schwartz, R. C. (2005). *The essentials of family therapy* (2nd ed.). Boston: Allyn & Bacon.

Noller, P., Conway, S., & Blakeley-Smith, A. (2008). Sibling relationships in adolescent and young adult twin and nontwin siblings: Managing competition and comparison. In J. P. Forgas & J. Fitness (Eds.), *Social relationships: Cognitive, affective, and motivational processes* (pp. 235–252). New York: Psychology Press.

Nuckolls, C. W. (1993). *Siblings in South Asia: Brothers and sisters in cultural context.* New York: Guilford Press.

Oliva, A., & Arranz, E. (2005). Sibling relationships during adolescence. *European Journal of Developmental Psychology, 2*(3), 253–270.

Papero, D. (1990). *Bowen family systems theory.* Needham Heights, MA: Allyn & Bacon.

Parke, R. D., & Buriel, R. (1998). Socialization in the family: Ethnic and ecological perspectives. In W. Damon & N. Eisenberg (Eds.), *Handbook of child psychology: Social, emotional, and personality development* (5th ed., Vol. 3, pp. 463–552). New York: Wiley.

Parsons, T., & Bales, R. F. (1955). *Family, socialization and interaction process.* New York: Psychology Press.

Patterson, G. R. (1986). Performance models for antisocial boys. *American Psychologist, 41*(4), 432–444.

Pike, A., & Kretschmer, T. (2009). Shared versus nonshared effects: Parenting and children's adjustment. *International Journal of Developmental Science, 3*(2), 115–130.

Rodríguez, C., & Moro, C. (2008). Coming to agreement: Object use by infants and adults. In J. Zlatev, T. Racine, C. Sinha, & E. Itkonen (Eds.), *The shared mind: Perspectives on intersubjectivity* (pp. 89–114). Amsterdam: John Benjamin.

Ryherd, L. M. (2011). Predictors of academic achievement: The role of older sibling and peer relationship factors (Unpublished master's thesis). Iowa State University, Ames.

Salmon, C. A., & Daly, M. (1998). Birth order and familial sentiment: Middleborns are different. *Evolution and Human Behavior, 19*(5), 299–312.

Sameroff, A. E. (2009). *The transactional model of development: How children and contexts shape each other.* Washington, DC: American Psychological Association.

Sameroff, A. J. (1975a). Early influences on development: Fact or fancy? *Merrill-Palmer Quarterly of Behavior and Development, 21*(4), 267–294.

Sameroff, A. J. (1975b). Transactional models in early social relations. *Human Development, 18*(1–2), 65–79.

Sameroff, A. J., & MacKenzie, M. J. (2003). Research strategies for capturing transactional models of development: The limits of the possible. *Development and Psychopathology, 15*, 613–640.

Samuels, H. R. (1980). The effect of an older sibling on infant locomotor exploration of a new environment. *Child Development, 51*(2), 607–609.

Scheithauer, H., Niebank, K., & Ittel, A. (2009). Developmental science: Integrating knowledge about dynamic processes in human development. In J. Valsiner, P. Molenaar, M. Lycra, & N. Chaudhary (Eds.), *Dynamic process methodology in the social and developmental sciences* (pp. 595–617). New York: Springer.

Shanahan, L., McHale, S. M., Crouter, A. C., & Osgood, D. W. (2008). Linkages between parents' differential treatment, youth depressive symptoms, and sibling relationships. *Journal of Marriage and Family, 70*(2), 480–494.

Shaver, P. R., & Mikulincer, M. (2002). Attachment-related psychodynamics. *Attachment and Human Development, 4*, 133–161.

Slomkowski, C., Rende, R., Conger, K. J., Simons, R. L., & Conger, R. D. (2001). Sisters, brothers, and delinquency: Evaluating social influence during early and middle adolescence. *Child Development, 72*(1), 271–283.

Stewart, R. B. (1983). Sibling attachment relationships: Child-infant interactions in the strange situation. *Developmental Psychology, 19*, 192–199.

Stocker, C., Dunn, J., & Plomin, R. (1989). Sibling relationships: Links with child temperament, maternal behavior, and family structure. *Child Development, 60*, 715–727.

Sturaro, C., Denissen, J. J., van Aken, M. A., & Asendorpf, J. B. (2008). Person-environment transactions during emerging adulthood. *European Psychologist, 13*(1), 1–11.

Sulloway, F. J. (1996). *Born to rebel: Birth order, family dynamics, and creative lives.* New York: Pantheon Books.

Sulloway, F. J. (2000). 'Born to Rebel' and its critics. *Politics and the Life Sciences, 19*(2), 181–202.

Sulloway, F. J. (2007). Birth order and sibling competition. In R. Dunbar & L. Barrett (Eds.), *The Oxford handbook of evolutionary psychology* (pp. 297–311). Oxford: Oxford University Press.

Sulloway, F. J. (2010). Why siblings are like Darwin's finches: Birth order, sibling competition, and adaptive divergence within the family. In D. M. Buss & P. H. Hawley (Eds.), *The evolution of personality and individual differences* (pp. 86–119). New York: Oxford University Press. doi:10.1093/acprof:oso/9780195372090.003.0004

Suls, J., Martin, R., & Wheeler, L. (2002). Social comparison: Why, with whom, and with what effect? *Current Directions in Psychological Science, 11*(5), 159–163.

Teti, D. M., & Ablard, K. E. (1989). Security of attachment and infant-sibling relationships: A laboratory study. *Child Development, 60*(6), 1519–1528.

Thibaut, J. W., & Kelley, H. H. (1959). *The social psychology of groups.* Oxford: John Wiley & Sons.

Tinbergen, N. (1951). *The study of instinct.* New York: Oxford University Press.

Volling, B. L. (1997). The family correlates of maternal and paternal perceptions of differential treatment in early childhood. *Family Relations, 46,* 227–236.

Volling, B. L. (2001). Early attachment relationships as predictors of preschool children's emotion regulation with a distressed sibling. *Early Education and Development, 12,* 185–207.

Volling, B. L., & Belsky, J. (1992). The contribution of mother-child and father-child relationships to the quality of sibling interaction: A longitudinal study. *Child Development, 63,* 1209–1222.

Von Bertalanffy, L. (1950). An outline of general system theory. *British Journal for the Philosophy of Science, 111,* 23–29.

Von Bertalanffy, L., Hempel, C. G., Bass, R. E., & Jonas, H. (1951). General systems theory: a new approach to unity of science. *Human Biology, 23*(4), 302–361.

Voorpostel, M., & Blieszner, R. (2008). Intergenerational solidarity and support between adult siblings. *Journal of Marriage and Family, 70*(1), 157–167.

Walster, E., Walster, G. W., & Berscheid, E. (1978). *Equity: Theory and research.* Boston: Allyn & Bacon.

Watts, R. E. (2003). Adlerian therapy as a relational constructivist approach. *The Family Journal, 11*(2), 139–147.

Weiner, B. (1979). A theory of motivation for some classroom experiences. *Journal of Educational Psychology, 71*(1), 3–25.

Weisner, T. S. (1993). Overview: Sibling similarity and difference in different cultures. In C. Nuckolls (Ed.), *Siblings in South Asia: Brothers and sisters in cultural context* (pp. 1–17). New York: Guilford Press.

White, L. (2001). Sibling relationships over the life course: A panel analysis. *Journal of Marriage and Family, 63*(2), 555–568.

Whiteman, S. D., Becerra, J. M., & Killoren, S. E. (2009). Mechanisms of sibling socialization in normative family development. *New Directions for Child and Adolescent Development, 126,* 29–43.

Whiteman, S. D., McHale, S. M., & Soli, A. (2011). Theoretical perspectives on sibling relationships. *Journal of Family Theory & Review, 3*(2), 124–139.

Wolter, S. C. (2003). *Sibling rivalry: A six country comparison* (IZA Discussion Paper Series, No. 734). Bonn, Germany: Institute for the Study of Labor (IZA).

Wong, T. M., Branje, S. J., VanderValk, I. E., Hawk, S. T., & Meeus, W. H. (2010). The role of siblings in identity development in adolescence and emerging adulthood. *Journal of Adolescence, 33*(5), 673–682.

Zlatev, J. (2008). The co-evolution of intersubjectivity and bodily mimesis. In J. Zlatev, T. Racine, C. Sinha, & E. Itkonen (Eds.), *The shared mind: Perspectives on intersubjectivity* (pp. 215–244). Amsterdam: John Benjamin.

Zlatev, J., Racine, T., Sinha, C., & Itkonen, E. (2008). *The shared mind: Perspectives on intersubjectivity.* Amsterdam: John Benjamin.

2

ADOLESCENT SIBLINGS AND WITHIN-FAMILY STUDY

Introduction

In this chapter, we survey the literature concerning adolescent siblings and within-family variation to open the conversation about the direct and indirect effects of family systems, parenting practices, and sibling dynamics within families. The nature of the family unit as a whole, the meaning of various subsystems, and their associated influences are ultimately highly informative in our comprehension of adolescent sibling relations. We offer a succinct overview of a within-family unit study, but refer to in-depth explication of relevant statistical techniques in Chapter 6 on methodology in sibling study.

The extant sibling literature typically inspects only the childhood sibling relationship or siblings in older age (Cicirelli, 1995, Derkman, Engels, Kuntsche, van
der Vorst, & Scholte, 2011). This paucity of adolescent inquiry has recently been
attended to by the likes of Scharf, Shulman, and Avigad-Spitz (2005) and extensive
work by McHale and colleagues (e.g. McHale, Kim, & Whiteman, 2006; McHale,
Updegraff, & Whiteman, 2012). A dearth of within-family studies specifically
plagues the systematic inquiry of the significance of brothers and sisters. Within-
family designs – in which two or more children from the same family are compared –
represent the sole way researchers can disentangle differential effects between siblings
(Whiteman, McHale, & Soli, 2011). Differences between siblings in the same family may result in differences in the rearing strategies, interaction styles, and overall
treatment of children, for instance, in the gender-based differential treatment of sons
and daughters (Pike & Kretschmer, 2009). As such, investigation of just how siblings'
parents interact in a particular family system is telling for both individual developmental outcomes and social relationships (Feinberg, Solmeyer, & McHale, 2012). In
fact, knowledge of subsystem interrelations and communication is ultimately necessary for any complete understanding of family relationships and functioning.

Not to discount the value of family systems readings, in this contribution we
privilege the sibling relationship, an all too often overlooked aspect of research,
whether viewed from familial or developmental subdisciplines (Edwards, Hadfield,
Lucey, & Mauthner, 2006). We do this by respecting the intersubjectivities and
multiple truths unique to each individual in the relational constellation (e.g. sister-
brother subsystem), while acknowledging that we expect significant overlap
between the whole family system, specific subsystem, and individual development
dynamics (Edwards, Hadfield, & Mauthner, 2005).

State of the research

Existing scholarship on sibling relationships has focused on their meaning as fundamental social partners within the larger network of relations (Buhrmester & Furman,
1990), on linkages to individual development (reviewed by Smetana, Campione-
Barr, & Metzger, 2006; Yeh & Lempers, 2004), as well as specific relationship patterns such as conflict (Raffaelli, 1997; Updegraff, Thayer, Whiteman, Denning &
McHale, 2005) and support (Branje, Van Lieshout, Van Aken & Haselager, 2004).
We know that conflict and aggression between siblings is common in multiple
contexts, but is certainly not the most prevalent interaction pattern (Newman,
1994), and certain researchers question claims of the long-held generalizability of
sibling rivalry (Edwards et al., 2006).

Siblings are furthermore key partners in the negotiation of relational dimensions like intimacy and companionship (Buhrmester & Fuhrman, 1990; Fuhrman
& Buhrmester, 1985), wielding direct influence on one another's development.
During early and middle childhood in particular, they enhance the development of
prosocial development (Dunn & Munn, 1986) and may act as confidants and sup-
porters (e.g. Jenkins, 1992). Within-family systems study shows that while siblings

can have moderately similar relational and attachment profiles, dissimilarity is surprisingly common (e.g. Van IJzendoorn *et al.*, 2000). As we will discuss, unique experience, meaning, that which is non-shared, is believed to account for large variations between siblings (e.g. Daniels, 1986; Plomin, 1994; Plomin & Daniels, 1987; Rowe, 1994). This has led to a concentration of empirical work to identify the ways in which siblings bear a resemblance to and, conversely, diverge from one another (e.g. Kretschmer & Pike, 2010).

The study of individual development should not be undertaken in isolation: all development occurs within variable environments, and the family system and composite relational subsystems should be examined with respect to the functioning of their components, their contingencies, and their linkages (Bukowski & Lisboa, 2007). It is in everyday social interaction – played out in the 'life space' where development occurs (Lewin, 1939) – that siblings directly engage one another and are engaged with other forces such as parents' economic hardships or expectations of an older sibling's new partner.

The family system depicts a salient context of particular importance for the adolescent's development (e.g. Rohan & Zanna, 1996; Younnis & Smollar, 1985). As Bukowski and Lisboa (2007) assert, it may be useful to view the context of development as residing in relationships themselves, as opposed to the traditional notion of relationships as a subclass of the environments in which children function (e.g. Kerr, Stattin, & Kiesner, 2007), an idea that stresses the social aspect in maturation. Such a perspective assists in filling the lacuna in knowledge of where exactly the person–environment interaction begins and ends (Lewin, 1939; Bukowski & Lisboa, 2007). It is with this that we begin our look at the sibling relationship within the family as one particular environment that affords significant relationship experiences for developing adolescents.

Within-family study

By studying multiple children within the same family, in a special form of sibling research methodology, developmental scientists gain the ability to identify the shared and non-shared family effects tied to sibling differentiation and sibling similarity (Pike & Kretschmer, 2009). Through statistical procedures like multilevel modelling, the separate influences of these effects can be represented and can thus elucidate links between family dynamics and individual children's behaviour. Unfortunately, most of the empirical work to date has consisted of investigations of families using only one child per family. The usefulness of this type of knowledge drawn from between-family groups is questionable insofar as variation in each family is not accounted for, although this source can be equally as important (e.g. Reiss, Neiderhiser, Hetherington, & Plomin, 2000) if not more so (Jenkins, Rasbash, Leckie, Gass, & Dunn, 2012). Vital to extending family research on the broader scale and sibling research in specific, studying siblings within the same family unit permits us to locate the source of origin of divergence and convergence by way of comparing and contrasting between- and within-family effects.

Exactly how can brothers and sisters reared under the same in the same household further our knowledge of family studies? The strength of sibling study designs lies in the ability for researchers to detect different children's contributions to within-family dynamics, enabling the comparison of each child's unique effects on the same parent (e.g. McGuire, Neiderhiser, Reiss, Hetherington, & Plomin, 1994). Behavioural geneticists contend that parenting operates according to a child-specific nature as opposed to a family-as-a-whole basis (Pike & Plomin, 1997). In end effect, parent–child interactions are thought to lead to disparate, child-specific trajectories of development, elicited in part by the children themselves – though this has been debated in the face of preceding claims of general family-wide effects such as authoritarian parenting style (Pike & Plomin, 1997; Pike, 2012a, 2012b).

The view of child-specific influence as contentious is based on the traditional socialization research which props up the notion of socialization from external agents (e.g. parents, teachers) through more top-down processes (Kuczynski & Hildebrandt, 1997; Kuczynski, Marshall, & Schell, 1997; Kuczynski & Parkin, 2007). Children's effects on parents and bidirectional influences are targeted to a much lesser degree versus the dominant work on parental influence and child outcomes (Pike & Kretschmer, 2009). Abundant literature sourced from cross-sectional and longitudinal research alike displays the wide and varied influence of parenting and children's outcomes (see Parke & Buriel, 2006). That notwithstanding, conceptualizing and studying children as active agents or co-constructors in their own socialization and development require that we adopt sibling designs (i.e., Pike & Plomin, 1997) that further a research programme geared at disentangling developmental influences.

Sibling designs additionally enable us to apportion the effect of family size and individual sibling characteristics into the family system mix (e.g. Olneck, 1977). The fourth chapter of this volume covers such within-family sibling designs from a behavioural genetics view of development. For the forthcoming sections, which present issues of family systems, parenting practices, and sibling relationship dynamics, we highlight a mix of research conducted under the auspices of both behavioural genetics studies of development and sibling studies in general. The reader is encouraged to supplant these empirical examples with additional coverage of family-wide impacts on sibling dynamics – but for brevity's sake, we restrict our sampling to a few issues of particular concern.

Family systems

The family systems framework attends to the greater context in which sibling relationships develop, namely, the family unit and its related influences. Derived from systems science and general systems theory, the tenets of family systems theory hold that families and their functioning are best understood through holistic examination (e.g. Guttman, 1991; Nichols & Schwartz, 2005). Resonant with Bronfenbrenner's (1979, 1986, 1989, 1992) ecological systems theory of development, family systems theory understands families as consisting of multiple levels, ranging from dyadic arrangements like the sibling pair to triadic parents–child groupings to more distal extended family networks (Whiteman *et al.*, 2011). The boundaries of these subsystems are malleable, which make allowances from other realms of influence, for instance, parents' occupational and educational status (Hess, Ittel, & Sisler, 2014). Desirable family functioning is believed to come from the maintenance of particular boundaries, like that of the spousal subsystem and its separation from children. Under this view were a parent to confide in a child about their marital dissatisfaction, forming a coalition of sorts, potential problems could arise for the family as a whole by straining other subsystems. However, it is worth noting that these assumptions of boundary importance predicate in part on notions of attachment, which are culturally variable (Keller, 2013). Certain roles may be encouraged within one family but not in others based on a host of factors, including cultural norms, although again, significant within-family variation may be more salient than between-family difference (Pike, 2012a).

Family structuring and role allowances call attention to the open systems nature of the familial unit: families, like organisms, can be thought to adapt and adjust to exterior and internal influences (Scheithauer, Niebank, & Ittel, 2009). The ability of a family to achieve 'equilibrium' after change and the resilience of a family to stressors may indicate 'ideal functioning' for the family as a whole and thus for constituent dyads, triads, and other subsystem arrangements. We can take the case of coalition-type arrangements within a family, as evidenced in a favoured child–parent dyad, to be symptomatic of dysfunctional families. In fact, research has shown that interfamilial coalitions are connected to troublesome sibling relations, purportedly due to parents' marital difficulties or exclusionary dynamics (McHale, Crouter, McGuire, & Updegraff, 1995; Volling, 1997). Again, these data were drawn from Western contexts, in accordance with most sibling study to date. Nevertheless, the general tenets of family system study, to which we now turn, state that family climates influence particular subsystems and vice versa, and certain influences external to the family itself are able to influence the system as a whole and its parts.

Family structure

Additional work that also considers family constellation factors such as structure, birth order, age spacing, size, and gender composition demonstrates differential outcomes for children. Siblings can exert indirect influence on each other in this way. Exemplary research in this area includes the finding that firstborn children often display the lowest levels of behavioural problems (Taanila, Ebeling, Kotimaa, Moilanen, & Järvelin, 2004), although for the eldest the initial impact of a new family addition may increase aggression, dependency, anxiety, and withdrawal (Dunn, 2006). Eldest children may also benefit from at least a 2-year gap between siblings (Buckles & Munnich, 2012), and the negative impact of not being firstborn can be mitigated with an approximate 3-year spacing, although this association may be confounded by maternal and socio-economic characteristics (Conde-Agudelo, Rosas-Bermúdez, & Kafury-Goeta, 2006).

Another family characteristic, sibship size, may exact a greater influence on individuals' academic achievement than birth order, once age, socio-economic background, religion, community size, and family size are accounted for (Blake, 1981). Likewise, only children share some of the cognitive advantages of firstborns (Maughan, 2011). Larger sibships might additionally link up with behavioural adjustment problems (Maughan, 2011), although other investigations suggest that this relationship disappears once social disadvantage is factored into account (Taanila et al., 2004). The same investigation additionally determined that larger families might be a protective factor for boys, and girls from single-parent families have a higher risk of emotional problems, though the gender dynamics here are not yet clear, and require further inquiry.

One of the foundations for this group of findings includes Downey's (2001) resource dilution hypothesis of differential parental treatment among siblings. Here parental resources such as personal attention, cultural objects, and money are seen as finite: each additional child spreads the demand for resources and so drives individuation processes as they fight for a piece of the parental pie. While the majority of parents do in fact display differential treatment of their children (Atzaba-Poria & Pike, 2008), it is generally tied to negative outcomes for both children and adolescents (e.g. Browne & Jenkins, 2012; Buist, Deković, & Prinzie, 2012; Coldwell, Pike, & Dunn, 2008). As siblings serve as prime figures for social comparison, perceptions of differential treatment impact self-esteem and sibling relationship dynamics (Boyle et al., 2004). Still, some researchers claim that this parental differentiation is a necessary condition for responsive parenting (Kowal & Kramer, 1997) based on child-specific attributes.

Further support from the resource dilution strand of work includes the relationship to economic resources also evident in the case of better academic performance for firstborns and only children (Case, Lin, & McLanahan, 2001; Nuttall, Nuttall, Polit, & Hunter, 1976; Travis & Kohli, 1995), lesser parental investment for step-children (Biblarz & Raftery, 1999; Case, Lin, & McLanahan, 2000; Case et al., 2001), and disruptive family events (Wu, 1996). At the same time, mothers who are depressed are not as attentive or sensitive to their children, and these negative effects are more pronounced among older children (Beardslee, 1998). It is highly likely that family dynamics vary systematically across family subsystem and structure such that, for instance, some step-parents do not feel they have the authority to discipline a step-child (Biblarz & Raftery, 1999; Sandefur & Wells, 1999). This is again important to bear in mind when considering wider influences and their interactive effects with individual sibling outcomes and bidirectional relationships.

Subsystem interactions: Parental and sibling relationships

On closer examination of the sibling subsystem and its associations, parental behaviour plays a sizable role in developmental and relationship outcomes (e.g. Meunier et al., 2011; Meunier, Wade, & Jenkins, 2012; Steinberg & Morris, 2001; Steinberg & Silk, 2002). Parental treatment and sibling relationships have been found to be significant sources of support in adolescence (e.g. Blyth, Hill, & Smith Thiel, 1982) with both tied to developing teens' well-being, social development, and self-esteem (e.g. Kim, McHale, Crouter, & Osgood, 2007; Levitt, GuacciFranco, & Levitt, 1993; Yeh & Lempers, 2004). Moreover, the quality of inter- and intra-subsystem interactions, specifically, those within parental or sibling subsystems and from parents to children and from children to parents, are closely interconnected (e.g. Brody, Stoneman, & McCoy, 1994; Oliva & Arranz, 2005). These linkages suggest reciprocal effects, whereby sibling relationships affect other subsystems just as other subsystems hold particular weight for siblings (e.g. Kim, McHale, Wayne Osgood, & Crouter, 2006; Yu & Gamble, 2008).

One can assume a number of theoretical perspectives in the assessment of family relations: the congruence hypothesis indicates a spillover effect from one relationship to the next, or conversely, the compensation hypothesis denotes the compensation of one particular relationship for another (e.g. McGuire, McHale, & Updegraff, 1996; Noller, 2005). This follows family systems theory which proposes families consist of interrelated subsystems that reciprocally influence one another (e.g. Epstein & Bishop, 1981; Whitchurch & Constantine, 1993), such that there are transactional loops between members and bidirectional relationships between parental behaviour and sibling relationship quality. This effect can be seen not only within coupled parents but also in single-parent households. Larson and Gillman (1999) investigated in a diverse sample the transmission of negative emotions like anxiety, stress, and sadness from single mothers to their adolescent children. The research generally supported the notion that family process variables like parenting style and mothers' time spent alone more accurately predicted the flow of mothers' negative emotions to adolescents rather than family structural factors like status or income, which regulated adjustment of individual family members.

Most research aligns with congruence theory and its positive associations between sibling and parent–child relationships (see Derkman et al., 2011). Attachment perspectives see children as forming internal working models of relationships based on their early parent–child bond experiences, that then guide and form the foundation of all other social relationships, including those with siblings (e.g. Ainsworth, Blehar, Waters, & Wall, 1978; Anders & Tucker, 2000; Bowlby, 1969; Kobak & Sceery, 1988). Additionally, social learning theory states that parents can serve as role models, modelling and shaping behaviour in line with key figure's own behaviour and attitudes (Bandura, 1977). Each child's own personal characteristics likely influence both their interactions with siblings and parents, leading to relationship concordance patterns (Brody et al., 1994; Pike & Kretschmer, 2009; Stoneman & Brody, 1993).

On the other hand, a few cross-sectional, as well as qualitative sibling and family, studies suggest that compensatory patterns of relationships may be particularly evident for disharmonious, conflict-ridden families, and that one positive relationship with a parent may offset negative ones with a sibling and vice versa (e.g. Abbey & Dallos, 2004; Jenkins, 1992; Voorpostel & Blieszner, 2008).

A longitudinal inquiry found maternal warmth to positively co-vary with sibling intimacy, whereas fathers' marital love was negatively linked to sibling intimacy, implicating compensation effects (Kim et al., 2006). Interestingly, father–child conflict co-varied positively with sibling conflict across time, depicting the complex multifaceted nature of family constellation dynamics. We investigate sibling conflict and rivalry in forthcoming sections.

The marital relationship is noted as being especially significant for (adolescent) siblings' relationships. Volatile relationships between spouses typically link up to not only more hostile parent–child exchanges, but also more negative sibling relationships, although in the face of troubled marital relationships some siblings depend on one another for support (Abbey & Dallos, 2004; Jenkins, 1992; Sheehan, Darlington, Noller, & Feeney, 2004). Another body of findings considers the parent–child attachment as a mediator in the connection between parental and sibling relationship characteristics (e.g. Brody et al., 1994; Dunn, Deater-Deckard, Pickering, & Golding, 1999; Solmeyer, McHale, & Crouter, 2014; Stocker & Youngblade, 1999; Whiteman et al., 2011). Edwards and colleagues (2006), however, challenge the assumption that intense sibling bonds operate merely as compensatory forms of attachment, as most research has failed to investigate the intrinsic value of sibling relationships in and of themselves.

Sensitive periods for change

Family systems theory makes claim to sensitive periods or times of transition during which relationships are especially subject to change (Whiteman et al., 2011). Conger and Little (2010) underscore the place of siblings in the transition to different life phases. If one family member faces a challenge, then all other subsystems and the family unit as a whole must likewise shift to make allowances for changes in that one individual's functioning. For instance, in the case of one sibling moving from elementary school to high school, difficulties in adjusting may not only prove a challenge for the family at present but may be a harbinger for younger siblings' difficulties with their own transitions. Conversely, an older sibling who models an adaptive switch may act as a bulwark and a source of support for younger siblings (Conger, Bryant, & Brennom, 2004; Cox, 2010).

The importance of sensitive periods is backed by evidence of sibling relationship change during divorce (Abbey & Dallos, 2004; Sheehan et al., 2004) and at the dynamic and formative pre-adolescent juncture between childhood and the teen years (Brody et al., 1994; Derkman, 2011; Kim et al., 2006). Moreover, researchers have found that students entering adolescence displayed a significant increase in attachment bonds with their siblings, presumably due to a sibling's entry into secondary school and the resulting new shared environment (Buist, Deković, Meeus, & van Aken, 2002). The authors of this study further conjectured that the increasing peer-like and voluntary nature of sibling relationships at this sensitive period promoted enhanced intimacy. The sibling relationship and its quality change not only during certain sensitive periods, but appears to continue to shift during the adolescent years (Conger et al., 2004), though the specific contingencies are not yet soundly grasped.

Relationship quality

The closeness in age of siblings appears to influence the relationship quality. Those who have a sibling around the same age are, for example, more likely to make the transition from elementary to high school together, or start dating at the same time, and so have the opportunity to engage in shared knowledge and experiences. Conversely, these similar circumstances can exacerbate social comparison processes when the sibling bond is marked by rivalry and conflict (Conger & Little, 2010). Here, it is important to take note of the individual perceptions of relationship quality among siblings in adolescence and later life stages, as they often vary (Riggio, 2006).

General trends indicate high sibling relationship quality during late childhood (approximately 10 years old) with a decline in early adolescence (ages 10–15), and then with subsequent upswings in quality from age 15 onwards (e.g. Cicirelli, 1995; McHale et al., 2006). More specifically, changes in sibling relationships throughout the course of adolescence appear to be dependent upon the specific gender and birth order of the sibling subsystem (Buhrmester & Furman, 1990; Cicirelli, 1995; Cole & Kerns, 2001; Kim et al., 2006). Younger siblings seem to benefit more than older siblings and maintain higher levels of intimacy with their more mature counterparts (Buhrmester, 1992; Tucker, Barber, & Eccles, 1997). Reflecting back on social learning theory and attachment tenets, older, warm, and accepting individuals perceived as relatively similar are more likely to serve both as role models and as attachment figures as seen in younger sibling admiration and mutual modelling processes (Whiteman, Jensen, & Maggs, 2014).

Warmth and conflict

Childhood sibling studies generally detect two behavioural dimensions of opposite valence: one dimension of positive quality, which captures warmth and affection, and a negative dimension marked by hostility or conflict (e.g. Brody, Stoneman, & Burke, 1987; Furman & Buhrmester, 1985). Conger et al.'s (2004) model of changing sibling relationships that examined adolescent siblings and their families included these behavioural dimensions, as they give indication of reciprocal influence and potential for change. The presence of warmth and the absence of hostility both contribute to optimal family relations within the whole family and bode well for its constituent relationships (e.g. Kim et al., 2006; Stocker, 1994; Yu & Gamble, 2008). For instance, children who experience low levels of warmth in mother *and* sibling ties generally have considerably greater difficulties with loneliness, behaviour problems, and self-worth (Stocker, 1994). Furthermore, longitudinal work supports the appreciation of differential effects over time for brother–sister dyads (Kim *et al.*, 2006).

The genders of siblings also impact their relationship in various ways such as life transition timing, sequencing, and quality (Bedford, Volling, & Avioli, 2000; Conley, 2004); these and other sibling effects fluctuate based on gendered socio-cultural expectations (e.g. Cauce & Domenech-Rodriguez, 2002; McHale, Updegraff, Shanahan, Crouter, & Killoren, 2005). For instance, in the case of Mexican-American and African-American families, sisters might be enlisted as caregivers for siblings as well as nieces and nephews, which leads to lowered developmental outcomes such as worse grades, yet social benefits like increased life satisfaction (East, 1998; East & Khoo, 2005; East, Weisner, & Reyes, 2006). On top of that, these sister caregivers experienced warmer sibling bonds and were more mature, though, in the presence of conflictual sibling relations, the younger sibling was at a greater risk of a host of both independent positive and negative outcomes. For instance, when care was seen as coerced (arguments between sisters, anger about providing care), sisters were more positive in their school orientation, less likely to drop out and become pregnant in their teenage years, yet were less happy and optimistic about their futures (East *et al.*, 2006). Collectively, this literature emphasizes the varied influence of sibling relationship dynamics on individual-level and gendered outcomes.

Other research provides evidence that based on absolute levels, same-sex sibling pairs report higher levels of intimacy and less hostility than opposite-sex pairs (Buhrmester & Furman, 1990; Pepler, Abramovitch, & Corter, 1981). Warmth was seen to decrease in mixed-sex dyads from middle childhood through early adolescence, with an increase in mid-adolescence, and was thought to increase following a presumed greater investment in friendships and romantic relationships in sister–brother dyads (Kim *et al.*, 2006). Mixed-sex dyads might well share advice and support about romantic relationships, although this supposition discounts same-sex attraction. Interestingly, both same- and mixed-sex dyads exhibited decreased conflict throughout adolescence. The authors postulated that as peers and romantic relationships become more salient and important to the early adolescent, sibling relationships adjust accordingly and so decline in warmth during these transitional years. As teens mature and start to invest more time and attention to significant others, scaffolding alternate social bonds, warmth may then increase with siblings' shared environments and developmental challenges (e.g. Derkman *et al.*, 2011).

While conflict is thought to be an intrinsic part of the sibling bond, particularly during early adolescence when issues of autonomy and individuation are at the fore (Erikson, 1968; Kroger, 2004; Marcia, 1980; Raffaelli, 1997), these levels are likely to shift over time. Conflict levels and related problem behaviours may increase (e.g. Ensor, Marks, Jacobs, & Hughes, 2010; Low, Snyder, & Shortt, 2012) or, alternately, decrease over the course of adolescence and may continue to do so into young adulthood depending on features of the relationship (Scharf *et al.*, 2005). As siblings transition to young adulthood from adolescence, their perception of the relationship may likewise become more balanced and mature and rest less on parental involvement and relationship characteristics (Scharf *et al.*, 2005).

Parental influence

Sibling relationship quality is influenced by family structure as well as family inter-action patterns like parenting behaviours (Conger & Conger, 1996; Furman, 1995; McHale, & Crouter, 1996). Some parents attempt to shape sibling interactions through direct means, but they also exert influence by serving as models for children and adolescents. Moreover, the parent–child relationship appears to mediate some of the links between spousal and sibling relationship qualities (e.g. Brody *et al.*, 1994; Noller, Feeney, Sheehan, & Peterson, 2000; Stocker & Youngblade, 1999). When we consider social learning and observation, positive, warm communicative couples can act as salient examples of prosocial relations for their children or, on the other hand, negative, cold couples with communication difficulties may promote more conflicted and antagonistic parent–child as well as sibling interactions (Bandura, 1977).

However, in the face of troubled marital relations, siblings can act as strong support networks (Jenkins, 1992), though divorce and remarriage can still have enduring effects for siblings (Hetherington, 1988). Adolescent siblings who have gone through divorce or parental separation report more emotionally intense relationships with higher levels of warmth and hostility as compared to children who have not (Sheehan *et al.*, 2004). In another examination of young people's perceptions of divorce and its impact on sibling relationships, Abbey and Dallos (2004) found again that siblings proffered emotional support and intimacy at times of parental emotional absence, as well as an overall increased closeness with their sibling. Additional family stressors such as financial difficulties can also impact on sibling bonds (Conger, Stocker, & McGuire, 2009). Conger and Little (2010) highlight that this line of work stresses 'potential reciprocal effects between families' socio-emotional climate and sibling relationship quality' (p. 90).

Parents may foster prosocial interaction qualities, such as the ability to see others' perspectives or by modelling effective conflict resolution within their own relationships; they may also act as a mediator, for example, in sibling spats over computer time allowance (Whiteman *et al.*, 2011; Perlman & Ross, 1997). In contrast to the positive effects of parents' interventional efforts in resolving childhood sibling conflict (e.g. Siddiqui & Ross, 2004; Tiedemann & Johnston, 1992), this approach is not as successful in adolescence (e.g. McHale, Updegraff, Tucker, & Crouter, 2000). Feasibly, those sibling pairs where frequent intervention is still necessary into adolescence might be characteristically more troubled than those where siblings get more or less along and do not demand constant regulatory attention (Whiteman *et al.*, 2011).

Kim *et al.* (2006) found that sibling conflict in childhood and adolescence was linked to both father–child and mother–child conflict, and sibling intimacy and conflict were linked more closely to fathers' than mothers' marital evaluations.

This is particularly interesting to note because foregoing research generally under-represents the contribution of fathers to children's development, though this is changing (e.g. S. N. Davis & Wills, 2010; Lamb, 2004). Further investigation of these within-family dynamics and the mechanisms by which they operate is needed to progress our understanding of the role of individual family members in conflict within the family system.

Overall, cohesion and harmony between adolescents and parents seem to be associated with more positive sibling affiliations (Jodi, Bridges, Kim, Mitchell, & Chan, 1999). On the other hand, aggressiveness towards siblings and peers appears to be tied to perceived parental rejection (MacKinnon-Lewis, Starnes, Volling, & Johnson, 1997), while perceived unjust parental treatment among children is linked to conflict between siblings (Brody *et al.*, 1987), sibling ill-health (Browne & Jenkins, 2012), as well as less close sibling relationships (Sutton, 1996). Siblings may act as moderator between differential parental treatment and externalizing problem behaviours whereby the sibling relationship can either exacerbate negative parental effects or act as a buffer (Scholte, Engels, de Kemp, Harakeh, & Overbeek, 2007). Furthermore, a recent meta-analysis of children and adolescents detected that decreased conflict in the sibling relationship and more warmth and lower levels of differential treatment on the part of parents all tied significantly to fewer internalizing and externalizing problem behaviours; the effect size was the largest for the last two influences (Buist *et al.*, 2012). Various characteristics of the sibling constellation moderated these effect sizes, with stronger effects for brother pairs, for smaller age gaps between siblings, and for children versus adolescents. The researchers underlined the importance of considering both sibling relationships in combination with parental and environmental influences in the development of psychopathology.

In tandem with differential parental treatment, parent–child relationship problems or family dysfunction are also pivotal factors in the aetiology of adolescent depression, a prime example of internalizing problems. A host of studies have examined depression-related variables including mother–child and father–child relationships, parents' spousal relationship, and sibling relationships (e.g. Puig-Antich *et al.*, 1993). Whereas warm, open, and caring parents instil confidence, mastery, and high self-esteem, and parental acceptance is related to internal or emotional adjustment variables (e.g. Steinberg & Morris, 2001; Steinberg & Silk, 2002), over-bearing parents seem to be associated with less mastery and greater levels of depression (Avison & McAlpine, 1992). Interestingly, new research on the part of Meunier and colleagues (2012) attempted to address potential links between parental differential treatment, children's externalizing behaviour, and sibling relations, in conjunction with mediating effects of children's perceptions of favouritism, personality, and parents' self-efficacy. Parental differential treatment was associated with externalizing behaviour as well as sibling levels of affection, yet perception of favouritism was predictive solely of sibling hostility levels. Children's externalizing behaviour was predictive of parental differential treatment, and this correlation was mediated by parents' self-efficacy. We see here the importance of considering the characteristics of the child, their sibling relationship, as well as parental factors in the child's well-being; again, the study of within-family dynamics helps us to complete the picture of both individual outcomes and sibling relationship influences.

Antisocial behaviour and difficulties in personal adjustment are further bound up with conflictive and violent sibling relations in adolescence (Berman, 1994; Conger, Conger, & Scaramella, 1997; Wolke & Skew, 2012). Conversely, positive intersibling interactions bolster levels of personal adjustment, with siblings often imparting greater effects than parents (Seginer, 1998; Yeh, 2001), though this might vary along particular gender constellations. Females have been found to exhibit stronger sibling–personal adjustment links (Bank, Patterson, & Reid, 1996; G. Davis, 2000; Sutton, 1996), and sister–sister dyads have been shown to have more intimate and less conflictual relationships (Cole & Kerns, 2001; Furman & Buhrmester, 1992), potentially due to gender-related relationship dynamics versus structural differences, though this speculation warrants deeper study (Feinberg *et al.*, 2012; Furman & Lanthier, 2002). In a related vein, Derkman and colleagues (2011) recently found a lack of differentiation based on the gender of sibling pairs: same- and mixed-sex dyads displayed similar results for the association between sibling relationships and parental support. This analysis was limited in that bidirectional associations could not be conducted for all four gender constellations within a sibling dyad (e.g. boy–boy, girl–boy, etc.). Future research is merited to investigate possible gender and age contingencies in sibling relationships in relation to additional factors like parental behaviour.

Whiteman *et al.*'s (2011) coverage of social comparison theory lends additional insight into the processes and mechanisms involved in conflict and rivalry between siblings in adolescence. As sibling rivalry is a topic particularly over-represented in the literature, we mention it only in passing. For further inquiry, we refer the reader to the aforementioned authors' explication on implicated theories of social comparison (Festinger, 1954) and equity (Adams, 1965; Walster, Walster, & Berscheid, 1978) and how they help to explain sibling rivalry and perceptions of fairness and justice in the presence of parental differential treatment (e.g. Boll, Ferring, & Filipp, 2003; Cicirelli, 1992; Kowal, Kramer, Krull, & Crick, 2002).

Another key contribution to sibling relationship dynamics expresses a new means of conceptualizing conflict and rivalry. Kramer (2010) expounds the role of the sibling relationship in providing experiences conducive to socio-emotional and cognitive development such as conflict management skills, identity formation, social competence, and the toleration of negative emotions. Importantly, both conflict, which was previously considered as purely negative, and positive experience can bring forth development in these areas for both siblings. As Cox states, '. . . intervention programs that aim to improve sibling relationships must consider carefully what the goals in behavioural change should be and recognize that the common goal of eliminating conflict may not be an appropriate goal. Interventions to improve family relationships therefore require high-quality basic research that illuminates the developmental function of different qualities of family relationships'

(Cox, 2010, p. 95). In the following chapter, we discuss more in-depth conflict's function within the sibling relationship which may aid in driving forth personality development through individuation processes. We now illustrate one central area of individual development and its role in the sibling relationship: academics.

Academics: A key domain

When considering later individual-level outcomes, academic achievement in youth stands out as a major indicator of adult adjustment and is rated as an important area for both parents and teens alike (Dagys Pajoluk, 2013). Indeed, 'during early adolescence, a student's scholastic record can initiate a trajectory of subsequent educational opportunities and choices that can either impede or enhance ultimate socioeconomic standing' (Bouchey, Shoulberg, Jodl, & Eccles, 2010). Much scholarship has covered the micro and macro contexts in which high academic achievement is promoted, particularly the familial milieu, although the majority of extant work focuses on parental impacts (e.g. Bean, Bush, McKenry, & Wilson, 2003; Wong, 2008). Our empirical base is limited in terms of siblings and their reciprocal impacts, and we know even less of the mediating and moderating conditions under which these effects differ, for example, gender-based differences stemming from qualities found in mixed-sex dyads.

In their study of prospective relations between older siblings' support, academic engagement, and younger siblings' academic adjustment in early adolescence, Bouchey and colleagues (2010) discovered an intriguing link between older siblings' academic support and younger siblings' socialization. Older siblings may serve as beneficial role models up to a point beyond which declines in scholastic adjustment may particularly impact mixed-sibling dyads. As parental and teacher beliefs and behaviours were not concomitantly measured, it is difficult to say with certainty the processes through which such a decrease may be operating. Again, perceptions and comparisons with siblings could be exerting influence, as well as the type of context associated with greater sibling academic support, for instance, in families where parents are not able to offer assistance.

Birth order has been found to relate to academic achievement (e.g. Healey & Ellis, 2007; Paulhus, Trapnell, & Chen, 1999), as has personality (Chamorro-Premuzic & Furnham, 2003; Chowdhury & Amin, 2006). Relating personality and academic achievement to sibling and familial characteristics like birth order, age spacing, and sibship size invokes various theoretical perspectives previously attended to, such as evolutionary psychology's resource dilution hypothesis (Downey, 2001) and social-ecological theory's confluence hypothesis (Zajonc & Markus, 1975). If birth order helps shape personality and cognitive achievement alike, then one should expect to see a relationship between these two factors.

The findings in this regard are, however, equivocal. Duration of academic studies has been linked to birth order within a middle class sample (Travis & Kohli, 1995), yet Edwards and Thacker (1979) and Hauser and Sewell (1985) both detected a non-correlation between ordinal position and academic indicators in their respective investigations. In a current study of birth order effects, personality, and academic achievement enlisting a Malaysian sample, the sole resulting association was between extraversion and achievement (Ha & Tam, 2011). The authors postulated that while immediate findings appeared to contradict the previous empirics attesting to distinctive niche effects and dethroning among older siblings, this may have been due to confounding variable influence and methodological differences. Between-family design was not utilized despite a within-family framework (e.g. Healey & Ellis, 2007) being necessary in considering, for example, sibship size, effects, socio-economic status, and parental personality traits.

While academic achievement may seem to be a contained area of inquiry, its related findings may serve as a (larger) model for sibling relations, as they are exemplary of inherent multidimensionality and the distinct mechanisms that characterize them (Whiteman *et al.*, 2011). Dagys Pajoluk (2013) has helped to clarify the contingencies and interrelations among implicated variables targeted in previous research like sibling intimacy, older sibling support, sibling perception, social learning processes, individuation, and differentiation. In fact, this research found that the older sibling's academic engagement was the most significant sibling relationship factor for the younger sibling's academic outcomes. Nonetheless, interactive effects and their relative contributions as embedded in the family system must be focused upon, as should the gender-based differentials (Milevsky & Levitt, 2005; Bouchey *et al.*, 2010). For instance, exactly why receiving support from brothers but not sisters was positive for boys begs further examination from a family systems perspective (Milevsky & Levitt, 2005). Again, within-family research designs are critical to these ends, as they enable multilevel analysis that allows researchers to unpick the comparative influence of different family members and family characteristics like sibship size (e.g. Jenkins *et al.*, 2012).

Some final remarks and suggestions

In summary, sibling relationships are multifaceted, as are the different dynamics and direct and indirect influences that affect various family members within the family system. We have seen evidence of the change in sibling relationships across time, as well as variance by gender, birth order, and ethnicity, among other factors. Insight into the differential experiences, meanings, and processes of individual family members can be gleaned from a family systems approach that investigates the bidirectional relations between specific subsystems such as the marital couple, the parent–child dyad, and the sibling dyad (Cox & Paley, 1997; Minuchin, 1985). Indeed, preliminary results speak to the differential effects among siblings as in varied reports of sibling conflict and peer experiences (Greer, Campione-Barr, Debrown, & Maupin, 2014). Moreover, we have set out theories and evidence from lesser-known frameworks in sibling study, such as postmodernist and feminist perspectives that challenge traditional accounts of sibling relationship features of rivalry and conflict.

The study of academic achievement and adjustment within a family is a prime display of the interaction of biological influences, for example, richer uterine environment and resource investment for firstborns, familial and environmental influences, as well as social influences like those of gender-differentials, social learning effects, and direct social support from siblings. Unpicking the relative influence of genetics and the social environment among siblings within their families is made possible via tools apparent in behavioural genetics study that we present in Chapter 4.

As no one theoretical perspective can attempt to cover the complexity that characterizes the family unit and its interrelated components, prospective research is well advised to incorporate multiple methods (e.g. discourse analysis and behavioural genetics) and theory in sibling study. Moreover, sibling researchers should compare only children, particularly with the trend towards more single-child households especially in North America and Western Europe and among certain ethnic groups. The field would gain strength if single-children households and diverse familial arrangements were included for comparisons; data collection of sibling pairs usually focuses on one target child and the sibling he or she feels closest to or is closest in age, although sibling relationship patterns might be quite different in families with three or more children (e.g. Whiteman *et al.*, 2011). Forthcoming sibling research would do well to compare different sibling dyads across time, combined with within-family methodological designs.

Alongside longitudinal investigations of within-family dynamics, the future study of brothers and sisters in adolescence ought to privilege developing sibling's perspectives, giving credence to the differential meanings and experiences of individuals. The development of a comprehensive model whereby the correlates and processes involved in siblinghood in adolescence could be more readily traced and elucidated would complement these diverse perspectives. We pose future researchers such a task in the final chapter of this volume.

References

Abbey, C., & Dallos, R. (2004). The experience of the impact of divorce on sibling relationships: A qualitative study. *Clinical Child Psychology and Psychiatry, 9*(2), 241–259.

Adams, J. S. (1965). Inequity in social exchange. *Advances in Experimental Social Psychology, 2,* 267–299.

Ainsworth, M. D., Blehar, M. C., Waters, E., & Wall, S. (1978). *Patterns of attachment: A psychological study of the strange situation.* Hillsdale, NJ: Lawrence Erlbaum Associates.

Anders, S. L., & Tucker, J. S. (2000). Adult attachment style, interpersonal communication competence, and social support. *Personal Relationships, 7*(4), 379–389.

Atzaba-Poria, N., & Pike, A. (2008). Correlates of parental differential treatment: Parental and contextual factors during middle childhood. *Child Development, 79*(1), 217–232.

Avison, W. R., & McAlpine, D. D. (1992). Gender differences in symptoms of depression among adolescents. *Journal of Health and Social Behavior, 33*(2), 77–96.

Bandura, A. (1977). *Social learning theory.* Englewood Cliffs, NJ: Prentice Hall.

Bank, L., Patterson, G., & Reid, J. (1996). Negative sibling interaction patterns as predictors of later adjustment problems in adolescent and young males. In G. H. Brody (Ed.), *Sibling relationships: Their causes and consequences* (pp. 197–229). Norwood, NJ: Ablex.

Bean, R. A., Bush, K. R., McKenry, P. C., & Wilson, S. M. (2003). The impact of parental support, behavioral control, and psychological control on the academic achievement and self-esteem of African American and European American adolescents. *Journal of Adolescent Research, 18*, 523–541.

Beardslee, W. R. (1998). Children of affectively ill parents: A review of the past 10 years. *Journal of the American Academy of Child & Adolescent Psychiatry, 37*, 1134–1141.

Bedford, V. H., Volling, B. L., & Avioli, P. S. (2000). Positive consequences of sibling conflict in childhood and adulthood. *International Journal of Aging & Human Development, 51*, 53–69.

Berman, S. (1994). Perceived conflict and violence in childhood sibling relationships and later emotional adjustment. *Journal of Family Psychology, 8*, 85–97.

Biblarz, T. J., & Raftery, A. E. (1999). Family structure, educational attainment, and socioeconomic success: Rethinking the 'pathology of matriarchy'. *American Journal of Sociology, 105*, 321–365.

Blake, J. (1981). Family size and quality of children. *Demography, 18*, 421–442.

Blyth, D. A., Hill, J. P., & Smith Thiel, K. (1982). Early adolescents' significant others: Grade and gender differences in perceived relationships with familial and nonfamilial adults and young people. *Journal of Youth and Adolescence, 11*, 425–450.

Boll, T., Ferring, D., & Filipp, S. H. (2003). Perceived parental differential treatment in middle adulthood: Curvilinear relations with individuals' experienced relationship quality to sibling and parents. *Journal of Family Psychology, 17*, 472–487.

Bouchey, H. A., Shoulberg, E. K., Jodl, K. M., & Eccles, J. S. (2010). Longitudinal links between older sibling features and younger siblings' academic adjustment during early adolescence. *Journal of Educational Psychology, 102*, 197–211.

Bowlby, J. (1969). *Attachment and loss: Attachment* (Vol. 1). New York: Basic Books.

Boyle, M. H., Jenkins, J. M., Georgiades, K., Cairney, J., Duku, E., & Racine, Y. (2004). Differential-maternal parenting behavior: Estimating within- and between-family effects on children. *Child Development, 75*, 1457–1476.

Branje, S. J., Van Lieshout, C. F., Van Aken, M. A., & Haselager, G. J. (2004). Perceived support in sibling relationships and adolescent adjustment. *Journal of Child Psychology and Psychiatry, 45*(8), 1385–1396.

Brody, G. H., Stoneman, Z., & Burke, M. (1987). Child temperaments, maternal differential behavior, and sibling relationships. *Developmental Psychology, 23*(3), 354–362.

Brody, G. H., Stoneman, Z., & McCoy, J. K. (1994). Contributions of family relationships and child temperaments to longitudinal variations in sibling relationship quality and sibling relationship styles. *Journal of Family Psychology, 8*, 274–286.

Bronfenbrenner, U. (1979). *The ecology of human development: Experiments by nature and design.* Cambridge, MA: Harvard University Press.

Bronfenbrenner, U. (1986). Ecology of the family as a context for human development: Research perspectives. *Developmental Psychology, 22*(6), 723–742.

Bronfenbrenner, U. (1989). Ecological systems theory. In R. Vasta (Ed.), *Annals of child development: Vol. 6. Theories of child development: Revised formulations and current issues* (pp. 187–249). Greenwich, CT: JAI Press.

Bronfenbrenner, U. (1992). Ecological systems theory. In R. Vasta (Ed.), *Six theories of child development: Revised formulations and current issues* (pp. 187–249). London: Jessica Kingsley.

Browne, D. T., & Jenkins, J. M. (2012). Health across early childhood and socioeconomic status: Examining the moderating effects of differential parenting. *Social Science & Medicine, 74*(10), 1622–1629.

Buckles, K. S., & Munnich, E. L. (2012). Birth spacing and sibling outcomes. *Journal of Human Resources, 47*(3), 613–642.

Buhrmester, D. (1992). The developmental courses of sibling and peer relationships. In F. Boer & J. Dunn (Eds.), *Children's sibling relationships: Developmental and clinical issues* (pp. 19–40). Hillsdale, NJ: Erlbaum.

Buhrmester, D., & Furman, W. (1990). Perceptions of sibling relationships during middle childhood and adolescence. *Child Development, 61*(5), 1387–1398.

Buist, K. L., Deković, M., Meeus, W., & van Aken, M. A. (2002). Developmental patterns in adolescent attachment to mother, father and sibling. *Journal of Youth and Adolescence, 31*(3), 167–176.

Buist, K. L., Deković, M., & Prinzie, P. (2012). Sibling relationship quality and psychopathology of children and adolescents: A meta-analysis. *Clinical Psychology Review, 33*, 97–106.

Bukowski, W., & Lisboa, C. (2007). Understanding the place of place in developmental psychology. In C. Rutger, E. Engels, & M. Kerr (Eds.), *Friends, lovers and groups: Key relationships in adolescence* (pp. 167–173). West Sussex: John Wiley & Sons.

Case, A., Lin, I.-F., & McLanahan, S. (2000). How hungry is the selfish gene? *Economic Journal, 110*, 781–804.

Case, A., Lin, I.-F., & McLanahan, S. (2001). Educational attainment of siblings in stepfamilies. *Evolution & Human Behavior, 22*(4), 269–289.

Cauce, A. M., & Domenech-Rodriguez, M. (2002). Latino families: Myths and realities. In J. M. Contreras, K. A. Kerns, & A. M. Neal-Barnett (Eds.), *Latino children and families in the United States* (pp. 5–25). Westport, CT: Praeger.

Chamorro-Premuzic, T., & Furnham, A. (2003). Personality traits and academic examination performance. *European Journal of Personality, 17*, 237–250.

Chowdhury, M. S., & Amin, M. N. (2006). Personality and students' academic achievement: Interactive effects of conscientiousness and agreeableness on students' performance in principles of economics. *Social Behaviour and Personality, 34*, 381–388.

Cicirelli, V. G. (1992). *Family caregiving: Autonomous and paternalistic decision-making.* Newbury Park, CA: Sage.

Cicirelli, V. G. (1995). *Sibling relationships across the life span.* New York: Plenum.

Coldwell, J., Pike, A., & Dunn, J. (2008). Maternal differential treatment and child adjustment: A multi-informant approach. *Social Development, 17*, 596–612.

Cole, A., & Kerns, K. A. (2001). Perceptions of sibling qualities and activities of early adolescents. *Journal of Early Adolescence, 21*, 204–227.

Conde-Agudelo, A., Rosas-Bermúdez, A., & Kafury-Goeta, A. C. (2006). Birth spacing and risk of adverse perinatal outcomes. *Journal of the American Medical Association, 295*(15), 1809–1823.

Conger, K. J., Bryant, C. M., & Brennom, J. M. (2004). The changing nature of adolescent sibling relationships. In R. D. Conger, F. O. Lorenz, & K. A. S. Wickrama (Eds.), *Continuity and change in family relations: Theory, methods, and empirical findings* (pp. 319–344). Hillsdale, NJ: Erlbaum.

Conger, K. J., & Conger, R. D. (1996). Sibling relationships. In R. L. Simons (Ed.), *Understanding differences between divorced and intact families: Stress, interaction, and child outcome* (pp. 104–121). Thousand Oaks, CA: Sage.

Conger, K. J., Conger, R., & Scaramella, L. (1997). Parents, siblings, psychological control and adolescent adjustment. *Journal of Adolescent Research, 12*, 113–138.

Conger, K. J., & Little, W. M. (2010). Sibling relationships during the transition to adulthood. *Child Development Perspectives, 4*(2), 87–94.

Conger, K. J., Stocker, C., & McGuire, S. (2009). Sibling socialization: The effects of stressful life events and experiences. *New Directions for Child and Adolescent Development, 126*, 45–60.

Conley, D. (2004). *The pecking order: Which siblings succeed and why.* New York: Pantheon.

Cox, M. J. (2010). Family systems and sibling relationships. *Child Development Perspectives, 4*(2), 95–96.

Cox, M. J., & Paley, B. (1997). Families as systems. *Annual Review of Psychology, 48,* 243–226.

Dagys Pajoluk, N. (2013). *Sibling relationship predictors of academic achievement in adolescents* (Unpublished PhD dissertation). University of California, Los Angeles.

Daniels, D. (1986). Differential experiences of siblings in the same family as predictors of adolescent sibling personality differences. *Journal of Personality and Social Psychology, 51*(2), 339–346.

Davis, G. (2000). Adolescent depression and the effect of sibling relationships. *Dissertation Abstracts International, 61*(2B), 1076.

Davis, S. N., & Wills, J. B. (2010). Adolescent gender ideology socialization: Direct and moderating effects of fathers' beliefs. *Sociological Spectrum, 30,* 580–604.

Derkman, M. (2011). Siblinks: The implications of siblings for adolescents' adjustment and parent-child relationships (Unpublished doctoral dissertation). University of Radboud, Nijmegen, The Netherlands.

Derkman, M. M., Engels, R. C., Kuntsche, E., van der Vorst, H., & Scholte, R. H. (2011). Bidirectional associations between sibling relationships and parental support during adolescence. *Journal of Youth and Adolescence, 40*(4), 490–501.

Downey, D. B. (2001). Number of siblings and intellectual development: The resource dilution explanation. *American Psychologist, 56*(6–7), 497–504.

Dunn, J., Deater-Deckard, K., Pickering, K., & Golding, J. (1999). Siblings, parents and partners: Family relationships within a longitudinal community study. *Journal of Child Psychology and Psychiatry, 40,* 1025–1037.

Dunn, J., & Munn, P. (1986). Siblings and the development of prosocial behaviour. *International Journal of Behavioral Development, 9*(3), 265–284.

Dunn, J. F. (2006). Siblings. In J. Grusec & D. Hastings (Eds.), *Handbook of socialization: Theory and research* (pp. 309–27). New York: Guilford Press.

East, P. L. (1998). Impact of adolescent childbearing on families and younger siblings: Effects that increase younger siblings' risk for early pregnancy. *Applied Developmental Science, 2,* 62–74.

East, P. L., & Khoo, S. K. (2005). Longitudinal pathways linking family factors and sibling relationship qualities to adolescence substance use and sexual risk behaviors. *Journal of Family Psychology, 19,* 571–580.

East, P. L., Weisner, T. S., & Reyes, B. T. (2006). Youths' caretaking of their adolescent sisters' children: Its costs and benefits for youths' development. *Applied Developmental Science, 10*(2), 86–95.

Edwards, R., Hadfield, L., Lucey, H., & Mauthner, M. (2006). *Sibling identity and relationships: Sisters and brothers.* Oxon: Routledge.

Edwards, R., Hadfield, L., & Mauthner, M. (2005). *Children's understandings of their sibling relationships.* London: National Children's Bureau/Joseph Rowntree Foundation.

Edwards, R. P., & Thacker, K. (1979). The relationship of birth-order, gender, and sibling gender in the two-child family to grade point average in college. *Adolescence, 14,* 111–114.

Ensor, R., Marks, A., Jacobs, L., & Hughes, C. (2010). Trajectories of antisocial behaviour towards siblings predict antisocial behaviour towards peers. *Journal of Child Psychology and Psychiatry, 51*(11), 1208–1216.

Epstein, N. B., & Bishop, D. S. (1981). Problem-centred systems therapy in the family. In A. S. Gurman & D. P. Kniskern (Eds.), *Handbook of family therapy* (pp. 23–31). New York: Brunner/Mazel.

Erikson, E. H. (1968). *Identity: Youth and crisis.* New York: W. W. Norton.

Feinberg, M. E., Solmeyer, A. R., & McHale, S. M. (2012). The third rail of family systems: Sibling relationships, mental and behavioral health, and preventive intervention in childhood and adolescence. *Clinical Child and Family Psychology Review, 15*(1), 43–57.

Festinger, L. (1954). A theory of social comparison processes. *Human Relations, 7*(2), 117–140.

Furman, W. (1995). Parenting siblings. In M. H. Bornstein (Ed.), *Handbook of parenting: Children and parenting* (Vol. 1, pp. 143–162). Mahwah, NJ: Erlbaum.

Furman, W., & Buhrmester, D. (1985). Children's perceptions of the qualities of sibling relationships. *Child Development, 56*, 448–461.

Furman, W., & Lanthier, R. (2002). Parenting siblings. In M. Bornstein (Ed.), *Handbook of parenting: Children and parenting* (2nd ed., Vol. 1, pp. 165–188). Mahwah, NJ: Lawrence Erlbaum Associates.

Greer, K. B., Campione-Barr, N., Debrown, B., & Maupin, C. (2014). Do differences make the heart grow fonder? Associations between differential peer experiences on adolescent sibling conflict and relationship quality. *Journal of Genetic Psychology, 175*(1), 16–34.

Guttman, H. A. (1991). Systems theory, cybernetics, and epistemology. In A. S. Gurman & D. P. Kniskern (Eds.), *Handbook of family therapy* (Vol. 2, pp. 41–61). New York: Brunner/Mazel.

Ha, T. S., & Tam, C. L. (2011). A study of birth order, academic performance, and personality (International Conference on Social Science and Humanity). *IPEDR, 5*, 28–32.

Hauser, R., & Sewell, W. (1985). Birth order and educational attainment in full sibships. *American Educational Research Journal, 22*, 1–23.

Healey, M. D., & Ellis, B. J. (2007). Birth order, conscientiousness, and openness to experience: Tests of the family-niche model of personality using a within-family methodology. *Evolution & Human Behavior, 28*, 55–59.

Hess, M., Ittel, A., & Sisler, A. (2014). Gender-specific macro- and micro-level processes in the transmission of gender role orientation in adolescence: The role of fathers. *European Journal of Developmental Psychology, 11*, 211–226.

Hetherington, E. M. (1988). Parents, children, and siblings: Six years after divorce. In R. A. Hinde & J. Stevenson-Hinde (Eds.), *Relationships within families: Mutual influences* (pp. 311–331). Oxford: Claredon.

Jenkins, J. (1992). Sibling relationships in disharmonious homes: Potential difficulties and protective effects. In F. Boer & J. Dunn (Eds.), *Children's sibling relationships* (pp. 125–138). Hillsdale, NJ: Erlbaum.

Jenkins, J., Rasbash, J., Leckie, G., Gass, K., & Dunn, J. (2012). The role of maternal factors in sibling relationship quality: A multilevel study of multiple dyads per family. *Journal of Child Psychology and Psychiatry, 53*, 622–629.

Jodi, K., Bridges, M., Kim, J., Mitchell, A., & Chan, R. (1999). Relations among relationships: A family systems perspective. In E. Hetherrington, S. Henderson, & D. Reiss (Eds.), Adolescent siblings in stepfamilies: Family functioning and adolescent adjustment. *Monographs of the Society for Research in Child Development, 64*, 150–183.

Keller, H. (2013). Attachment and culture. *Journal of Cross-Cultural Psychology, 44*(2), 175–194.

Kerr, M., Stattin, H., & Kiesner, J. (2007). Peers and problem behavior: Have we missed something. In C. Rutger, E., Engels, & M. Kerr (Eds.), *Friends, lovers and groups: Key relationships in adolescence* (pp. 125–153). West Sussex: John Wiley & Sons.

Kim, J. Y., McHale, S. M., Crouter, A. C., & Osgood, W. (2007). Longitudinal linkages between sibling relationships and adjustment from middle childhood through adolescence. *Developmental Psychology, 43*, 960–973.

Kim, J. Y., McHale, S. M., Wayne Osgood, D., & Crouter, A. C. (2006). Longitudinal course and family correlates of sibling relationships from childhood through adolescence. *Child Development, 77*(6), 1746–1761.

Kobak, R. R., & Sceery, A. (1988). Attachment in late adolescence: Working models, affect regulation, and representations of self and others. *Child Development, 59,* 135–146.

Kowal, A., & Kramer, L. (1997). Children's understanding of parental differential treatment. *Child Development, 68*(1), 113–126.

Kowal, A., Kramer, L., Krull, J. L., & Crick, N. R. (2002). Children's perceptions of the fairness of parental preferential treatment and their socioemotional well-being. *Journal of Family Psychology, 16*(3): 297–306.

Kramer, L. (2010). The essential ingredients of successful sibling relations: An emerging framework for advancing theory and practice. *Child Development Perspectives, 4,* 80–86.

Kretschmer, T., & Pike, A. (2010). Links between nonshared friendship experiences and adolescent siblings' differences in aspirations. *Journal of Adolescence, 33*(1), 101–110.

Kroger, J. (2004). *Identity in adolescence.* New York: Routledge.

Kuczynski, L., & Hildebrandt, N. (1997). Models of conformity and resistance in socialization theory. In J. E. Grusec & L. Kuczynski (Eds.), *Parenting and children's internalization of values: A handbook of contemporary theory* (pp. 227–256). New York: Wiley.

Kuczynski, L., Marshall, S., & Schell, K. (1997). Value socialization in a bidirectional context. In J. E. Grusec & L. Kuczynski (Eds.), *Parenting and children's internalization of values: A handbook of contemporary theory* (pp. 23–50). New York: Wiley.

Kuczynski, L., & Parkin, C. M. (2007). Agency and bidirectionality in socialization: Interactions, transactions, and relational dialectics. In J. E. Grusec & P. D. Hastings (Eds.), *Handbook of socialization: Theory and research* (pp. 259–283). New York: Guilford Press.

Lamb, M. E. (Ed.). (2004). *The role of the father in child development.* Hoboken, NJ: John Wiley & Sons.

Larson, R. W., & Gillman, S. (1999). Transmission of emotions in the daily interactions of single-mother families. *Journal of Marriage and the Family, 61,* 21–37.

Levitt, M. J., GuacciFranco, N., & Levitt, J. L. (1993). Convoys of social support in childhood and early adolescence: Structure and function. *Developmental Psychology, 29*(5), 811–818.

Lewin, K. (1939). The field theory approach to adolescence. *American Journal of Sociology, 44,* 868–897.

Low, S., Snyder, J., & Shortt, J. W. (2012). The drift toward problem behavior during the transition to adolescence: The contributions of youth disclosure, parenting, and older siblings. *Journal of Research on Adolescence, 22*(1), 65–79.

MacKinnon-Lewis, C., Starnes, R., Volling, B., & Johnson, S. (1997). Perceptions of parenting as predictors of boys' sibling and peer relations. *Developmental Psychology, 33,* 1024–1031.

Marcia, J. E. (1980). Identity in adolescence. In J. Adelson (Ed.), *Handbook of adolescent psychology* (pp. 159–187). New York: Wiley.

Maughan, B. (2011). Family and systemic influences. In D. Skuse, H. Bruce, L. Dowdney, & D. Mrazek (Eds.), *Child psychology and psychiatry: Frameworks for practice* (2nd ed., pp. 3–7). West Sussex: John Wiley & Sons.

McGuire, S., McHale, S. M., & Updegraff, K. (1996). Children's perceptions of the sibling relationship in middle childhood: Connections within and between family relationship. *Personal Relationships, 3,* 229–239.

McGuire, S., Neiderhiser, J. M., Reiss, D., Hetherington, E. M., & Plomin, R. (1994). Genetic and environmental influences on perceptions of self-worth and competence in adolescence: A study of twins, full siblings, and step-siblings. *Child Development, 65*(3), 785–799.

McHale, S. M., & Crouter, A. C. (1996). The family contexts of children's sibling relationships. In G. H. Brody (Ed.), *Sibling relationships: Their causes and consequences* (pp. 173–198). Norwood, NJ: Ablex.

McHale, S. M., Crouter, A. C., McGuire, S. A., & Updegraff, K. A. (1995). Congruence between mothers' and fathers' differential treatment of siblings: Links with family relations and children's well-being. *Child Development, 66*(1), 116–128.

McHale, S. M., Kim, J., & Whiteman, S. D. (2006). Sibling relationships in childhood and adolescence. In P. Noller & J. A. Feeney (Eds.), *Close relationships: Functions, forms, and processes* (pp. 128–149). New York: Psychology Press.

McHale, S. M., Updegraff, K. A., Shanahan, L., Crouter, A. C., & Killoren, S. E. (2005). Gender, culture, and family dynamics: Differential treatment of siblings in Mexican American families. *Journal of Marriage and Family, 67*, 1259–1274.

McHale, S. M., Updegraff, K. A., Tucker, C. J., & Crouter, A. C. (2000). Step in or stay out? Parents' roles in adolescent siblings' relationships. *Journal of Marriage and the Family, 62*(3), 746–760.

McHale, S. M., Updegraff, K. A., & Whiteman, S. D. (2012). Sibling relationships and influences in childhood and adolescence. *Journal of Marriage and Family, 74*(5), 913–930.

Meunier, J. C., Roskam, I., Stievenart, M., van de Moortele, G., Brown, D. T., & Kumar, A. (2011). Externalizing behavior trajectories: The role of parenting, sibling relationships and child personality. *Journal of Applied Developmental Psychology, 32*, 20–33.

Meunier, J. C., Wade, M., & Jenkins, J. M. (2012). Mothers' differential parenting and children's behavioural outcomes: Exploring the moderating role of family and social context. *Infant and Child Development, 21*(1), 107–133.

Milevsky, A., & Levitt, M. J. (2005). Sibling support in early adolescence: Buffering and compensation across relationships. *European Journal of Developmental Psychology, 2*, 299–320.

Minuchin, P. (1985). Families and individual development: Provocations from the field of family therapy. *Child Development, 56*, 289–302.

Newman, J. (1994). Conflict and friendship in sibling relationships: A review. *Child Study Journal, 24*, 119–153.

Nichols, M. P., & Schwartz, R. C. (2005). *The essentials of family therapy* (2nd ed.). Boston: Allyn & Bacon.

Noller, P. (2005). Sibling relationships in adolescence: Learning and growing together. *Personal Relationships, 12*, 1–22.

Noller, P., Feeney, J. A., Sheehan, G., & Peterson, C. (2000). Marital conflict patterns: Links with family conflict and family members' perceptions of one another. *Personal Relationships, 7*, 79–94.

Nuttall, E. V., Nuttall, R. L., Polit, D., & Hunter, J. B. (1976). The effects of family size, birth order, siblings separation and crowding on the academic achievement of boys and girls. *American Educational Research Journal, 13*, 217–223.

Oliva, A., & Arranz, E. (2005). Sibling relationships during adolescence. *European Journal of Developmental Psychology, 2*(3), 253–270.

Olneck, M. (1977). On the use of sibling data to estimate the effects of family background, cognitive skills, and schooling: Results from the Kalamazoo brothers study. In P. Taubman (Ed.), *Kinometrics: Determinants of socioeconomic success within and between families* (pp. 125–163). New York: North-Holland.

Parke, R. D., & Buriel, R. (2006). Socialization in the family: Ethnic and ecological perspectives. In N. Eisenberg (Ed.), *Handbook of child psychology: Social, emotional, and personality development* (Vol. 3, pp. 429–504). Hoboken, NJ: Wiley.

Paulhus, D. L., Trapnell, P. D., & Chen, D. (1999). Birth order effect on personality and achievement within families. *Psychological Sciences, 10*, 482–488.

Pepler, D. J., Abramovitch, R., & Corter, C. (1981). Sibling interaction in the home: A longitudinal study. *Child Development, 52*, 1344–1347.

Perlman, M., & Ross, H. (1997). The benefits of parent intervention in children's disputes: An examination of concurrent changes in children's fighting styles. *Child Development, 64*, 690–700.

Pike, A. (2012a). Commentary: Are siblings birds of a feather? – Reflections on Jenkins *et al.* (2012). *Journal of Child Psychology and Psychiatry, 53*(6), 630–631.

Pike, A. (2012b). The importance of behavioural genetics for developmental science. *International Journal of Developmental Science, 6*(1–2), 13–15.

Pike, A., & Kretschmer, T. (2009). Shared versus nonshared effects: Parenting and children's adjustment. *International Journal of Developmental Science, 3*(2), 115–130.

Pike, A., & Plomin, R. (1997). A behavioural genetic perspective on close relationships. *International Journal of Behavioral Development, 21*(4), 647–668.

Plomin, R. (1994). Genetics and experience. *Current Opinion in Psychiatry, 7*(4), 297–299.

Plomin, R., & Daniels, D. (1987). Why are children in the same family so different from one another? *Behavior and Brain Sciences, 10*, 1–60.

Puig-Antich, J., Kaufman, J., Ryan, N., Williamson, D., Dahl, R., Lukens, E., *et al.* (1993). The psychological functioning and family environment of depressed adolescents. *Journal of the American Academy of Child & Adolescent Psychiatry, 32*, 244–253

Raffaelli, M. (1997). Young adolescents' conflicts with siblings and friends. *Journal of Youth and Adolescence, 26*(5), 539–558.

Reiss, D., Neiderhiser, J., Hetherington, E. M., & Plomin, R. (2000). *The relationship code: Deciphering genetic and social patterns in adolescent development.* Cambridge, MA: Harvard University Press.

Riggio, H. R. (2006). Structural features of sibling dyads and attitudes toward sibling relationships in young adulthood. *Journal of Family Issues, 27*, 1233–1254.

Rohan, M. J., & Zanna, M. P. (1996). Value transmission in families. In C. Seligman, J. M. Olson, & M. P. Zanna (Eds.), *The psychology of values: The Ontario symposium* (Vol. 8, pp. 253–276). Mahwah, NJ: Erlbaum.

Rowe, D. C. (1994). *The limits of family influence: Genes, experience, and behavior.* New York: Guilford Press.

Sandefur, G. D., & Wells, T. (1999). Does family structure really influence educational attainment? *Social Science Research, 28*(4), 331–357.

Scharf, M., Shulman, S., & Avigad-Spitz, L. (2005). Sibling relationships in emerging adulthood and in adolescence. *Journal of Adolescent Research, 20*(1), 64–90.

Scheithauer, H., Niebank, K., & Ittel, A. (2009). Developmental science: Integrating knowledge about dynamic processes in human development. In J. Valsiner, P. Molenaar, M. Lycra, & N. Chaudhary (Eds.), *Dynamic process methodology in the social and developmental sciences* (pp. 595–617). New York: Springer.

Scholte, R. H. J., Engels, R. C. M. E., de Kemp, R. A. T., Harakeh, Z., & Overbeek, G. (2007). Differential parental treatment, sibling relationships and delinquency in adolescence. *Journal of Youth and Adolescence, 36*, 661–671. doi:10.1007/s10964-006-9155-1

Seginer, R. (1998). Adolescents' perceptions of relationships with older sibling in the context of other close relationships. *Journal of Research on Adolescence, 8*, 287–308.

Sheehan, G., Darlington, Y., Noller, P., & Feeney, J. (2004). Children's perceptions of their sibling relationships during parental separation and divorce. *Journal of Divorce & Remarriage, 41*(1–2), 69–94.

Siddiqui, A., & Ross, H. S. (2004). Mediation as a method of parent intervention in children's disputes. *Journal of Family Psychology, 18*, 147–159.

Smetana, J. G., Campione-Barr, N., & Metzger, A. (2006). Adolescent development in interpersonal and societal contexts. *Annual Review of Psychology, 57,* 255–284.

Solmeyer, A. R., McHale, S. M., & Crouter, A. C. (2014). Longitudinal associations between sibling relationship qualities and risky behavior across adolescence. *Developmental Psychology, 50*(2), 600–610. doi:10.1037/a0033207

Steinberg, L., & Morris, A. S. (2001). Adolescent development. *Annual Review of Psychology, 52,* 83–110.

Steinberg, L., & Silk, J. S. (2002). Parenting adolescents. In M. Bornstein (Ed.), *Handbook of parenting: Children and parenting* (Vol. 1, pp. 103–133). Mahwah, NJ: Lawrence Erlbaum Associates.

Stocker, C. M. (1994) Children's perceptions of relationships with siblings, friends and mothers: Compensatory processes and links with adjustment. *Journal of Child Psychology and Psychiatry, 35,* 1447–1459.

Stocker, C. M., & Youngblade, L. (1999). Marital conflict and parental hostility: Links with children's sibling and peer relationships. *Journal of Family Psychology, 13,* 598–609.

Stoneman, Z., & Brody, G. H. (1993). Sibling temperaments, conflict, warmth, and role asymmetry. *Child Development, 64,* 1786–1800.

Sutton, L. (1996). Gender differences in sibling/parent relationships and adjustment. *Dissertation Abstracts International, 57*(3B), 2183.

Taanila, A., Ebeling, H., Kotimaa, A., Moilanen, I., & Järvelin, M. R. (2004). Is a large family a protective factor against behavioural and emotional problems at the age of 8 years? *Acta Paediatrica, 93*(4), 508–517.

Tiedemann, G. L., & Johnston, C. (1992). Evaluation of a parent training program to promote sharing between young siblings. *Behavior Therapy, 23,* 299–318.

Travis, R., & Kohli, V. (1995). The birth order factor: Ordinal position, social strata, and education achievement. *Journal of Social Psychology, 135,* 499–507.

Tucker, C., Barber, B., & Eccles, J. (1997). Advice about life plans and personal problems in late adolescent sibling relationships. *Journal of Youth and Adolescence, 26,* 63–76.

Updegraff, K. A., Thayer, S. M., Whiteman, S. D., Denning, D. J., & McHale, S. M. (2005). Relational aggression in adolescents' sibling relationships: Links to sibling and parent-adolescent relationship quality. *Family Relations, 54*(3), 373–385.

Van IJzendoorn, M. H., Moran, G., Belsky, J., Pederson, D., Bakermans-Kranenburg, M. J., & Kneppers, K. (2000). The similarity of siblings' attachments to their mother. *Child Development, 71*(4), 1086–1098.

Volling, B. L. (1997). The family correlates of maternal and paternal perceptions of differential treatment in early childhood. *Family Relations, 46,* 227–236.

Voorpostel, M., & Blieszner, R. (2008). Intergenerational solidarity and support between adult siblings. *Journal of Marriage and Family, 70,* 157–167.

Walster, E., Walster, G. W., & Berscheid, E. (1978). *Equity: Theory and research.* Boston: Allyn & Bacon.

Whitchurch, G. G., & Constantine, L. L. (1993). Systems theory. In P. G. Boss, W. J. Doherty, R. LaRossa, W. R. Schumm, & S. K. Steinmetz (Eds.), *Sourcebook of family theories and methods: A contextual approach* (pp. 325–355). New York: Plenum.

Whiteman, S. D., Jensen, A. C., & Maggs, J. L. (2014). Similarities and differences in Adolescent siblings' alcohol-related attitudes, use, and delinquency: Evidence for convergent and divergent influence processes. *Journal of Youth and Adolescence, 43*(5), 687–697.

Whiteman, S. D., McHale, S. M., & Soli, A. (2011). Theoretical perspectives on sibling relationships. *Journal of Family Theory & Review, 3*(2), 124–139.

Wolke, D., & Skew, A. J. (2012). Bullying among siblings. *International Journal of Adolescent Medicine and Health, 24*(1), 17–25.

Wong, M. M. (2008). Perceptions of parental involvement and autonomy support: Their relations with self-regulation, academic performance, substance use and resilience among adolescents. *North American Journal of Psychology, 10,* 497–518. doi:10.1177/0272431699019002003

Wu, L. L. (1996). Effects of family structure and income risks of premarital birth. *American Sociological Review, 61,* 386–406.

Yeh, H. C. (2001). The influences of sibling relationships in adolescence. *Dissertation Abstracts International, 62*(2A), 794.

Yeh, H., & Lempers, J. D. (2004). Perceived sibling relationships and adolescent development. *Journal of Youth and Adolescence, 33,* 133–147.

Younnis, J., & Smollar, J. (1985). *Adolescents' relations with mothers, fathers, and friends.* Chicago: University of Chicago Press.

Yu, J., & Gamble, W. C. (2008). Pathways of influence: Marital relationships and their association with parenting styles and sibling relationship quality. *Journal of Child and Family Studies, 17,* 757–778.

Zajonc, R. B., & Markus, G. B. (1975). Birth order and intellectual development. *Psychological Review, 82,* 74–88.

3

SIBLINGS AND THEIR RELATIONSHIPS

Correlates and effects

In exploring the varied literature on adolescent siblings and their relationships, we look at some of the social processes at play between siblings and discuss a variety of effects and correlates, including social developmental, transitional behaviours, as well as a selection of outcomes. This contribution enlists an appraisal of empirical work from various strands of research including large-scale cross-sectional and longitudinal studies in tandem with explications of underpinning theory. We make use of comprehensive foregoing reviews of the sibling corpus by the likes of Whiteman, McHale, and Soli (2011); McHale, Updegraff, and Whiteman (2012); and Feinberg, Solmeyer, and McHale (2012) while endeavouring to cover associative new ground. We finish off with an examination of wider socio-environmental influences and their meaning for the sibling relationship.

Despite the abundance of general work on adolescence, relatively few systematic studies exist that focus exclusively on the relationship between siblings. Still, researchers have made considerable gains in closing the gap by mounting novel explorations and reframing old portraits (East, 2009). Most prior research has been undertaken within the context of larger assessments of families, family systems, or individual-level outcomes as in the prediction of health-related or problem behaviours (e.g. Adams & Berzonsky, 2003; Heaven, 1994). We seek to connect some of these disparate findings by synthesizing meaningful developmental correlates, effects, and processes between brothers and sisters. The results are grouped accordingly: micro-level influences in socio-emotional development; identity, individuation, and personality development; sexual development; and health and risk behaviours including illness and disability as well as substance use will be examined, as will macro-level variables of socio-economic status, societal structures, and the environment at-large. We save discussion of cultural variability and related dynamics implicated in sibling development for the fifth chapter, where cross-cultural issues are attended to at length.

After the presentation of highlighted micro-level and macro-level influences, a comprehensive research programme – depicted in the seventh chapter – is briefly introduced. Here, we frame the findings within a developmental model, for clarity's sake, forming a coherent depiction of sibling interrelationships and some of the bidirectional effects involved in one another's development.

Sibling developmental correlates

A relationship with a sibling may well be the longest in an individual's life (Cicirelli, 1995). Adolescence, a sensitive period in development perhaps second only to infancy (Carnegie Council on Adolescent Development, 1996), signals a time of great physiological and socio-emotional change. What better relationship than that of the sibling bond to examine the qualities and machinations of intimate ties. Knowledge garnered from brothers and sisters across the teenage years ferments and furthers research not only on individual-level outcomes, but also the stability and change in close relations (Whiteman et al., 2011). To begin the inquest into variables central to adolescent siblings, we start by exploring an individual's core personality and identity development. Thereafter, we survey various elements bound up with adolescent sibling relationships: socio-emotional development, sexual development, health and risk behaviour, as well as other associated factors like academic adjustment and macro-social influences.

State of the research

Existing scholarship on sibling relationships has focused on their meaning as partners within the larger network of social relations (Buhrmester & Furman, 1990) and on linkages to individual development and outcomes (reviewed by Smetana, Campione-Barr, & Metzger, 2006; Yeh & Lempers, 2004), in addition to specific relationship patterns such as conflict (Raffaelli, 1997; Updegraff, Thayer, Whiteman, Denning, & McHale, 2005) and support (Branje, Van Lieshout, Van Aken, & Haselager, 2004). We do know that conflict and rivalry between siblings are common in multiple contexts, although certainly not the most prevalent interaction pattern (Newman, 1994). But some researchers now question claims of the damaging effects of sibling conflict and instead opt for the notion that not only positive interactions but accompanying conflicts with siblings can be valuable, if not vital, instigator and context of developmental change (Kramer, 2010).

Siblings are furthermore key social partners (Dunn, 1998). Within the context of their often ubiquitous relationship, brothers and sisters offer experiences which support the attainment of skills critical for socio-emotional and cognitive development (Howe, Ross, & Recchia, 2010). Some of these skills involve conflict regulation, identity development, negative emotion management, empathic and social awareness, and negotiation relational dimensions like intimacy and companionship (Furman & Buhrmester, 1992; Kramer, 2010). During early and middle childhood in particular, they enhance the advance of prosocial development (Dunn & Munn, 1986) and may act as confidants and supports (e.g. Jenkins, 1992) in their everyday emotionally rich interactions.

Alternately, within-family systems study shows that while siblings can have moderately similar relational and attachment profiles, dissimilarity is surprisingly common (e.g. Van IJzendoorn *et al.*, 2000). As we discuss in the second chapter on within-family sibling study, unique experience, meaning, that which is non-shared, is believed to account for large variations between siblings (e.g. Daniels, 1986; Plomin, 1994; Plomin & Daniels, 1987). This has led to a concentration of empirical work aiming to identify the ways in which siblings bear a resemblance to and, conversely, are dissimilar to one another through convergent and divergent processes (e.g. Feinberg, McHale, Crouter, & Cumsille, 2003; Pike & Kretschmer, 2009, 2010).

Beyond similarity in physical appearance, siblings resemble one another *vis-à-vis* a variety of dimensions like gender role orientations (Hess, Ittel, & Sisler, 2014), delinquency and related behaviours (e.g. Bank, Patterson, & Reid, 1996; Craine, Tanaka, Nishina, & Conger, 2009; Slomkowski, Rende, Conger, Simons, & Conger, 2001), substance use (e.g. Brook & Brook, 1990; Crabbe, McSwigan, & Belknap, 1985; Slomkowski, Rende, Novak, Lloyd-Richardson, & Niaura, 2005), sexual behaviour (e.g. McHale, Bissell, & Kim, 2009; Rodgers & Rowe, 1988), peer acceptance and social competence (Bank, Burraston, & Snyder, 2004; Kim, McHale, Crouter, & Osgood, 2007; Stormshak, Bellanti, & Bierman, 1996), and certain academic domains (Dagys Pajoluk, 2013; Watzlawik, 2009). On the other hand, brothers and sisters may look quite different with respect to areas such as personality (Daniels, 1986); friendship experiences and aspirations for self-acceptance, affiliation, and financial success (Pike & Kretschmer, 2010); adjustment and psychopathological disorders in childhood and adolescence (see Turkheimer &

Waldron's (2000) review); and, dependent on birth order and gender, academic achievement (Bouchey, Shoulberg, Jodl, & Eccles, 2010; Milevsky & Levitt, 2005).

As we have seen from studies on the impact of non-shared environment, unique experiences occupy a significant role in the above examples of sibling differentiation. Although born into the same family, raised in the same neighbourhood, and drawn from the same genetic pool, siblings can vary greatly along, for instance, individual characteristic continuums (Michalski & Shackelford, 2001), intelligence quotients (Boomsma et al., 2008), and familial sentiment (Salmon, 1998, 1999; Salmon & Daly, 1998). Differential parental treatment, family milieus, family system constellations, access to resources related to age order and spacing, and other unique experiences are thought to contribute to sibling differentiation (e.g. Conley, 2004; Dunn & Stocker, 1989; Kowal, Krull, & Kramer, 2006; Meunier et al., 2012; Rosenzweig, 1986; Stocker, Dunn, & Plomin, 1989).

Among critical factors which influence differences in individual-level outcomes, within-family effects are cited as central for child and adolescent outcomes. As such, birth order effects, for example, may serve as a proxy for age, status, power, and access to resources (Sulloway, 2007). This has led authors like Salmon (2003) to state, 'The sibships into which humans are born are crucial social environments with associated opportunities, costs, and "niches",' . . . 'it would be remarkable if our evolved social psyches did not contain features adapted to the peculiarities of sibling relationships' (p. 82). In turn, we explore theory behind personality development and individuation processes in relation to other factors like birth order effects.

Personality, individuation, and birth order

Sibling similarity and difference have typically encompassed psychoanalytic explanations from the likes of Adler's birth order effects on individual development (Ansbacher & Ansbacher, 1956) to Eysenck's highly specific analysis of personality structure and temperamental difference (Eysenck & Eysenck, 1975). Furthermore, explications abound of just how it is that siblings from the same family can, in some cases, so closely resemble one another, and in others, show great disparity and seeming non-relatedness. Observational learning as per social learning theory (Bandura, 1977) plus interactive processes in the family unit are further implicated yet rarely directly targeted in empirical investigations. In a unique analysis of the underpinning mechanisms involved in sibling de-identification, Whiteman, McHale, and Crouter (2007) considered the effects of observational learning and patterns of sibling similarity and difference. The findings drawn from two-stage cluster analyses suggested that three profiles were evident for depicting sibling influence: modelling, deidentificaiton, and non-reference. Moreover, differences were detected based on birth order as well as within ordinal rank, such that younger-born siblings who engaged in modelling appeared qualitatively distinguishable from those who indicated de-identification. These results are important in that they begin to add rich information on the differences between siblings' personal qualities and relationship qualities, thus refining processes of sibling influence.

Additionally, there is a growing corpus of evidence to suggest that certain birth orders play a role in individual personality development. The perspective that a family's composition is fundamental to individual development processes is a common thread running through evolutionary, psychoanalytic, and social psychology, as well as family systems theory. Frequent depictions of high-achieving firstborns, baby-like last borns, and the forgotten middle child are prevalent in the literature, lay belief, and empirical research alike. While cases of siblicide are thankfully more prevalent in the animal kingdom than in our own species, competition between human brothers and sisters is thought to prevail all the same. As Sulloway (2007) opines,

> ordinal position is associated with disparities in parental investment, which can lead to differences in behavior, health, and mortality. In addition, siblings in our own species typically occupy disparate niches within the family system and, in mutual competition, generally use different tactics based on age, size, and sex. (p. 162)

He goes on to claim that these disparate strategies for survival success in conjunction with experiences then shape personality and bring out disparities in attitudes, motivations, and sentiments regarding family. What is more, some research seems to suggest that during adolescence, competition may spike while outright conflict and aggressions lessens, as teens engage in more social comparative processes (East, 2009). The specifics of these dynamics and the differences between certain sibling constellations are interesting future lines of investigation.

Alfred Adler's pioneering personality research privileged the family's role and sibling dynamics in particular in his psychoanalytic theory that firstborns seek parental approval through conventional achievement in academics and conscientious behaviours. Middle children may particularly grapple with issues tied to sibling rivalry and exhibit feelings of inferiority, deemed as part of a greater inferiority complex, and the competition for parents' attention and resources. Rivalry is thought to stem from this need to overcome threats to self-esteem; siblings then differentiate, developing personal characteristics and selecting different areas to occupy, as in the so-called niche theory. Adler postulated that younger siblings attempt to differentiate themselves upon detecting the higher status of the eldest child, even amounting to maladaptive adjustment and differentiation strategies.

But just how is it that individuals carve out their own niches, and why do siblings look so different in many regards? A number of theories hone in on individuation in families. From psychoanalytic schools of thought, firstborns are said to develop dominant, conscientious, and conforming personalities, and to exhibit feelings of dislike or ambivalence towards their younger siblings, whereas younger children are creative and adventuresome, and middle children are mediators (e.g. Mitchell, 2000; Sulloway, 1996, 2001). Dethronement theory likewise conjectures that upon losing the monopoly on parental attention, an eldest child would subsequently develop qualities like conscientiousness, independence, and competence to regain positive accord (Adams, 1972; Paulhus, Trapnell, & Chen, 1999; Sulloway, 1996). Indeed, eldest children do appear to possess in consequence certain advantages; according to some studies, they come out wealthier and more intelligent (Behrman & Taubman, 1986).

Yet another view sees differential niches within the familial milieu as paramount in personality development (Sulloway, 1996). Children develop and carve out distinctive niches in order to maximize parental investment. For instance, firstborns might exhibit less agreeableness in order to dominate younger siblings and maximize parental attention. Additionally, later-borns might be less likely to mirror parental values and characteristics like the eldest children, which may lead to more openness, creativity, and an adventuresome nature (Sulloway, 1996). In a test of this theoretical standpoint, Healey and Ellis (2007) have in fact found that within a university sample, older siblings were more likely to be conscientious and less open than their younger counterparts. Similarly, although there is a distinct lack of research on adolescent sibling effects, differentiation might be particularly prominent at this stage when identity formation is at the forefront (e.g. Marcia, 1980; Kroger, 2004). Experiences and the testing of different social niches and accompanying roles during adolescence and their reception in relation to siblings and other family members are likely to have lasting impacts on the developing teen.

Such socio-biological accounts of human development have not gone without criticism, frequently being deemed too reductionistic or disproportionally weighted to the biological, with a lack of focus on social forces. Edwards, Hadfield, Lucey, and Mauthner (2006) have shown that conventional conceptions related to birth order and age hierarchy, and their implicated power dynamics, were not the universal imperatives evoked in evolutionary accounts, but are rather flexible and contestable. Nonetheless, considerable overlap can be found between the areas of interest common to disparate interpretative lenses. Personality, social attitudes, health, cognitive characteristics, and behaviour may be related, in part, to birth order effects and familial dynamics in a given family; still, the extent and mechanisms of these relationships are disputed. It is likely the case that these effects may be more salient in certain family contexts – and less so in others. Next, we discuss one important feature of the sibling relationship within the family context and its role in development: individuation.

Sibling dynamics and individuation

The sibling relationship embedded in the family system can assist in driving the process of developing an independent, differentiated individual. One of adolescence's prime developmental tasks includes this process of individuation (Blos, 1967). Teens engage in the so-called second individuation process following the initial task in early childhood in ' . . . which a person becomes increasingly differentiated from a past or present relational context' (Karpel, 1976, p. 66). Here, the adolescent must move beyond early internalized representations of parental figures and instead develop 'a sense of self that is distinct and individuated' (Lapsley

& Stey, 2010, p. 3). The adolescent tries out and takes on an assortment of roles, experimenting socially and moving beyond familial constraints and expectations. These divergent processes occur alongside convergent ones, like modelling and increasing sibling similarity (e.g. Grotevant, 1978). Feinberg and colleagues adopt a theory of sibling de-identification in their insightful examination of sibling dynamics, where both convergence and divergence in parent–child and sibling relationships are counterbalanced throughout adolescence and its task of individuation.

According to Adlerian psychology, siblings dovetail in their development in order to create separate distinct niches, thus gaining parents' warmth and care (Ansbacher & Ansbacher, 1956). This process of sibling de-identification is thought to promote positive relations by decreasing conflict stemming from competition for parental resources. More similar siblings presumably engage in stronger de-identification processes, like those of the same gender or closer in age, for example (Schachter, Gilutz, Shore, & Adler, 1978). Evidence attesting to sibling de-individuation effects includes more pronounced difference on self-reported measures of personality between the two firstborn children in a family versus second- and third-born siblings (Schachter, Shore, Feldman-Rotman, Marquis, & Campbell, 1976). Likewise, greater age spacing between siblings has been tied to increased similarity in adjustment (Feinberg & Hetherington, 2000). Sibling de-identification might be particularly active in adolescence, a time when teenagers attempt to carve out a particular identity, in contrast to childhood youngsters, where sibling similarity in sex-typed qualities increases (McHale, Updegraff, Helms-Erikson, & Crouter, 2001).

Indeed, we can now apply Kramer's (2010) position that the sibling relationship offers a unique opportunity for individuals to develop unique senses of selves to the process of individuation. Siblings and their shared experiences promote social, emotional, and cognitive development through both amiable and antagonistic experiences (Kramer, 2010). Feinberg and researchers' study on sibling divergence and convergence supports this view, showing that rising sibling differences across time in parent–child warmth were linked to less conflict in the sibling bond among firstborn accounts, and more warmth in both first- and second-born sibling accounts (Feinberg et al., 2003). The authors propose that sibling rivalry and conflict are negotiated through processes like sibling de-individuation.

In addition, research on adolescent separation-individuation processes further reveals the constructive role of siblings in the family context (Kroger, 2004). A critical component of individuation includes an adolescent's reception of a 'family blessing' (Blos, 1985). Here, a blessing is defined as the acknowledgment and acceptance of a child's adult status: for instance, for a son, his adult masculinity. Bjornsen (2000) found evidence that most female and male college students (71.5%) received some form of blessing from a parent and further ascribed great meaning to the event. Importantly, in the loss of a father figure, 'big brothers' can serve as key figures to promote male adolescents' individuation process in single-mother families (Saintonge, Achille, & Lachance, 1998). Whether the quality and nature of the blessing varies between siblings and families based on family structure and sibling relationship characteristics awaits additional investigation.

Our final note on conflict, rivalry, and individuation requires us to consider the changing nature of conceptualizations of 'healthy' identity development and socio-emotional relating. Most past and modern day accounts give ascendancy to the notion of individuation and autonomy seeking as a necessary, intrinsic part of growing up. Following this, conflict and rivalry, differential parental treatment, and individuation are all tied to the emphasis on defining oneself as an individual, carving out a particular niche within the family and other social contexts, and asserting one's agency on others, all paramount features in an individualistic social landscape (e.g. Hofstede, 1980).

Some of the assumptions concerning formerly negativistic views of sibling conflict, however, have been challenged by the likes of Edwards and colleagues (2006) who write on the increasingly transactional formulations of social relationships in diverse socio-environmental contexts. Indeed, distinctive features of sibling relationships encompass their hierarchical and reciprocal substance, and the quality of seriality: 'that is, the ability to be one among a series of more than one (a sibling group) while at the same time remaining aware of uniqueness (Mitchell, 2003)' (cited in Edwards *et al.*, 2006). Sibling relationship study signals a shift in intimate relationship conceptualizations to more interdependent identities, transactional practices, and interactions borrowed from intersubjective and feminist traditions (e.g. Feinberg *et al.*, 2003; Murray, 2006). The furtherance of our comprehension of the mechanisms at play in sibling rivalry, individuation processes, and parental treatment in adolescence awaits inquiry into the deeper *differential* meaning and experiences of sibling relationships from a more qualitative perspective. We consider cultural differences in these constructs in the final chapter.

Beyond birth order effects, individuation and relational dynamics between siblings depend on factors like the individual characteristics of the child, social comparison processes, perceptions of fairness and equity in the face of potential differential parental treatment, sensitive periods in development, and past experiences (e.g. Connidis, 2007; Noller, Conway, & Blakeley-Smith, 2008; Tesser, 1980). For instance, individual-specific qualities of the child and adolescent greatly influence sibling relationship dynamics. Important personality features like base levels of agreeableness impact on siblings and how they will get along in the future (Furman & Lanthier, 2002), just as siblings without mental health difficulties report fewer cases of conflict with their brothers and sisters (Cicirelli, 1989). More conscientious siblings might make life transitions in a more normative, planned way in comparison with siblings who tend to be less controlled (K. J. Conger & Little, 2010).

An illustration of some of the structural features that impact sibling development includes evidence that upward social comparison might be particularly damaging for siblings who are close in age and often in conflict (Noller *et al.*, 2008). Likewise, siblings may be more or less likely to assimilate certain aspects of older siblings into their own identity; bidirectional influence of siblings varies based on features like gender or affinity (e.g. Derkman, Engels, Kuntsche, van der Vorst, & Scholte, 2011; Kim, McHale, Wayne Osgood, & Crouter, 2006). Complicating the issue further, children's individual adjustment has been found to relate more closely to how they compare to their siblings versus the absolute levels of behaviour (Feinberg, Niederhiser, Simmens, Reiss, & Hetherington, 2000). We examine other such relational dynamics next.

Social and relational dynamics

Social trends towards smaller family sizes and family blending resulting from events like divorce and parental separation may position siblings as ever-greater influences in individual development (Bank & Kahn, 1982; East, 2009; Mitchell, 2003). They can exert greater force in the shaping of personality with 'increased access' (one sibling, cohabiting, playing together, narrow age difference, etc.) and are critical in areas of socio-emotional development like learning to be prosocial (Dunn, 2007; Whiteman et al., 2007). Furthermore, parents are arguably less available to their children with increasing numbers of dual-income households and the great demands of work. In fact, siblings spend more time with one another than with parents (McHale & Crouter, 1996). Extending past the biological, step-, half-, and adopted siblings serve as valuable relational partners, in the case of mixed/blended families which are becoming more commonplace (Cox, 2010; Mitchell, 2003).

Over developmental time, adolescent relationships move from the prescribed and involuntary, for example, parent/caregiver–child relationship, to selected reciprocal ties wherein mutual receptiveness and engagement become increasingly salient (e.g. Dunn, 2007). A prime example of chosen relations is the shift towards increasingly important peers and friendships in adolescence (e.g. Furman & Buhrmester, 1992; Scholte, Van Lieshout, & Van Aken, 2001). Even as the family's influence wanes in many respects during the course of adolescence (Scharf, Shulman, & Avigad-Spitz, 2005), sibling relationships may remain central in multiple arenas of a teen's development (e.g. Dunn, 2007; East, 2009; McHale, Kim, & Whiteman, 2006).

As interaction over the teen years becomes increasingly voluntary rather than subject to parental constraints or other external conditions, this may relate to decreased conflict and aggression, and increased intimacy and egalitarian relating (East, 2009; Stewart et al., 2001). Furthermore, Stewart and colleagues (2001) assert that the sibling relationship transitions qualitatively, in that emerging adults report less conflict demonstrated in decreased amounts of competition, power struggles, antagonism, and argumentation than in adolescence. Scharf et al. (2005) found additional evidence for diminished intensity of rivalry and conflict in emerging adulthood as compared to adolescence, plus greater links between the parent–child relationship and sibling relationship. Moreover, siblings influence one another's externalizing (aggression, oppositional, and conduct behaviours) and internalizing (anxiety, depression, worry-related behaviours), despite their age rank (Dunn, 2007; Garcia, Shaw, Winslow, & Yaggi, 2000; Pike, Coldwell, & Dunn, 2006). While siblings can develop a prosocial orientation in the context of their relationship (e.g. Kramer, 2010), low levels of caring, empathetic and otherwise assistive behaviour has been tied to sibling hostility and later conduct disorder problems

(Garcia *et al.*, 2000). What is more, these associations hold over and above strained parent–child relations, indicating the direct influence siblings have on one another's social development.

Socialization in the context of sibling relationships

Research indicates that siblings have significant influence over one another, and that the sibling relationship is laden with emotion (Dunn, 2007). In this dynamic context, important social learning occurs through a number of processes (Bandura, 1977; Cox, 2010). Over and above direct relational exchanges and dynamics, brothers and sisters can serve as social models (e.g. Brook & Brook, 1990; Derkman *et al.*, 2011). Learning theories and social learning perspectives also point to direct shaping of behaviour, and both younger and older siblings take part in this process. Parents might assign caregiving duties to an older sibling, or a younger sibling might assist an older sibling with a disability. Siblings further practise and learn key negotiation and cooperation skills through skirmishes, constructive exchanges, or in outright backyard battles; Kramer (2010) sheds light on how this particular intimate relationship invites and encourages social, emotional, and cognitive development, not only through the so-called adaptive interactions, but also through conflictual interactions.

Siblings can serve as direct role models. Whether it is in the athletic, scholastic, or social realm, brothers and sisters offer examples of how and what to do in certain circumstances and can proffer advice, assistance, or support. Conversely, siblings can coerce or display risky behaviours (e.g. Brook, Whiteman, Gordon, & Brook, 1990), and, often times, the sibling similarity for certain behaviours is greater than that of parent–child (Ary, Tildesley, Hops, & Andrews, 1993; Fagan & Najman, 2005). In the case of the onset of substance use in adolescence, older siblings' usage was found to impart a direct effect on younger sibling use, as were relationship dynamics and reinforcement (Low, Shortt, & Snyder, 2012). In the same study, collusion and conflict within the sibling bond exerted indirect effects via younger siblings' peer affiliation. These results draw attention to siblings' complex yet critical influence in one another's socialization and offer researchers an entry point for intervention, as changing sibling social dynamics seems to be a more effective strategy than concentrating on substance use alone (Kim *et al.*, 2007). Here, as in other work, sibling constellation composition is thought to be important in depicting processes involved in social modelling.

Additional examples of how siblings socialize one another into various behaviours and orientations include evidence of the sibling relationship as a 'training ground' for aggression (Patterson, 1984, 1986; Patterson, Dishion, & Bank, 1984). In this research, which depicts a sibling-training model for (physical) aggression, siblings are seen to engage in coercive cycles of escalating negative interactions that occur when one sibling concedes to the other, rewarding and thus maintaining negative behavioural patterns. In a longitudinal study, Dunn and Munn (1986) likewise looked into the link between sibling conflict, conflict resolution strategies, and physical aggression. In this study, physical aggression of one sibling was negatively correlated to child conciliation and positively correlated with sibling physical aggression measured 6 months later. Such longitudinal investigations allow researchers to track individual sibling outcomes in relation to their sibling within their developmental milieus.

To further contextualize sibling socialization and its wider impacts on individual outcomes, we first turn to a review of four separate examinations of bullying between siblings. In their analysis of both sibling and peer bullying, Wolke and Skew (2012) determined that sibling-based bullying is widespread, with close to 50 per cent of siblings involved in bullying per month. In reference to the reciprocal nature of the sibling relationship, being both perpetrator and victim was the most frequent pattern in sibling bullying, whereas peer-based instances tend towards either victim or bully roles. Furthermore, while sibling bully/victims and rates of victimization appear to decrease over adolescence, sibling bullying seems to stabilize between ages 10 and 15 years. Importantly, when bullying occurs at home, this translates to bullying within the peer and school context, and both bullying at home and school are uniquely linked to behavioural and emotional problems. Children unfortunate enough to experience bullying in both contexts are almost at a 14-fold increased chance of behavioural and emotional difficulties versus those who experience bullying in school, at home, or none at all. These results seem to support the sibling relationship as a training ground for certain negative behaviours and have strong implications for each sibling's developmental outcomes.

An additional study to contextualize individual well-being and sibling patterns of behaviour examined 296 sibling pairs with average ages of 10 and 13 years alongside their caregivers, complemented with census data (Brody et al., 2003). Parents' harsh-inconsistent rearing styles and low nurturant-involved parenting were linked to younger siblings' conduct disorder symptoms and older siblings' problematic behaviour and attitudes. Importantly, these associations were most potent for families living in the most impoverished neighbourhoods. These examples illustrate the complex and strong effects siblings can have on one another's socialization into various behaviours. However, as sibling risk factors tend to covary, some of these influences might actually have more to do with parenting behaviour, deviant peers, or family and community climates than direct sibling effects per se (Feinber et al., 2012). Nonetheless, it is important to then note that bolstering family support in addition to parents' and siblings' relationship skills is a favourable route for improving individual outcomes.

Socio-emotional adjustment

Siblings aid one another in acquiring the core developmental abilities of a sense of mind, taking perspective, and understanding other's emotional and mental states. This social understanding involves the sharing and practising of relating to others through conversation, play, and cooperative, negotiated, and conflictual behaviour alike. A warm sibling bond bolsters the attainment of social comprehension

(Dunn, 2011). Indeed, siblings can even aid their brothers and sisters with severe difficulties in social relating, as with siblings who have autism spectrum disorder (ASD), scaffolding their social understanding and supporting individual adjustment (Kaminsky & Dewey, 2002; Knott, Lewis, & Williams, 1995; Tsao & Odom, 2006). Adolescent boys with ASDs who had at least two siblings were at a decreased risk of loneliness, and the link between close friend support and loneliness was no longer significant once controlled for number of siblings, underscoring the central role of siblings in facilitating healthy social adjustment and development (Lasgaard, Nielsen, Eriksen, & Goossens, 2010).

Oliva and Arranz (2005) additionally examined sibling relationships during adolescence, within the context of parent and peer relationships, and their link with socio-emotional adjustment. They found important gender-based differences in the meaning and importance that sibling adjustment holds for adolescents. These researchers detected differential effects by gender: for girls, a good relationship with their siblings was connected to similarly positive relationships with their parents and peers, as well as increased self-esteem and life satisfaction, whereas for boys, sibling relationships had no relation with other family or personal factors. In their discussion of potential explanatory roots for the gender-based differential, the authors cite sex role socialization theory. According to this perspective, boys emphasize domination and exploration of their world, while girls are more encouraged to develop social relationships (Harter, 1999). That girls seem to demonstrate greater congruence with their internal working models, in relation to their parents as well as their siblings and peers, is in accordance with attachment theory (Bowlby, 1980; Sroufe & Fleeson, 1986). Interestingly, an additive or accumulative model was also displayed for girls in which positive relations between parents and siblings had independent beneficial effects. Gender-based differences and implicated processes, and the gender composition of the sibling dyad are fruitful areas to pursue in next research steps.

Sexual development: Sexuality and sexual orientation

Adolescence is a time of first sexual experimentations with oneself and others (Andrew Collins & Steinberger, 2008). While sibling relationships generally become more egalitarian, with a movement away from pervasive emotionally intense experiences as adolescents spend more time with peers, they remain important influences in romantic attachment and sexual activity (Buhrmester & Furman, 1990; Hetherington *et al.*, 1999). Siblings resemble one another in the age of first intercourse, early sexual behaviour, teenage pregnancy, and related attitudes and beliefs (e.g. East, 1998; East & Jacobson, 2001; Widmer, 1997). In adolescence, the psychosocial task of sexuality, meaning, 'adjusting to a sexually maturing body, managing sexual desires, forming sexual attitudes and values and learning about others' expectations, experimenting with sexual behaviours, and integrating these dimensions into one's sense of self' (Andrew Collins & Steinberger, 2008, p. 573; see Crockett, Raffaelli, & Moilanen, 2003), is strongly influenced by socialization processes like those at play in sibling relationships (East, 1998; McHale *et al.*, 2009; McHale *et al.*, 2012). McHale *et al.* (2012) state, as per social learning theory, that sibling influence in the development of ideas around sexuality and childbearing may be all the more evident when siblings share a warm rapport and are the same sex (McHale *et al.*, 2009). Siblings may act as viable models, transmit information on contraception, sexual behaviour, and even directly encourage sexual activity and certain relationship partners, especially when siblings' peer groups overlap (East, 1998; Rodgers, Rowe, & Harris, 1992). Furthermore, significant ethnic and racial differences in psychosocial sexuality exist in, for example, the sequence, timing, and prevalence of sexual behaviour, contraceptive usage, patterns of sexually transmitted diseases, and pregnancy (Blum *et al.*, 2000; Smith & Udry, 1985; Yana, 1998). As such, contextualized understanding of sibling influences on sexual development takes the recognition and further investigation of culturally specific expectations in and around adolescent sexuality, intimate relationships, and attachment.

Both socialization and biological factors and their likely interaction are evoked in explications of sexual orientation and its dynamic development. In an investigation of sexual orientation development using the National Longitudinal Study of Adolescent Health (Add Health), a nationally representative sample of adolescents in the United States (Udry, 2003), longitudinal results taken at 20–24 years, shed light on implicated family-demographic factors (Francis, 2008). The biodemographic findings ran in contrast to the maternal immune hypothesis that holds male homosexuality is linked solely to the number of older brothers, while female homosexuality lacks biodemographic correlates. Francis detected, however, that having older brothers did not significantly raise the likelihood of being homosexual for men and that having older sisters lowered homosexual or bisexual identity. In addition, for women, possessing an older brother or sisters of any age decreased the chances of being homosexual. Over and above this across time data, family structure, ethnicity, and education are further related to male and female sexual orientations.

Sexual minority siblings as compared to their heterosexual siblings are subject to greater amounts of childhood psychological and physical abuse by caretakers, more childhood sexual abuse, as well as, in later years, more sexual assaults and partner psychological and physical victimization (Balsam, Rothblum, & Beauchaine, 2005). Furthermore, sexual minority youth who had disclosed their identity to their families reported more verbal and physical abuse from family members (D'Augelli, Hershberger, & Pilkington, 1998). 'Coming out' to a sibling can offer an intergenerational and societal bridge or a questioning voice. In one qualitative study of disclosing one's sexual minority orientation to a sibling (Gottesman, 2012), common elements included silence and secrecy, sense of relief, honesty, and self-discovery, attesting to the close and often emotionally ambiguous ties between siblings (East, 2009). The multiplicities of sexual minority youth experiences within the context of their sibling and familial relationships are great, yet largely absent from current scholarship (Gottesman, 2012).

Same-sex and non-heterosexual sexuality among ethnic minority communities is thought to be even more stigmatized than in modern Western society (e.g. Chan,

1995; Diamond & Savin-Williams, 2003). Nonetheless, both dominant and minority culture's notions of sexuality, sexual expression, and sexual identity are ultimately bound up with stereotypes about gender and race (Chan, 1995; Stephens & Phillips, 2003). Multiple minority status may intersect to produce the most negative outcomes for adolescents in many cases (Consolacion, Russell, & Sue, 2004), although certain groups of individuals can respond in resilient ways in the face of prejudice and discrimination (e.g. Bowleg, Huang, Brooks, Black, & Burkholder, 2003). Ethnic-minority adolescents and youth frequently develop in contexts devoid of any representation of non-heterosexual relationships, and their identities and experiences are likely impacted by this vacuum (Savin-Williams, 1996); for instance, no positive or neutral terms for 'lesbian', 'gay', or 'bisexual' exists in many languages (Espin, 1997, cited in Diamond & Savin-Williams, 2003). The variegated socio-cultural constructions of sexuality are worth bearing in mind for future cross-cultural research of sibling and familial influences on sexuality in particular during adolescence. Again, considering biological and social theories of sexual orientation in tandem proffers more nuanced perspectives of the interactive effects at play.

Health and risk behaviours

Despite the influence of the sibling context on development, not much is known of the processes implicated in the role of siblings in psychopathology and other health and risk behaviours (Solmeyer, McHale, & Crouter, 2013). All the same, investigations of siblings across adolescence reveal their importance in teenagers' health and well-being (Kramer & Bank, 2005). Most other prevailing work has examined configurations of sibling outcomes and inferred sibling influence based upon concordance rates (see McHale et al., 2012). However, such analyses (1) may underestimate sibling influence due to separate processes that operate in differentiation and likeness and (2) do not explicate the mechanisms by which such patterns emerge.

One recent meta-analysis conducted by Buist, Deković, and Prinzie (2012) did tackle meditational processes implicated in the link between sibling relationships and the development of psychopathology in children and adolescence. Results of 34 studies underscored the positive effects of sibling warmth, lowered sibling conflict, and less parental differential treatment that manifested in less internalizing and externalizing problems. These effect sizes were further moderated by sibling gender arrangement with stronger effects for brother pairs, age difference between siblings with stronger effects for smaller age gaps, and developmental period with stronger effects for children than adolescents. The researchers attributed the findings to a number of theoretical explanations: (1) attachment processes between siblings may relate to healthy relational emotional regulation (Guttmann-Steinmetz & Crowell, 2006) and lessen the risk for developing anxiety, depression, and aggressive behaviour; (2) siblings may promote the attainment of social skills through positive relational dynamics (Yeh & Lempers, 2004) and so mitigate the potential for depression, loneliness, or antisocial behaviour; and (3) social competence and confidence might be bolstered in warm, supportive sibling relationships, thus offsetting the development of psychopathology (Sherman, Lansford, & Volling, 2006). A final key takeaway from this meta-analysis highlighted the greater impact of negative (sibling conflict) influence in comparison with sibling warmth and parental differential treatment, though the exact processes by which this observation arises await further investigation.

Disability, illness, and coping strategies

A special subfield in sibling research investigates how families deal with chronic illness or disability. What does it mean when a sibling has a disease or disability? How does this affect family dynamics more generally, and the relationship between siblings in particular? In the film *What's Eating Gilbert Grape*, themes such as caregiving, independence and autonomy, and familial expectations are explored in the relationship between an older brother and his younger brother with autism to great effect. A number of projects have assessed the impact of having a sibling with a disability on siblings, the family as a whole, and the individual itself. Some evidence suggests that sibling relationship dynamics differ in families with a child with a disability. Although parents might be perceived to treat the child with the disability in a more preferential manner, this differential treatment does not necessarily proscribe sibling conflict or adjustment difficulties as in other family types (McHale & Pawletko, 1992). Parental differential treatment perceived as fair by siblings such as in the case of a brother or sister with a disability may relate to overall positive relations (Kowal & Kramer, 1997). In fact, the presence of one sibling with a disability or illness has been correlated with more positive affect and warmth in some investigations (Begum & Blacher, 2011; Stoneman, 2001). Conversely, having a brother or sister with ASD was found to be related to the development of internalizing behaviour in the non-affected sibling, although the mechanisms and processes at work are unclear (Ross & Cuskelly, 2006) As McHale and colleagues project, having a sibling with a disability or illness may make for greater variability in a typical sibling's life, and so it is important to further understand individual and disability or illness-specific factors involved in adjustment for both siblings (McHale *et al.*, 2012).

Coping strategies and the impact on individual development of siblings are of current interest to Beth Manke from California State University, USA, who explores illness-related and common developmental stressors among children with Type 2 diabetes (*Diabetes – Children and Their Siblings (D-CATS)*) (e.g. Eriksen & Manke, 2011). Manke's cross-sectional study includes families with at least two children between the ages of 8 and 18 years, of which one was diagnosed with Type 2 diabetes. Participating siblings are interviewed regarding their social relationships, stressors, coping strategies, and mental health, and participate in regular telephone interviews to report on their daily activities across the past 2 weeks. Furthermore, parents complete questionnaires about their children's medical history and mental health, family life events, as well as family relations. The project aims to determine which aspects of illness are most stressful and delineate typical coping strategies used to deal with these stressors. Manke also analyses whether sibling-related coping mitigates the association between stress and depression and anxiety, and if older siblings who are successful themselves in coping with stressful circumstances may serve as positive role models for children with chronic illness. We look forward to the results of project like this one, which highlight the role of siblings in health and risk behaviours and coping strategies.

Substance initiation and use

In understanding initiation into substance use, two broad categories are typically employed: genetic predispositions and psychosocial influences (Marlatt, Baer, Donovan, & Kivlahan, 1988). With respect to the former, two predicating assumptions are laid out with the implications of genetic heritability in addition to epigenetic factors. That is, epigenetic forces operate by way of heritability interacting with certain environmental features (Holliday, 2006). Again, studies on twins, adopted children, and half-brothers and half-sisters are useful in disentangling these complex interactions (Adityanjee & Murray, 1991). Alcoholism has been thought to be largely genetically based; higher than expected concordance rates between identical twins versus their fraternal counterparts, for instance, can attest to this view (Adityanjee & Murray, 1991). Investigations of half-siblings and adoptees additionally suggest strong genetic influence in alcohol abuse (Adityanjee & Murray, 1991; Crabbe et al., 1985). Finally, sons of alcoholics have shown initial tolerance for alcohol as well as unique neuropsychological profiles (Marlatt et al., 1988). This research underscores evidence for the genetic predispositions implicated in substance use typically initiated in the teen years (Heaven, 1994).

While exploring the key psychosocial facets that determine drug use, Brook et al. (1990) discovered sibling factors constituted a considerable influence. As per social learning theory, older siblings can serve as powerful role models in the relationship to substance usage. If both youths have positive attitudes towards deviance, for example, this could translate to drug use later on. For interventional purposes, it is important to consider younger siblings' perception of older siblings, as those who are viewed as similar and have a relationship characterized by warmth and positivity are more likely to be modelled (e.g. Bandura, 1977; Festinger, 1954). The social environment in which sibling relationships transpire additionally colours attitudes and shapes behaviours of both siblings through bidirectional effects (Derkman et al., 2011). We examine environmental influences next.

Socio-environmental influences on the sibling relationship

Siblings develop and interact with one another within wider intersecting familial and systemic contexts (Maughan, 2011). The transactional nature of the person–environment interrelationship implies that each sibling brings in their individual-level qualities that influence and are influenced by the environment in which they are intricately embedded (Scheithauer, Niebank, & Ittel, 2009). Like Bronfenbrenner (1979, 1986) expounds in his ecological theory of social development, or in Kurt Lewin's (1939) privileging of both person and context in his writings on the importance of 'life space', forces outside the family household shape adolescent sibling interactions. Shared and unique environmental powers such as socio-economic setting, school context, or neighbourhood ecosocial environment influence siblings, alone and together; they comprise the physical and social realities in which bidirectional relationships occur.

According to the ecological systems view of development, multiple interacting levels of influence guide developmental courses and relationships (see Figure 3.1). Within the most proximal microsystem, including the adolescent's daily life setting, the household is of utmost importance. More distal meso- and macro-level factors such as the local neighbourhood playground, school-based extracurricular organizations, or cultural influences likewise play critical roles in adolescents' growth. In the case of the potency of school-based characteristics in development, consider that the average time spent within this institution's walls falls in the range of some 14,000 hours; school is the place where children spend the majority of their time outside the home (Elmore, 2009). Impacts from early childhood class effects (Pellegrine & Perlmutter, 1989) and extracurricular activities (Mahoney & Cairns, 1997) attest to the power of place in shaping relationships and development.

A few studies have considered ecological factors from Bronfenbrenner's (1979, 1986) meso- and macro-levels, thus incorporating analysis of social forces outside the familial sphere. This is important in that differential access to forms of social, economic, and cultural capital impact development. From a behavioural standpoint, problem behaviours are linked to economic disadvantage (that is in turn often linked to lack of social supports and infrastructure), particularly for boys, and implicate stress in the familial context, which then influences family system and sibling relationships (e.g. Brody *et al.*, 2003; Maughan, 2011). Single-parent and blended families likely face increased economic pressures as well as social stigmatization and decreased support, which add to increased stress; however, once controlled, there are no differences by family type (Maughan, 2011). In other examinations, lower social economic satus (SES) has been linked with negative sibling relationships (e.g. R. D. Conger *et al.*, 1992; Dunn, Slomkowski, & Beardsall, 1994). Furthermore, residential instability and poor-quality housing were the most consistent and strongest predictors of emotional and behavioural problems in low-SES children and youth in another investigation, due to the strain placed on parents and accompanying anxiety and depression in the family system (Coley, Leventhal, Lynch, & Kull, 2013). Yet evidence to the contrary underscores the lack of clarity of the relationship between socio-economic indicators and familial and sibling relationship quality (McHale, Whiteman, Kim, & Crouter, 2007).

Some researchers have taken to studying the effects of neighbourhoods on the sibling relationship. Families and their subsystems may act as mediators and moderators of such community-level effects, where 'families and neighbourhoods jointly influence youth outcomes' (Duncan & Raudenbush, 2001, p. 116). Updegraff and

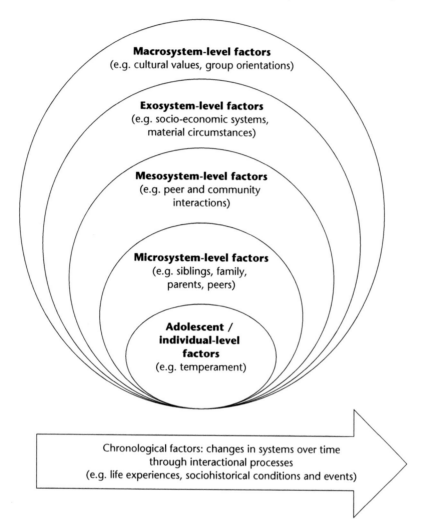

FIGURE 3.1 Depiction of adolescent development ecology

Source: Based on Bronfenbrenner (1986).

Obeidallah (1999) found that adolescents who lived in areas with high accessibility to common play areas like playgrounds were more likely to develop intimate relationships with their peers than with their siblings. In another analysis, Kerr, Stattin, and Kiesner (2007) assessed everyone and everyplace in an adolescent's 'life space' in the argumentation for examination of relationship effects, in this case, that of peer relations. Complete evaluation of environmental influence needs to go beyond assessment of the typical actors; these researchers' study of all children in a town allowed them to view the adolescent in each afforded context. Future examination should consider such holistic framing beyond the confines of family home and school contexts in the understanding of siblings' bidirectional impacts (e.g. Bukowski & Lisboa, 2007; Greer, Campione-Barr, Debrown, & Maupin, 2014; Hopfer, 2014).

Summing up

In this chapter, we sought to give a brief overview of some of the correlates and processes implicated in the adolescent sibling relationship and the impact siblings have on one another during this key developmental period. We began by delineating personality, individuation, and birth order influences; we then moved to social relational dynamics, health and risk behaviours, and ended with a focus on external influences on the sibling relationship. Additional examination of the exact mechanisms, convergent and divergent processes, and their contingencies, particularly among under-studied groups of siblings (e.g. Whiteman, Zeiders, Killoren, Rodriguez, & Updegraff, 2014), embedded within their socio-environmental context, are necessary to best guide researchers in their quest for effective interventional science.

References

Adams, B. N. (1972). Birth order: A critical review. *Sociometry, 35*, 411–439. Adams, G. R., & Berzonsky, M. D. (2003). *Blackwell handbook of adolescence.* Oxford: Blackwell.

Adityanjee, M., & Murray, R. (1991). The role of genetic predisposition in alcoholism. In I. Glass (Ed.), *The international handbook of addiction behavior* (pp. 41–47). London: Routledge.

Andrew Collins, W., & Steinberger, L. (2008). Adolescent development in interpersonal context. In W. Damon & R. Lerner (Eds.), *Child and adolescent development: An advanced course* (pp. 551–590). Hoboken, NJ: John Wiley & Sons.

Ansbacher, M. L., & Ansbacher, R. (1956). *The individual psychology of Alfred Adler.* New York: Basic Books.

Ary, D. V., Tildesley, E., Hops, H., & Andrews, J. (1993). The influence of parent, sibling, and peer modeling and attitudes on adolescent use of alcohol. *Substance Use & Misuse, 28*, 853–880.

Balsam, K. F., Rothblum, E. D., & Beauchaine, T. P. (2005). Victimization over the life span: A comparison of lesbian, gay, bisexual, and heterosexual siblings. *Journal of Consulting and Clinical Psychology, 73*(3), 477–487.

Bandura, A. (1977). *Social learning theory.* Englewood Cliffs, NJ: Prentice Hall.

Bank, L., Burraston, B., & Snyder, J. (2004). Sibling conflict and ineffective parenting as predictors of adolescent boys' antisocial behavior and peer difficulties: Additive and interactional effects. *Journal of Research on Adolescence, 14*(1), 99–125.

Bank, L., Patterson, G. R., & Reid, J. B. (1996). Negative sibling interaction patterns as predictors of later adjustment problems in adolescent and young adult males. In G. H. Brody (Ed.), *Sibling relationships: Their causes and consequences* (pp. 197–229). Westport, CT: Ablex.

Bank, S. P., & Kahn, M. D. (1982). *The sibling bond.* New York: Basic Books.

Begum, G., & Blacher, J. (2011). The siblings relationship of adolescents with and without intellectual disabilities. *Research in Developmental Disabilities, 32*(5), 1580–1588.

Behrman, J. R., & Taubman, P. (1986). Birth order, schooling, and earnings. *Journal of Labor Economics, 4*, S121–S145.

Bjornsen, C. A. (2000). The blessing as a rite of passage in adolescence. *Adolescence, 35,* 357–363.

Blos, P. (1967). The second individuation process of adolescence. *Psychoanalytic Study of the Child, 22,* 162–186.

Blos, P. (1985). *Son and father: Before and beyond the Oedipus complex.* New York: Free Press.

Blum, R. W., Beuhring, T., Shew, M. L., Bearinger, L. H., Sieving, R. E., & Resnick, M. D. (2000). The effects of race/ethnicity, income, and family structure on adolescent risk behaviors. *American Journal of Public Health, 90*(12), 1879–1884.

Boomsma, D. I., van Beijsterveld, T. C. E. M., Beem, A. L., Hoekstra, R. A., Polderman, T. J. C., & Bartels, M. (2008). Intelligence and birth order in boys and girls. *Intelligence, 36,* 630–634.

Bouchey, H. A., Shoulberg, E. K., Jodl, K. M., & Eccles, J. S. (2010). Longitudinal links between older sibling features and younger siblings' academic adjustment during early adolescence. *Journal of Educational Psychology, 102,* 197–211. doi:10.1037/aa0017487

Bowlby, J. (1980). *Attachment and loss: Loss, sadness, and depression* (Vol. 3). New York: Basic Books.

Bowleg, L., Huang, J., Brooks, K., Black, A., & Burkholder, G. (2003). Triple jeopardy and beyond: Multiple minority stress and resilience among Black lesbians. *Journal of Lesbian Studies, 7*(4), 87–108.

Branje, S. J., Van Lieshout, C. F., Van Aken, M. A., & Haselager, G. J. (2004). Perceived support in sibling relationships and adolescent adjustment. *Journal of Child Psychology and Psychiatry, 45*(8), 1385–1396.

Brody, G. H., Ge, X., Kim, S. Y., Murry, V. M., Simons, R. L., Gibbons, F. X., *et al.* (2003). Neighborhood disadvantage moderates associations of parenting and older sibling problem attitudes and behavior with conduct disorders in African American children. *Journal of Consulting and Clinical Psychology, 71,* 211–222.

Bronfenbrenner, U. (1979). *The ecology of human development: Experiments by nature and design.* Cambridge, MA: Harvard University Press.

Bronfenbrenner, U. (1986). Ecology of the family as a context for human development: Research perspectives. *Developmental Psychology, 22*(6), 723–742.

Brook, D., & Brook, J. (1990). The etiology and consequences of adolescent drug use. In R. Watson (Ed.), *Drug and alcohol abuse prevention* (pp. 339–362). Clifton, NJ: Humana Press.

Brook, J. S., Whiteman, M., Gordon, A. S., & Brook, D. W. (1990). The role of older brothers in younger brothers' drug use viewed in the context of parent and peer influences. *The Journal of Genetic Psychology, 151*(1), 59–75.

Buhrmester, D., & Furman, W. (1990). Perceptions of sibling relationships during middle childhood and adolescence. *Child Development, 61*(5), 1387–1398.

Buist, K. L., Deković, M., & Prinzie, P. (2012). Sibling relationship quality and psychopathology of children and adolescents: A meta-analysis. *Clinical Psychology Review, 33,* 97–106.

Bukowski, W., & Lisboa, C. (2007). Understanding the place of place in developmental psychology. In C. Rutger, E. Engels, & M. Kerr (Eds.), *Friends, lovers and groups: Key relationships in adolescence* (pp. 167–173). West Sussex: John Wiley & Sons.

Carnegie Council on Adolescent Development. (1996). *Great transitions: Preparing adolescents for a new century.* New York: Carnegie Corporation.

Chan, C. S. (1995). Issues of sexual identity in an ethnic minority: The case of Chinese American lesbians, gay men, and bisexual people. In A. R. D'Augelli & C. J. Petterson (Eds.), *Lesbian, gay, and bisexual identities over the lifespan* (pp. 87–101). New York: Oxford University Press.

Cicirelli, V. G. (1989). Feelings of attachment to siblings and well-being in later life. *Psychology and Aging, 4*(2), 211–216.

Cicirelli, V. G. (1995). *Sibling relationships across the life span.* New York: Plenum.

Coley, R. L., Leventhal, T., Lynch, A., & Kull, M. (2013). Relations between housing characteristics and the well-being of low-income children and adolescents. *Developmental Psychology, 49*(9), 1775–1789. doi:10.1037/a0031033

Conger, K. J., & Little, W. M. (2010). Sibling relationships during the transition to adulthood. *Child Development Perspectives, 4*(2), 87–94.

Conger, R. D., Conger, K. J., Elder, G. H., Lorenz, F. O., Simons, R. L., & Whitbeck, L. B. (1992). A family process model of economic hardship and adjustment of early adolescent boys. *Child Development, 63*(3), 526–541.

Conley, D. (2004). *The pecking order: Which siblings succeed and why.* New York: Pantheon.

Connidis, I. A. (2007). Negotiating inequality among adult siblings: Two case studies. *Journal of Marriage and Family, 69,* 482–499.

Consolacion, T. B., Russell, S. T., & Sue, S. (2004). Sex, race/ethnicity, and romantic attractions: Multiple minority status adolescents and mental health. *Cultural Diversity & Ethnic Minority Psychology, 10*(3), 200–214.

Cox, M. J. (2010). Family systems and sibling relationships. *Child Development Perspectives, 4*(2), 95–96.

Crabbe, J., McSwigan, J., & Belknap, J. (1985). The role of genetics in substance abuse. In M. Galizio & S. Maisto (Eds.), *Determinants of substance abuse treatment: Biological, psychological, and environmental factors* (pp. 13–64). New York: Plenum.

Craine, J. L., Tanaka, T. A., Nishina, A., & Conger, K. J. (2009). Understanding adolescent delinquency: The role of older siblings' delinquency and popularity with peers. *Merrill-Palmer Quarterly, 55*(4), 436–453.

Crockett, L. J., Raffaelli, M., & Moilanen, K. L. (2003). Adolescent sexuality: Behavior and meaning. In G. R. Adams & M. D. Berzonsky (Eds.), *Blackwell handbook of adolescence* (pp. 371–392). Malden, MA: Blackwell.

Dagys Pajoluk, N. (2013). Sibling relationship predictors of academic achievement in adolescents (Unpublished PhD dissertation). University of California, Los Angeles.

Daniels, D. (1986). Differential experiences of siblings in the same family as predictors of adolescent sibling personality differences. *Journal of Personality and Social Psychology, 51*(2), 339–346.

D'Augelli, A. R., Hershberger, S., & Pilkington, N. (1998). Lesbian, gay and bisexual youth and their families: Disclosure of sexual orientation and its consequences. *American Journal of Orthopsychiatry, 68*(3), 361–371.

Derkman, M. M., Engels, R. C., Kuntsche, E., van der Vorst, H., & Scholte, R. H. (2011). Bidirectional associations between sibling relationships and parental support during adolescence. *Journal of Youth and Adolescence, 40*(4), 490–501.

Diamond, L. M., & Savin-Williams, R. C. (2003). The intimate relationships of sexual-minority youths. In M. D. Berzonsky & G. R. Adams (Eds.), *Handbook of adolescence* (pp. 393–412). Malden, MA: Blackwell.

Duncan, G. J., & Raudenbush, S. W. (2001). Neighborhoods and adolescent development: How can we determine the links. In A. Booth & N. Crouter (Eds.), *Does it take a village? Community effects on children, adolescents, and families state college* (pp. 105–136). University Park, PA: Pennsylvania State University Press.

Dunn, J. (1998). Siblings, emotion, and development of understanding. In S. Braten (Ed.), *Intersubjective communication and emotion in early ontogeny: Studies in emotion and social interaction* (pp. 158–168). New York: Cambridge University Press.

Dunn, J. (2007). Siblings and socialization. In J. Grusec & P. D. Hastings (Eds.), *Handbook of socialization: Theory and research* (pp. 309–327). New York: Guilford Press.

Dunn, J. (2011). Sibling influences. In D. Skuse, H. Bruce, L. Dowdney, & D. Mrazek (Eds.), *Child psychology and psychiatry: Frameworks for practice* (2nd ed., pp. 8–12). West Sussex: John Wiley & Sons.

Dunn, J., & Munn, P. (1986). Siblings and the development of prosocial behaviour. *International Journal of Behavioral Development, 9*(3), 265–284.

Dunn, J., Slomkowski, C., & Beardsall, L. (1994). Sibling relationships from the preschool period through middle childhood and early adolescence. *Developmental Psychology, 30,* 315–324.

Dunn, J., & Stocker, C. M. (1989). The significance of differences in siblings' experiences within the family. In K. Kreppner & R. Lerner (Eds.), *Family systems and life-span development* (pp. 289–301). Hillsdale, NJ: Erlbaum.

East, P. L. (1998). Impact of adolescent childbearing on families and younger siblings: Effects that increase younger siblings' risk for early pregnancy. *Applied Developmental Science, 2,* 62–74. doi:10.1207/s1532480xads0202_1

East, P. L. (2009). Adolescents' relationships with siblings. In R. Lerner & L. Steinberg (Eds.), *Handbook on adolescent psychology: Contextual influences on adolescent psychology* (3rd ed., Vol. 2, pp. 43–73). Hoboken, NJ: Wiley.

East, P. L., & Jacobson, L. J. (2001). The younger siblings of teenage mothers: A follow-up of their pregnancy risk. *Developmental Psychology, 37*(2), 254–264.

Edwards, R., Hadfield, L., Lucey, H., & Mauthner, M. (2006). *Sibling identity and relationships: Sisters and brothers.* Oxon: Routledge.

Elmore, R. (2009). Schooling Adolescents. In R. Lerner & L. Steinberg (Eds.), *Handbook of adolescent psychology* (Vol. 2, pp. 193–227). Hoboken, NJ: John Wiley & Sons.

Eriksen, S. J., & Manke, B. (2011). 'Because being fat means being sick': Children at risk of type 2 diabetes. *Sociological Inquiry, 81*(4), 549–569.

Espin, O. M. (1997). Crossing borders and boundaries: The life narratives of immigrant lesbians. In B. Greene (Ed.), *Ethnic and cultural diversity among lesbians and gay men* (pp. 191–215). Thousand Oaks, CA: Sage.

Eysenck, H., & Eysenck, S. (1975). *Manual of the Eysenck Personality Questionnaire.* London: Hodder & Stoughton.

Fagan, A. A., & Najman, J. M. (2005). The relative contributions of parental and sibling substance use to adolescent tobacco, alcohol, and other drug use. *Journal of Drug Issues, 35,* 869–884.

Feinberg, M. E., & Hetherington, E. M. (2000). Sibling differentiation in adolescence: Implications for behavioral genetic theory. *Child Development, 71*(6), 1512–1524.

Feinberg, M. E., McHale, S., Crouter, A., & Cumsille, P. (2003). Sibling differentiation: Sibling and parent relationship trajectories in adolescence. *Child Development, 74,* 1261–1274.

Feinberg, M. E., Neiderhiser, J. M., Simmens, S., Reiss, D., & Hetherington, E. M. (2000). Sibling comparison of differential parental treatment in adolescence: Gender, self-esteem, and emotionality as mediators of the parenting-adjustment association. *Child Development, 71*(6), 1611–1628.

Feinberg, M. E., Solmeyer, A. R., & McHale, S. M. (2012). The third rail of family systems: Sibling relationships, mental and behavioral health, and preventive intervention in childhood and adolescence. *Clinical Child and Family Psychology Review, 15*(1), 43–57.

Festinger, L. (1954). A theory of social comparison processes. *Human Relations, 7*(2), 117–140.

Francis, A. M. (2008). Family and sexual orientation: The family-demographic correlates of homosexuality in men and women. *Journal of Sex Research, 45*(4), 371–377.

Furman, W., & Buhrmester, D. (1992). Age and sex in perceptions of networks of personal relationships. *Child Development, 63,* 103–115.

Furman, W., & Lanthier, R. (2002). Parenting siblings. In M. Bornstein (Ed.), *Handbook of parenting: Children and parenting* (2nd ed., Vol. 1, pp. 165–188). Mahwah, NJ: Lawrence Erlbaum Associates.

Garcia, M. M., Shaw, D. S., Winslow, E. B., & Yaggi, K. E. (2000). Destructive sibling conflict and the development of conduct problems in young boys. *Developmental Psychology, 36*, 44–53.

Gottesman, R. M. (2012). Coming out: Sexual orientation disclosure to siblings (Unpublished master's dissertation). Smith College School for Social Work, Northampton, MA.

Greer, K. B., Campione-Barr, N., Debrown, B., & Maupin, C. (2014). Do differences make the heart grow fonder? Associations between differential peer experiences on adolescent sibling conflict and relationship quality. *The Journal of Genetic Psychology, 175*(1), 16–34.

Grotevant, H. (1978). Sibling constellations and sex-typing of interests in adolescence. *Child Development, 49*, 540–542.

Guttmann-Steinmetz, S., & Crowell, J. A. (2006). Attachment and externalizing disorders: A developmental psychopathology perspective. *Journal of the American Academy of Child & Adolescent Psychiatry, 45*, 440–451. doi:10.1097/01.chi.0000196422.42599.63

Harter, S. (1999). *The construction of the self: A developmental perspective.* New York: Guilford Press.

Healey, M. D., & Ellis, B. J. (2007). Birth order, conscientiousness, and openness to experience: Tests of the family-niche model of personality using a within-family methodology. *Evolution and Human Behavior, 28*, 55–59.

Heaven, P. (1994). *Contemporary adolescence: A social psychological approach.* Melbourne: Macmillan.

Hess, M., Ittel, A., & Sisler, A. (2014). Gender-specific macro- and micro-level processes in the transmission of gender role orientation in adolescence: The role of fathers. *European Journal of Developmental Psychology, 11*, 211–226.

Hetherington, E. M., Henderson, S. H., Reiss, D., Anderson, E. R., Bridges, M., Chan, R. W., *et al.* (1999). Adolescent siblings in stepfamilies: Family functioning and adolescent adjustment. *Monographs of the Society for Research in Child Development, 64*, 1–222.

Hofstede, G. (1980). *Culture's consequences: International differences in work-related values.* Beverly Hills, CA: Sage.

Holliday, R. (2006). Epigenetics: A historical overview. *Epigenetics, 1*(2), 76–80.

Hopfer, C. (2014). Community, siblings, heritability and the risk for drug abuse. *American Journal of Psychiatry, 171*(2), 140–141.

Howe, N., Ross, H., & Recchia, H. (2010). Sibling relations in early childhood. In C. Hart & P. K. Smith (Eds.), *Wiley-Blackwell handbook of childhood Social development* (pp. 356–372). New York: Wiley.

Jenkins, J. (1992). Sibling relationships in disharmonious homes: Potential difficulties and protective effects. In F. Boer & J. Dunn (Eds.), *Children's sibling relationships* (pp. 125–138). Hillsdale, NJ: Erlbaum.

Kaminsky, L., & Dewey, D. (2002). Psychosocial adjustment in siblings of children with autism. *Journal of Child Psychology and Psychiatry, 43*, 225–232.

Karpel, M. (1976). Individuation: From fusion to dialogue. *Family Process, 15*, 65–82.

Kerr, M., Stattin, H., & Kiesner, J. (2007). Peers and problem behavior: Have we missed something. In C. Rutger, E. Engels, & M. Kerr (Eds.), *Friends, lovers and groups: Key relationships in adolescence* (pp. 125–153). West Sussex: John Wiley & Sons.

Kim, J. Y., McHale, S. M., Crouter, A. C., & Osgood, D. W. (2007). Longitudinal linkages between sibling relationships and adjustment from middle childhood through adolescence. *Developmental Psychology, 43*, 960–973.

Kim, J. Y., McHale, S. M., Wayne Osgood, D., & Crouter, A. C. (2006). Longitudinal course and family correlates of sibling relationships from childhood through adolescence. *Child Development, 77*(6), 1746–1761.

Knott, F., Lewis, C., & Williams, T. (1995). Sibling interaction of children with learning disabilities: A comparison of autism and Down's syndrome. *Journal of Child Psychology and Psychiatry, 36*, 965–976.

Kowal, A. K., & Kramer, L. (1997). Children's understanding of parental differential treatment. *Child Development, 68,* 113–126. doi:10.2307/1131929

Kowal, A. K., Krull, J. L., & Kramer, L. (2006). Shared understanding of parental differential treatment in families. *Social Development, 15*(2), 276–295.

Kramer, L. (2010). The essential ingredients of successful sibling relations: An emerging framework for advancing theory and practice. *Child Development Perspectives, 4,* 80–86.

Kramer, L., & Bank, L. (2005). Sibling relationship contributions to individual and family well-being: Introduction to the special issue. *Journal of Family Psychology, 19*(4), 483–485.

Kroger, J. (2004). *Identity in adolescence.* New York: Routledge.

Lapsley, D., & Stey, P. (2010). Separation-individuation. In I. Weiner & E. Craighead (Eds.), *Corsini's encyclopedia of psychology.* New York: Wiley.

Lasgaard, M., Nielsen, A., Eriksen, M. E., & Goossens, L. (2010). Loneliness and social support in adolescent boys with autism spectrum disorders. *Journal of Autism and Developmental Disorders, 40*(2), 218–226.

Lewin, K. (1939). The field theory approach to adolescence. *American Journal of Sociology, 44,* 868–897.

Low, S., Shortt, J. W., & Snyder, J. (2012). Sibling influences on adolescent substance use: The role of modeling, collusion, and conflict. *Development and Psychopathology, 24,* 287–300. doi:10.1017/S0954579411000836

Mahoney, J. L., & Cairns, R. B. (1997). Do extracurricular activities protect against early school dropout? *Developmental Psychology, 33,* 241–253.

Marcia, J. E. (1980). Identity in adolescence. In J. Adelson (Ed.), *Handbook of adolescent psychology* (pp. 159–187). New York: Wiley.

Marlatt, G. A., Baer, J. S., Donovan, D. M., & Kivlahan, D. R. (1988). Addictive behaviors: Etiology and treatment. *Annual Review of Psychology, 39*(1), 223–252.

Maughan, B. (2011). Family and systemic influences. In D. Skuse, H. Bruce, L. Dowdney, & D. Mrazek (Eds.), *Child psychology and psychiatry: Frameworks for practice* (2nd ed., pp. 3–7). West Sussex: John Wiley & Sons.

McHale, S. M., Bissell, J., & Kim, J. (2009). Sibling relationship, family, and genetic factors in sibling similarity in sexual risk. *Journal of Family Psychology, 23,* 562–572. doi:10.1037/a0014982

McHale, S. M., & Crouter, A. C. (1996). The family contexts of sibling relationships. In G. Brody (Ed.), *Sibling relationships: Their causes and consequences* (pp. 173–196). Norwood, NJ: Ablex.

McHale, S. M., Kim, J., & Whiteman, S. D. (2006). Sibling relationships in childhood and adolescence. In P. Noller & J. A. Feeney (Eds.), *Close relationships: Functions, forms, and processes* (pp. 128–149). New York: Psychology Press.

McHale, S. M., & Pawletko, T. (1992). Differential treatment of siblings in two family contexts. *Child Development, 63,* 68–81.

McHale, S. M., Updegraff, K. A., Helms-Erikson, H., & Crouter, A. C. (2001). Sibling influences on gender development in middle childhood and early adolescence: A longitudinal study. *Developmental Psychology, 37*(1), 115–125.

McHale, S. M., Updegraff, K. A., & Whiteman, S. D. (2012). Sibling relationships and influences in childhood and adolescence. *Journal of Marriage and Family, 74*(5), 913–930.

McHale, S. M., Whiteman, S. D., Kim, J., & Crouter, A. C. (2007). Characteristics and correlates of sibling relationships in two-parent African American families. *Journal of Family Psychology, 21,* 227–235.

Meunier, J. C., Roskam, I., Stievenart, M., Van De Moortele, G., Browne, D. T., & Wade, M. (2012). Parental differential treatment, child's externalizing behavior and sibling relationships: Bridging links with child's perception of favoritism and personality, and parents' self-efficacy. *Journal of Social and Personal Relationships, 29*(5), 612–638.

Michalski, R. L., & Shackelford, T. K. (2001). Methodology, birth order, intelligence, and personality. *American Psychologist, 56*, 520–521.

Milevsky, A., & Levitt, M. J. (2005). Sibling support in early adolescence: Buffering and compensation across relationships. *European Journal of Developmental Psychology, 2*, 299–320.

Mitchell, J. (2000). *Mad men and medusas: Reclaiming hysteria and the effects of Sibling relationships on the human condition.* London: Penguin Books.

Mitchell, J. (2003). *Siblings, sex and violence.* Cambridge: Polity Press.

Murray, C. E. (2006). Controversy, constraints, and context: Understanding family violence through family systems theory. *The Family Journal: Counseling and Therapy for Couples and Families, 14*(3), 234–239.

Newman, J. (1994). Conflict and friendship in sibling relationships: A review. *Child Study Journal, 24*, 119–152.

Noller, P., Conway, S., & Blakeley-Smith, A. (2008). Sibling relationships in adolescent and young adult twin and nontwin siblings: Managing competition and comparison. In J. P. Forgas & J. Fitness (Eds.), *Social relationships: Cognitive, affective, and motivational processes* (pp. 235–252). New York: Psychology Press.

Oliva, A., & Arranz, E. (2005). Sibling relationships during adolescence. *European Journal of Developmental Psychology, 2*(3), 253–270.

Patterson, G. R. (1984). Siblings: Fellow travelers in coercive family processes. *Advances in the Study of Aggression, 1*, 173–215.

Patterson, G. R. (1986). The contribution of siblings to training for fighting: A microsocial analysis. In J. Block, D. Olweus, & M. Radke-Yarrow (Eds.), *Development of antisocial and prosocial behavior* (pp. 235–261). New York: Academic Press.

Patterson, G. R., Dishion, T. J., & Bank, L. (1984). Family interaction: A process model of deviancy training. *Aggressive Behavior, 10*(3), 253–267.

Paulhus, D. L., Trapnell, P. D., & Chen, D. (1999). Birth order effects on personality and achievement within families. *Psychological Science, 10*(6), 482–488.

Pellegrine, A. D., & Perlmutter, J. C. (1989). Classroom contextual effects on children's play. *Developmental Psychology, 25*(2), 289–296.

Pike, A., Coldwell, J., & Dunn, J. (2006). *Family relationships in middle childhood.* York: York Publishing/Joseph Rowntree Foundation.

Pike, A., & Kretschmer, T. (2009). Shared versus nonshared effects: Parenting and children's adjustment. *International Journal of Developmental Science, 3*(2), 115–130.

Pike, A., & Kretschmer, T. (2010). Links between nonshared friendship experiences and adolescent siblings' differences in aspirations. *Journal of Adolescence, 33*, 101–110.

Plomin, R. (1994). Genetics and experience. *Current Opinion in Psychiatry, 7*(4), 297–299.

Plomin, R., & Daniels, D. (1987). Why are children in the same family so different from one another? *Behaviour and Brain Sciences, 10*, 1–60.

Raffaelli, M. (1997). Young adolescents' conflicts with siblings and friends. *Journal of Youth and Adolescence, 26*(5), 539–558.

Rodgers, J. L., & Rowe, D. C. (1988). Influence of siblings on adolescent sexual behavior. *Developmental Psychology, 24*, 722–728.

Rodgers, J. L., Rowe, D. C., & Harris, D. F. (1992). Sibling differences in adolescent sexual behavior: Inferring process models from family composition patterns. *Journal of Marriage and the Family, 54*, 142–152. doi:10.2307/353282

Rosenzweig, M. R. (1986). Birth spacing and sibling inequality: Asymmetric information within the family. *International Economic Review, 27*(1), 55–76.

Ross, P., & Cuskelly, M. (2006). Adjustment, sibling problems and coping strategies of brothers and sisters of children with autistic spectrum disorder. *Journal of Intellectual & Developmental Disability, 31*(2), 77–86.

Saintonge, S., Achille, P. A., & Lachance, L. (1998). The influence of big brothers on the separation–individuation of adolescents from single parent families. *Adolescence, 33*, 343–353.

Salmon, C. A. (1998). The evocative nature of kin terminology in political rhetoric. *Politics and the Life Sciences, 17*, 51–57.

Salmon, C. A. (1999). On the impact of sex and birth order on contact with kin. *Human Nature, 10*, 183–197.

Salmon, C. A. (2003). Birth order and relationships. *Human Nature, 14*(1), 73–88.

Salmon, C. A., & Daly, M. (1998). Birth order and familial sentiment: Middleborns are different. *Evolution and Human Behavior, 19*(5), 299–312.

Savin-Williams, R. C. (1996). Ethnic- and sexual-minority youth. In R. C. Savin-Williams & K. M. Cohen (Eds.), *The lives of lesbians, gays, and bisexuals: Children to adults* (pp. 152–165). Fort Worth, TX: Harcourt Brace.

Schachter, F. F., Gilutz, G., Shore, E., & Adler, M. (1978). Sibling deidentification judged by mothers: Cross-validation and developmental studies. *Child Development, 49*, 543–546.

Schachter, F. F., Shore, E., Feldman-Rotman, S., Marquis, R. E., & Campbell, S. (1976). Sibling deidentification. *Developmental Psychology, 12*, 418–427.

Scharf, M., Shulman, S., & Avigad-Spitz, L. (2005). Sibling relationships in emerging adulthood and in adolescence. *Journal of Adolescent Research, 20*(1), 64–90.

Scheithauer, H., Niebank, K., & Ittel, A. (2009). Developmental science: Integrating knowledge about dynamic processes in human development. In J. Valsiner, P. Molenaar, M. Lycra, & N. Chaudhary (Eds.), *Dynamic process methodology in the social and developmental sciences* (pp. 595–617). New York: Springer.

Scholte, R. H., Van Lieshout, C. F., & Van Aken, M. A. (2001). Perceived relational support in adolescence: Dimensions, configurations, and adolescent adjustment. *Journal of Research on Adolescence, 11*(1), 71–94.

Sherman, A. M., Lansford, J. E., & Volling, B. L. (2006). Sibling relationships and best friendships in young adulthood: Warmth, conflict, and well-being. *Personal Relationships, 13*, 151–165. doi:10.1111/j.1475-6811.2006.00110.x

Slomkowski, C., Rende, R., Conger, K. J., Simons, R. L., & Conger, R. D. (2001). Sisters, brothers, and delinquency: Evaluating social influence during early and middle adolescence. *Child Development, 72*, 271–283. doi:10.1111/1467-8624.00278

Slomkowski, C., Rende, R., Novak, S., Lloyd-Richardson, E., & Niaura, R. (2005). Sibling effects on smoking in adolescence: Evidence for social influence from a genetically informative design. *Addiction, 100*(4), 430–438.

Smetana, J. G., Campione-Barr, N., & Metzger, A. (2006). Adolescent development in interpersonal and societal contexts. *Annual Review Psychology, 57*, 255–284.

Smith, E., & Udry, J. R. (1985). Coital and noncoital sexual behaviors of White and Black adolescents. *American Journal of Public Health, 75*, 1200–1203.

Solmeyer, A. R., McHale, S. M., & Crouter, A. C. (2013). Longitudinal associations between sibling relationship qualities and risky behavior across adolescence. *Developmental Psychology, 50*(2), 600–610. doi:10.1037/a0033207

Sroufe, L. A., & Fleeson, J. (1986). Attachment and the construction of relationships. In W. Hartup & Z. Rubin (Eds.), *Relationships and development* (pp. 51–71). Hillsdale, NJ: Lawrence Erlbaum Associates.

Stephens, D. P., & Phillips, L. D. (2003). Freaks, gold diggers, divas, and dykes: The sociohistorical development of adolescent African American women's sexual scripts. *Sexuality & Culture, 7*(1), 3–49.

Stewart, R. B., Kozak, A. L., Tingley, L. M., Goddard, J. M., Blake, E. M., & Cassel, W. A. (2001). Adult sibling relationships: Validation of a typology. *Personal Relationships, 8*, 299–324.

Stocker, C., Dunn, J., & Plomin, R. (1989). Sibling relationships: Links with child temperament, maternal behavior, and family structure. *Child Development, 60*, 715–727.

Stoneman, Z. (2001). Supporting positive sibling relationships during childhood. *Mental Retardation and Developmental Disabilities Research Reviews, 7*(2), 134–142.

Stormshak, E. A., Bellanti, C. J., & Bierman, K. L. (1996). The quality of sibling relationships and the development of social competence and behavioral control in aggressive children. *Developmental Psychology, 32*(1), 79–89.

Sulloway, F. J. (1996). *Born to rebel: Birth order, family dynamics, and creative lives.* New York: Pantheon.

Sulloway, F. J. (2001). Birth order, sibling competition, and human behavior. In H. R. Holcomb III (Ed.), *Conceptual challenges in evolutionary psychology: Innovative research strategies* (pp. 39–83). Boston: Kluwer Academic Publishers.

Sulloway, F. J. (2007). Birth order. In C. Salmon & T. Shackelford (Eds.), *Evolutionary family psychology* (pp. 162–182). Oxford: Oxford University Press.

Tesser, A. (1980). Self-esteem maintenance in family dynamics. *Journal of Personality and Social Psychology, 39*, 77–91.

Tsao, L., & Odom, S. L. (2006). Sibling-mediated social interaction intervention for young children with autism. *Topics in Early Childhood Special Education, 26*, 106–123.

Turkheimer, E., & Waldron, M. (2000). Nonshared environment: A theoretical, methodological, and quantitative review. *Psychological Bulletin, 126*, 78–108.

Udry, J. R. (2003). *The National Longitudinal Study of Adolescent Health (Add Health), Wave III, 2001–2002.* Chapel Hill, NC: Carolina Population Center, University of North Carolina at Chapel Hill.

Updegraff, K. A., & Obeidallah, D. A. (1999). Young adolescents' patterns of involvement with siblings and friends. *Social Development, 8*, 52–69.

Updegraff, K. A., Thayer, S. M., Whiteman, S. D., Denning, D. J., & McHale, S. M. (2005). Relational aggression in adolescents' sibling relationships: Links to sibling and parent adolescent relationship quality. *Family Relations, 54*(3), 373–385.

Van IJzendoorn, M. H., Moran, G., Belsky, J., Pederson, D., Bakermans Kranenburg, M. J., & Kneppers, K. (2000). The similarity of siblings' attachments to their mother. *Child Development, 71*(4), 1086–1098.

Watzlawik, M. (2009). The perception of similarities and differences among adolescent siblings: Identification and deidentification of twins and nontwins. *Journal of Adolescent Research, 24*(5), 561–578.

Whiteman, S. D., McHale, S. M., & Crouter, A. C. (2007). Competing processes of sibling influence: Observational learning and sibling deidentification. *Social Development, 16*, 642–661. doi:10.1111/j.1467-9507.2007.00409.x

Whiteman, S. D., McHale, S. M., & Soli, A. (2011). Theoretical perspectives on sibling relationships. *Journal of Family Theory & Review, 3*(2), 124–139.

Whiteman, S. D., Zeiders, K. H., Killoren, S. E., Rodriguez, S. A., & Updegraff, K. A. (2014). Sibling influence on Mexican-origin adolescents' deviant and sexual risk behaviors: The role of sibling modeling. *Journal of Adolescent Health, 54*(5), 587–592.

Widmer, E. D. (1997). Influence of older siblings on initiation of sexual intercourse. *Journal of Marriage and the Family, 59*, 928–938. doi:10. 2307/353793

Wolke, D., & Skew, A. J. (2012). Bullying among siblings. *International Journal of Adolescent Medicine and Health, 24*(1), 17–25.

Yana, S. (1998). Sexuality and procreation among the Bamileke and Beti. In B. Kuate-Defo (Ed.), *Sexuality and reproductive health during adolescence in Africa* (pp. 91–107). Ottawa: University of Ottawa Press.

Yeh, H., & Lempers, J. D. (2004). Perceived sibling relationships and adolescent development. *Journal of Youth and Adolescence, 33*, 133–147.

4

BEHAVIOURAL GENETICS AND SIBLING RESEARCH

Introducing behavioural genetics and sibling research

The study of the behavioural genetics of siblings offers a unique window through which genetic and environmental influences can be unravelled and their relative significance appraised. Some of the largest systematic studies of adolescent siblings have utilized behavioural genetic methods. Conversely, other behaviour genetics investigations enlist specific sibling types such as identical and fraternal twins and adopted children as methodological tools. We overview here the theory and assumptions behind genetically sensitive research, the classic methodological strategies applied in the field, of which twin and adoption designs take centre stage, examples of behavioural genetics research, and, finally, the implications for adolescent siblings.

Specifically, in this chapter, we describe the theory and methods of this approach and outline the relevant results. We discuss, for instance, the importance of within-family variation, that is, nonshared environmental leverage, and the work that this has generated. We then illustrate with recent surveys the inheritance of behavioural traits and their environmental interplay regarding their role in adolescent transitional behaviours and activities, personality development, mental health, and social relationships with family members and others. In addition, the topics of child-specific effects and within-family study are addressed. To conclude, we touch upon issues of controversy and necessary directives for the advancement of the field and our understanding of siblings in adolescence.

> My sister and I, you will recollect, were twins, and you know how subtle are the links which bind two souls which are so closely allied.
> — *Sir Arthur Conan Doyle, The Adventure of the Speckled Band*

Behavioural genetics: A primer

The highly interdisciplinary field of behavioural genetics researches the contribution of genetics to animal and human behaviour (Jablonka & Lamb, 2005). Primary to the study of individual differences in traits and behaviours, this approach holds that the expression of human diversity is influenced by the dynamic interplay of genetic variation, different environments, and individuals' experiences within them (Pike, 2012b; Plomin, 1989). Heritability, a key construct, gives an indication of the amount of trait variance attributable to genetic factors considering development as it takes place within particular environmental conditions. Like two cherries sprouted from the same twig, the one receiving sun with regularity, the other shaded by her twin's overhanging leaf, ripened fruit from the same tree of heritage yet differentially exposed to the elements gives indication of heritable contributions and ecological effects.

But what of the age-old nature–nurture controversy? Is the diversity of humanity simply inherited through our unique genes or is development subject to purely environmental forces? According to current consensus, this false dichotomy has been settled; biology and the environment co-act in complex ways (e.g. Turkheimer, 2000; Turkheimer & Waldron, 2000). Rather, the top focus for investigations lies in identifying reciprocal bi-directional processes that elucidate development. Additionally, researchers now seek to identify the environmental variables involved in the 'nonshared' residual variance that remains once shared environmental and genetic effects have been considered (Rodgers & Bard, 2003). In this way, the area of behavioural genetics can be deemed unbalanced in its title, as environmental influences are just as critical to the comprehension of development.

Viewed from an epigenetic framework and its series of assumptions, the field does not rely solely on any particular normative model of human development and generally does not scrutinize group level difference. Rather, behavioural geneticists delve into the partitioning out of the relative influence of genes and experiences of particular environments. Variation in certain relational styles or relationship schemata, for instance, can be explored by looking at the difference between genetically similar siblings along with their shared and nonshared environmental influences. Just as Panksepp and Biven (2012) emphasize, ' . . . it is within the complexities of such differential gene-expression and epigenetic processes within the brain that *primary process* nomothetic abilities diverge into idiographic developmental landscapes of learning and cognition . . . ' (p. 151).

At its most fundamental, behavioural genetics aims to further the study of development by dividing and ascribing variation in individuals to biological versus environmental experiences, supported by the increasing usage of dual idiographic-nomothetic precepts, which importantly both specify and generalize, for the study of development (Kendall & Comer, 2013; Panksepp & Biven, 2012; Pike, 2012b).

This popular, albeit often-times controversial, methodology has been employed within developmental study and traditionally recruited in investigations of genetic variance and influence for over a century (Winerman, 2004). When one asks of the weight of 'nature versus nurture' in an individual's genesis, as one of the founding fathers of the field Sir Francis Galton (1875) did in his treatise *Inquiries into the Human Faculty and Its Development*, underpinning issues that lay at the intersection of biology, genetics, epigenetics, ethology, statistics, and psychology are raised, issues that are best explored, Galton already understands, by studying twins:

> The exceedingly close resemblance attributed to twins has been the subject of many novels and plays, and most persons have felt a desire to know upon what basis of truth those works of fiction may rest. But twins have a special claim upon our attention; it is, that their history affords means of distinguishing between the effects of tendencies received at birth, and of those that were imposed by the special circumstances of their after lives. The objection to statistical evidence in proof of the inheritance of peculiar faculties has always been: 'The persons whom you compare may have lived under similar social conditions and have had similar advantages of education, but such prominent conditions are only a small part of those that determine the future of each man's life'. (Galton, 1875, p. 156)

Along with Galton, foremost early theorists such as Weinberg (1910) and Siemens (1924) believed twins to be valuable in the study of human development, personality, behaviour, and psychopathology (Gedda, 1961; Rende, Plomin, & Vandenberg, 1990). While all these scholars privileged the biological, and in varying degrees, the environmental, in an individual's development, not all recognized the separability of twins into monozygotic (MZ) and dizygotic (DZ) categories. MZ or 'identical' twins possess duplicate genotypes, while DZ or fraternal twins have exactly half of their genetic material in common. Herein lies the value of the twin study: by examining similarities and differences in characteristics between twins, we can attribute the distribution of those characteristics to either the environment or genes and determine the heritability of a given trait with relative accuracy.

The distinction between identical twins, who share all of their alleles and their ovum of origin, and fraternal twins, who having germinated from two separate eggs and two separate sperm cells share approximately 50 per cent of their alleles, is a central issue not only in the study of twins, but in the theoretical assumptions of sibling research in general. Important to note is that non-twin siblings share the same percentage of their polymorphic alleles as their fraternal twin counterparts, which enables valuable comparative study.

But adoption studies and within-family studies of non-twin siblings also offer additional points of investigation and share similar issues of contention. In the following, we cover the classical twin and adoption research designs employed in behavioural genetics and the study of siblings.

Classic methods

Traditionally, genetically sensitive quantitative research has incorporated the usage of the twin and adoption study designs (Pike, 2012b). Both represent quasi-experimental frameworks for researching siblings who possess varying degrees of genetic similarity, for example, MZ twins versus non-twin siblings. Another key avenue of research is the examination of nonshared environmental influence: those environmental forces unique to each sibling are studied alongside the forces shared within a family. Basic univariate models of genetic variety break down the variance of traits on the basis of genetic, shared, and nonshared environmental components (DeThorne & Hart, 2009). Moreover, covariance investigation between a number of traits or behaviours also conscripts this schema (Pike & Kretschmer, 2009). To demonstrate, shared environmental characteristics could encompass parental warmth, for instance, although if parents differentially allocate warmth to a daughter and a son, then this would count as a unique nonshared force. For illustrative purposes, Figure 4.1 outlines a behavioural genetic common factors model whereby the ACE model (described later) is depicted using the influences common to harsh parenting and antisocial behaviour (in Pike & Kretschmer, 2009). The next section describes two common research designs which enlist siblings to detect developmental influences.

The twin study design

Since the times of Hippocrates and other Roman and Greek philosophers, twins have taken a prominent role in the understanding of human development (Gedda, 1961). The systematic study of twins, epitomized by the Minnesota Twin Family Study (MTFS), whose records go back nearly a century and a half, provides researchers with multiple points of analysis (McGue, 2010). Through behavioural genetic means using genetically sensitive sampling procedures, researchers are able to parse out shared (e.g. the family home climate) and nonshared (e.g. one sibling's

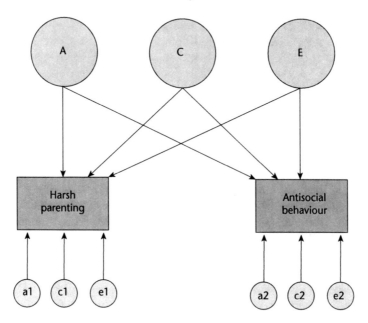

A = genetic, C = shared environmental, E = nonshared environmental influences common to parenting and antisocial behaviour; a1 = genetic, c1 = shared environmental, e1 = nonshared environmental influences unique to harsh parenting; a2 = genetic, c2 = shared environmental, e2 = nonshared environmental influences unique to antisocial behaviour.

FIGURE 4.1   ACE model

Source: Pike and Kretschmer (2009, p. 118); with kind permission from Springer.

exceptional kindergarten teacher) environmental influence (e.g. Pike & Plomin, 1996). In the comparison of great numbers of twins and their families, developmentalists can look at the level to which identical MZ twins are more similar than their DZ counterparts; they are then able to see if, in fact, genetic influence is central for a specific human trait or characteristic. If genetic influence is high, MZ twins should, based on twin study tenets, be more similar. Similarity beyond genetic factors is then ascribed to the shared environment such as brother and sister living in the same single-father household. Furthermore, unique, nonshared environmental forces can be modelled alongside measurement error and is exhibited in the difference between MZ pairs.

The investigation of twin pairs estimates the variance of a behaviour or phenotype within a large sample by modelling the genetic effects (heritability, denoted as A for additive genetics), shared environments (common environment, expressed as C), and unique environment (unshared influence, expressed as E). This relatively simple 'ACE' model can be further amended to incorporate non-additive genetics effects (D for dominance), in the 'ADE' model, involved in complex twin study designs; these effects are modelled almost universally by researchers via maximum likelihood methodologies and point to the power of twin designs (Martin & Eaves, 1977; Martin, Eaves, Kearsey, & Davies, 1978). Multivariate, panel study or multiple measurement investigations are generally the most common methods of inquiry, as in growth curve modelling, which can address issues of causality, and allows for across-time analysis. For instance, recent work by the likes of Boeldt *et al.* (2012) on externalizing behaviour and positive parenting shows how behaviour genetic modelling can inform the extent to which individual differences are attributable to genetic and environmental pull.

Contemporary twin studies have displayed the ubiquitous influence of genetics on all human traits (e.g. Bard & Rodgers, 2003). However, the degree of influence depends upon the characteristic in question (Bouchard, 2004). Height and eye colour exhibit strong genetic heritability, whereas the inheritance of schizophrenia and autism appear to be much more complex, implicating the importance of gene–environment epigenetic interactions in the expression of a particular phenotype. Even IQ inheritance estimates vary markedly as the environment's role is hotly debated in multiple twin studies and their subsequent critiques (e.g. Bouchard, Lykken, McGue, Segal, & Tellegen, 1990; Richardson & Norgate, 2006; Turkheimer, Haley, Waldron, Onofio, & Gottesman, 2003). The onus now falls on researchers to abandon the former nature versus nurture debate and develop a better understanding of their relative importance, their complexity, and their interactive processes (Plomin, 1989).

The twin design bears a number of limitations. At face value, it does not lend itself to the systematic investigation of shared environmental influence and non-additive genetic influence in tandem; explanatory power is limited in the traditional twin set-up as it does not directly measure but instead models family environment influence (Rose, 2007). However, within-family designs utilizing additional non-twin siblings can mitigate this drawback (Ehringer, Rhee, Young, Corley, & Hewitt, 2006). Additionally, the gene–environment relationship is not readily isolated and requires serious contemplation of its meaning (e.g. an 'exactly what are we measuring here' assessment) on the part of scientists. Adoption models paired with children-of-twins designs can begin to counteract the lack of knowledge on family effects unrelated to shared heritable effects.

The adoption study design

Conversely, the extent to which non-biologically related adoptive siblings are similar lends insight into the power of shared experience. The differences between the adoptee and the biological parent(s) are granted to genetics, while similarities are declared to be environmentally centred (Plomin, Fulker, Corley, & DeFries, 1997). In terms of sibling studies then, similarity between adoptive siblings is credited to shared environmental influence and its experience. Adoptive studies are oft cited in the investigation of psychopathology and its development, for instance, in the displayed heritability of schizophrenia (Ingraham & Kety, 2000) and mood and psychiatric disorders (Shih, Belmonte, & Zandi, 2004; Smoller & Finn, 2003), although issues regarding the reliability and completeness of data drawn from biological and adoptive parents and adoptees are frequently questionable (Roth &

Finley, 1998). All the same, the initial findings of adoptive studies generally converge on one theme: environmental effects are widespread and potent, but they are more involved in determining difference versus similarities of individuals raised together (Plomin & Daniels, 1987).

Taking twins reared apart into account blends together multiple advantages from twin and adoptive research. Drawing from the rich data provided by the MTFS, researchers were able to ascertain the marked similarity between twins brought up in separate households along a variety of features, including inborn abilities and propensities, physical appearance, attributes, and personality (Bouchard *et al.*, 1990; Iacono & McGue, 2002). That is to say that children raised in situations apart from their biological parents carry with them their biological propensities, but the particular environments they are exposed to and interact with then turn on or off the likelihood that a certain phenotype is expressed. Individuals act within the bounds of their genetic scripts (Moore, 2006).

As this chapter seeks to contribute to new areas of discussion in adolescent sibling study, classic results of twin and adoptive studies like that of the genetic heritability of cognitive abilities, for example, IQ (for a review, see Pike, 2012b), physical growth (e.g. Turkheimer, 1998), and psychopathology (e.g. schizophrenia, Cardno & Gottesman, 2000) are not reviewed. Rather, in the forthcoming sections, we delve into new fruitful arenas currently being assessed in developmental science and their implications for adolescent brothers and sisters. For these purposes, we make use of past and current behaviour genetic research on adolescence.

Recent research and its implications

But before we explore recent advances, a classic study of twins will shed light on some central issues. Loehlin and Nichols (1976) conducted a mass-scale adolescent twin study nearly 40 years ago that fundamentally changed the tone of the nature–nurture debate. Their findings showed that genetic inheritance accounted for roughly half the variance of self-reported measures for personality-related factors, yet the shared environment's role was found to be puzzlingly low: 'At least for dimensions of self-reported personality, neither parental rearing practices, the home atmosphere parents created, nor differences in family structure and status influenced the relative similarity of adolescent co-twins' (Rose, 2007, p. 106). This is not to say that shared environment is negligible in development. Instead, additional evidence has augmented these initial findings and converges on the premise that common environment is thought to exert strong influence in terms of aptitudes and capabilities, and even has effects for some dimensions of self-reported personality (Rose, 2007). For instance, Anderson and colleagues found nonshared and shared parenting to be roughly equal in their influence on adolescent siblings' adjustment and social competence and that these associations were similar between genders and diverse family types (Anderson, Hetherington, Reiss, & Howe, 1994). Further to note, observational assessment of siblings, length of co-habitation, and contact after separation in the case of twins all give indication of the need for refinement of behavioural genetics and sibling study.

Adolescence and transitional behaviours

The use of behaviour genetics methodology should come with an awareness of the topic at hand, in this case adolescence, and add to its understanding. As Bard and Rodgers state, the study of adolescent behavioural genetics has been held back by the lack of an integrative framework for study. Accordingly, they outline three possible perspectives or 'motivating orientations' with which we can frame the process of adolescent development in behavioural genetic terms (Rodgers & Bard, 2003). The Transition Behaviour Perspective (e.g. Rodgers & Rowe, 1993), which considers adolescence as a time for widened behavioural opportunity; Problem Behaviour Theory (Jessor & Jessor, 1977), which considers clusters of problem behaviour and further subdivides them into 'adolescence-limited' and 'life course persistent' behavioural clusters (Moffit, 1993); and the Life Course Perspective (Elder, 1975), which considers age-appropriate socio-cultural norms surrounding specific life course trajectories, all help shape discourse around adolescent development. Just as well, a biological perspective that inspects adolescent 'hormonal influences that affect both physiological changes and behavioural changes' serves to guide current research (Rodgers & Bard, 2003). We do not go into these perspectives in depth here, but rather adopt their premises to guide the presentation of related empirical data on adolescent siblings.

The extent of genetic variance in adolescent transition behaviours like smoking, drinking, sexual behaviour, and other (risk-taking) practices has been well established through behavioural genetics (Adams & Berzonsky, 2003). When one begins with the assumption that reciprocal effects of siblings are augmented among same age and gender siblings, twins should then exert potent reciprocal effects through mutual social learning and modelling (Bandura, 1977). Carey's (1986) model for mapping out twin effects regarding criminality offers a good example. In this framework, behavioural variance between twins resides in the level of reciprocal interactions and their covariance. Dichotomous behavioural outcomes like criminal involvement can be deduced based on genetic modelling of identical twins or sex-limited models of same-sex siblings. The impacts of cooperative social modelling in the sibling relationship can be examined through this lens (Rose, 2007), and indeed, findings from 16-year-old Finnish twins and their initiation to drinking attest to cooperative sibling effects (Rose, Kaprio, Winter, Koskenvuo, & Viken, 1999). We can continue to gather information on such mutual influences through elucidation of convergent and divergent processes at play in sibling relationships as in Whiteman, Jensen, and Maggs (2013, 2014) who look at differences and similarities in adolescent siblings' alcohol-related consumption, beliefs, and delinquency.

Other classic adolescent twin studies impart knowledge of wider substance use. Drawing from an adolescent Dutch sample, Koopmans and colleagues detected evidence of the separate albeit likely overlapping spheres of the initiation of smoking and the subsequent amount of smoking (Koopmans, Slutske, Heath, Neale, & Boomsma, 1999). Again, considering alcohol intake, studies of Finnish twins indicated that shared environmental influences were critical in initiation, but that additive factors were more paramount in depicting the subsequent frequency of alcohol ingestion (Viken, Kaprio, Koskenvuo, & Rose, 1999). This was exhibited within an additional investigation of female adolescents who displayed strong genetic propensities towards light and heavy drinking behaviour (Buster & Rodgers, 2000). Sophisticated modelling procedures add to this picture the suggestion that onset is socially driven whereas subsequent consumption amount is genetically driven (Adams & Berzonsky, 2003).

On the other hand, commencement of sexual relations and subsequent sexual behaviour becomes increasingly normative across adolescence with age, and significant genetic ties between age of first sexual intercourse are evident across cultures (e.g. Dunne *et al.*, 1997; Miller, 2002; Weisfeld, 1979). Interestingly, a dopamine receptor age of first sexual intercourse correlation pinpoints to potential precise genetic mechanisms (Miller, Pasta, MacMurray, Chiu, Wu, & Comings, 1999). These findings speak to an evolutionary analysis of adolescent development that sees reproductive maturation and gaining independence from parents as fundamental universal activities (Weisfeld, 1979). Reproductive maturation is believed to coincide with adaptive morphological and behavioural changes that are differentially encouraged across cultures. Sexual activities and attitudes during adolescence can be then perceived, at evolutionary behavioural genetics' extreme, as natural selection's influence on developmental sequences. Conversely, for a more social-constructivist take on adolescent sexuality and siblinghood, we refer the reader to Chapter 3 that covers social transmission processes.

In consideration of positive effects, Boeldt and colleagues (2012) detected the value of positive parenting on externalizing behaviours in a behaviour genetics study across time. Specifically, the effects of mothers' positive parenting in early childhood were put against the expression of externalizing behaviours in later childhood and adolescence. Importantly, when a child exhibits aggressive, delinquent, and hyperactive externalizing behaviours, they perturb their own and their siblings' development and family functioning (e.g. Fossum, Morch, Handegård, & Drugli, 2007; Frick & Jackson, 1993). The results confirmed that children whose mothers displayed positive parenting were less likely to exhibit externalizing behaviour later on in development. These findings are significant in that adolescence is often thought to be the gateholder for specific or general problem behaviour clusters, and so early influence is critical (Moffit, 1993). Unfortunately, the study lacked power due to a restrictive sample size and was unable to partition out the effects of shared, nonshared, and genetic influence.

Conversely, Gjone and researchers were able to assess problem behaviours, as broken into both internalizing and externalizing components, and determine significant heritability among same-sex Norwegian twins (Gjone, Stevenson, Sundet, & Eilertsen, 1996). The picture is complex, however, with competing claims from other studies whereby gendered effects and differentiation between internalizing and externalizing behaviour was found; however, similar aetiology might underlie these apparent gender differences (e.g. Deković, Buist, & Reitz, 2004; van den Oord, Boomsma, & Verhulst, 1994). Adding to the conversation on problem behaviour and its contingencies, van den Oord and Rowe's (1997) data are suggestive of a 'liability model' of sorts, where an underpinning latent third variable might explain the connection among later levels of problem behaviours. Development of research in this area has immediate import for applied fields like the study of juvenile criminology, which lacks a framework for assessing the genetic and environmental influences involved in severe problem behaviours (McCartan, 2007).

Personality, social attitudes, and mental health

Results derived from biometric modelling indicate the strong link between heritability and personality. For instance, twins display genetic similarity in Eysenckian personality dimensions (psychoticism, extraversion, neuroticism, and lie) as measured in adolescence (Gillespie et al., 2008), genetic bases for non-family life events (e.g. unique friendship experience) and its covariance with personality (Billig, Hershberger, Iacono, & McGue, 1996; Rowe, Woulbroun, & Gulley, 2013), and stability in personality structure itself (McGue, Bacon, & Lykken, 1993). In the last study cited, environmental influence was also ascribed to change in personality structure. In terms of social attitudes, conservatism and liberalism have been found to be more attributable to shared environmental influence up to young adulthood and more to genetics for older twin pairs (Eaves et al., 1997; Hatemi et al., 2009).

A new wave of research into the genetic inheritance of particular social attitudes and personality has recently gained much steam, although the exact meaning and any immediate applications remain contentious (e.g. Charney & English, 2012; Fowler & Dawes, 2013; Hatemi et al., 2011; McGue, 2010). This strand of work originates in the attempt to locate the origin of political beliefs and behaviours and how they are influenced by genetic and environmental factors and their interplay. Hatemi and colleagues (2009) attempted to track the course of political orientation development over the life span using longitudinal methods. From a sample of twins with data from childhood through to adolescence, in addition to cross-sectional data from adult twin pairs, results suggested a lack of genetic influence prior to young adulthood. Specifically, researchers conjectured that during the early years, individual differences in political attitudes are accounted for largely by environmental influence found in shared family effects, such as parental socialization. At the onset of early adulthood though, strong genetic influence on political attitudes and its stability indicate a pattern of familial and environmental transmission in adolescence, with a later genetic take-over as family effects wane. To address some of the mechanisms at play, we explore the transmission of a set of values between adolescent brothers and sisters within the same family in the third chapter. This exciting field anticipates additional inquiry, using adolescent samples to inform adolescent and life course development, in turn.

Like personality, mental and social health has been tied to genetically based biometric models (Pike, McGuire, Hetherington, Reiss, & Plomin, 1996). In particular, the study of adolescent twins and their parents helped make recent inroads into the structure of psychopathology. Tackett and colleagues (2013) tested and found strong evidence for a model of a dual-factor general psychopathology and the dispositional trait of negative emotionality based on the spectrum hypothesis of personality and psychopathology. Concerning depression specifically, heritability is strongly implicated, although extreme depression appears to map onto the same model, indicating a lack of additive genetic pathways (Rende, Plomin, Reiss, & Hetherington, 1993). Signs that depression, neuroticism, anxiety, and somatic distress are genetically co-morbid were gleaned from a sample of adolescent and young adult twins (Hansell et al., 2012). In a meta-analysis of the methodology of childhood and adolescent behaviour genetics studies addressing heritable models of anxiety and depression, Franić, Middeldorp, Dolan, Ligthart, and Boomsma (2010) found evidence for the minimal effects of gender in the genetic aetiology of childhood anxiety and depression and the strong role of genetic factors in temporal stability of anxiety and depression. Furthermore, they found a partial genetic link between depression and anxiety, the potential genotype–environment interaction affecting their liability, the role of genotype–environment relationships, and a minimal, possibly negligible role of sibling interaction. Taken together, these findings highlight the importance of genetic factors in the aetiology and temporal stability of child-specific differences in the early development of anxiety and depression.

Likewise, Pike and colleagues (1996) discovered that in a sample of twins, half-siblings, and unrelated siblings, depressive symptomology was found to be substantially tied to genetics factors, little to shared environmental influence, and moderately to nonshared environmental influence. In the same study, parental negativity was associated with depression through nonshared environment, apart from the genes and the shared environment. Specific gender contingencies are implicated in the relation between social connectedness and adolescent depression with varying models between boys and girls, where females, for instance, exhibit stronger genetic effects for depression (Jacobson & Rowe, 1999).

Pike et al. (1996) also unearthed evidence that antisocial behaviour displayed more shared environmental variance versus that of depression, although genetic and nonshared environmental influences made additional contributions. The negativity of mothers was again implicated in this discovery. An adoption study of late childhood and early adolescence points to tenable parental effects on children's antisocial behaviour; the child did not elicit covariation between their antisocial behaviour and negative parenting (O'Connor, Deater-Deckard, Fulker, Rutter, & Plomin, 1998). This finding, however, adds nuance to the general position that nonshared environment is largely attributable to unique child characteristics, currently held in acclaim by scholars including the likes of Scarr (1992) and Pike (2012b).

Social relationships with family members and others

Each culture enforces certain constraints and expectations on the developing adolescent. Transition from childhood to young adulthood necessitates a wide number of variable culturally bounded social norms set within the confines of physiological imperatives (Arnett, 2003). This sensitive period for social influences, often fraught with strained relationships, makes for important developmental analyses when we bear in mind the immediate and projected trajectories for the adolescent. Resounding evidence from a recent meta-analysis underscores the increasing influence of genetics and the weakening of environmental effects particularly during the transition from adolescence to young adulthood (Bergen, Gardner, & Kendler, 2007). Presumably, this is due to greater personal control and selection of genetically 'favoured' environments (Scarr & McCartney, 1983).

The Nonshared Environment in Adolescent Development (NEAD) project, which draws from samples of adolescents from both non-divorced and stepfamilies in the USA, has helped enlighten specific family dynamics and the genetic and environment overlap. For instance, surveyed same-sex siblings displayed a strong genetic link regarding parental and child maladjustment, in addition to the finding that adolescent perceptions of parenting mediates parent conflict measures and adolescent antisocial measures (Neiderhiser, Pike, Hetherington, & Reiss, 1998).

Enlisting the same data set, Bussell and colleagues (1999) found that most of the covariance in the quality of mother–child relationship and adolescent sibling relationship was ascribable to shared environment (i.e., similar patterns of interaction), although genetic and nonshared contributions were also present. This discovery goes against that of child-centred behaviour genetic work that generally maintains individual genetic influence is foremost in relationship quality (e.g. Pike & Atzaba-Poria, 2003; Pike & Eley, 2009). Furthermore, Neale (1999) supports family systems theory in acknowledging the criticality of shared environments for both sibling and parent–child relations. The NEAD project additionally explores the previously underestimated amount of variance to be found in the family environment that is attributable to genetic variation. That is, genetic variation among adolescents and their siblings is clearly significant, yet not well understood (Plomin, Reiss, Hetherington, & Howe, 1994). We explore this statement in the following.

Family effects: Are they (mostly) child specific?

> I may be a twin but I'm one of a kind.
>
> – *Author Unknown*

Behaviour genetics queries individual differences as well as broader socialization effects and need not necessarily enlist traditional twin or adoption research designs (Pike, 2012b). Methods of within-family study conscript sibling data as an instrument that juxtaposes brothers and sisters with different levels of genetic similarity in a family unit to test the gene–environment relationship and its implications for development. Relevant data continue to accumulate that contributes to the growing corpus of nonshared environmental influence in sibling differentiation effects and, thus, individual development (e.g. Daniels, 1986; Pike & Plomin, 1997).

The seminal article by Plomin and Daniels (1987) expounded the role of child-specific nonshared familial influence in siblings and sparked subsequent research (1987). Furthermore, Daniels (1986) outlined the importance of differential experiences between siblings from the same family in prediction of adolescent siblings personality dissimilarities. Pike and Plomin have both gone on to identify the over-attribution of parenting effects in sibling differentiation and call attention to nonshared influences such as peers and friendships in particular. In fact, multiple areas of import for siblings are revealed through studies depicting nonshared influence (e.g. Anderson et al., 1994; Pike & Plomin, 1997; Plomin & Daniels, 1987). Within-family research of siblings underscores, among other variables, the key roles of ordinal position of siblings, hierarchy, and differential parenting between siblings (McHale, Updegraff, & Whiteman, 2012; Plomin & Daniels, 1987).

Recent research that links parenting styles and children's self-esteem, which are both influenced by genes and nonshared environmental forces, has revealed the role of child-specific parenting and the elicitation of such parenting in relation to the child's genetic propensities and biological characteristics (Pike, 2012a, 2012b; Pike & Kretschmer, 2009). This means that siblings can be reared quite differently based in part on their own temperament, for instance. Critically, researchers have begun to take into consideration all children within family systems as a whole, allowing the utilization of within-family designs to partition out between-family (or shared environmental) and within-family (nonshared environmental) effects (Jenkins et al., 2012).

This promising line of research, while not genetically focused, accounts for the uniqueness of individuals and their interactions with their environment in a child-specific, person-centred research programme. This echoes Pike's (2012b) sentiments that past behavioural genetic findings are strongly suggestive of the limited influence of general parenting effects. Citing Scarr and McCartney's (1983) emphasis on the role of children as active constructors of their experienced environments, contemporary research on sibling relationships, their relations with peers and other family members, and behaviour in varying contexts (e.g. the classroom environment) affirms and communicates the influence of children themselves (e.g. Oliver, Pike, & Plomin, 2008; Pike & Atzaba-Poria, 2003; Pike & Eley, 2009).

Further research to unpick the relative share of genetic, shared, and nonshared influence reveals the importance of different relational qualities and contexts on children's and adolescents' lasting development. Pike and Atzaba-Poria's (2003) study of sibling relationships and friendship illustrates three themes to this effect: the congruent temperamental nature across relationship context, the disparity of relationship profiles (child-specific for friendships and reciprocal for siblings), and the commonality of influence between temperament and relationship quality. Considered together, these themes are suggestive of the importance of unique nonshared experiences and environment for adolescent development in siblings.

Specifically, analyses of adolescent relationships suggest that negative aspects of both types of bonds tie to emotionality, while the positive links to sociability and activity. Whereas nonshared environmental influence accounts for moderate variance in the sibling relationship and the larger share in friendship, genetics and shared environment alone cover much of the variance in the sibling relationship. Last, temperament-close relationship covariance spotlights the strong influence of nonshared environmental effects for adolescents.

One final example of the value of sibling study designs for illuminating shared versus nonshared environmental effects examined the link between nonshared friendship experiences and differences in aspirations among adolescent siblings (Kretschmer & Pike, 2010). Specifically, the degree of similarity among a sample of 102 same-sex sibling pairs of roughly 14–16 years were found to be only mildly similar among sibling dyads for both aspirations of self-acceptance, affiliation, financial success, and friendship experiences. Through bivariate modelling techniques, the researchers revealed that unique child-specific processes informed the aspiration–friendship association. Once more, these results add to the research which tells of the importance of considering differential influences among siblings reared within the family.

Issues of controversy

Behavioural genetic studies have been criticized for the general trend towards reporting 'moderate heritability', the lack of shared environmental effects, and relatively greater amounts of nonshared environmental effects and measurement error (see Turkheimer, 2000). But as Adams and Berzonsky (2003) show, such studies can nevertheless assist in highlighting key processes in development, hint at genetic-environment linkages worth further exploration, suggest gender and ethnic/racial variances, and inform human development and behaviour as a whole. Both environment and genetics are elucidated in genetically sensitive inquiry into behaviour, although the former tends to receive less emphasis. Again, at best, heritability indicates how much of the variation in a specific trait can be accounted for by genetic factors when development occurs within a specific set of environmental circumstances. Although now researchers can make use of advanced statistical modelling techniques such as structural equation modelling that assist in more clearly apportioning out variance in heritability (McGue, 2010).

In terms of research designs basic to behaviour genetics study in humans, as with all methodologies, quantitative twin and adoption designs are not without their drawbacks and limitations, namely, their quasi-experimental nature and reductionistic suppositions about the dynamic gene–environment interplay (e.g. Charney, 2012; Gottlieb, 1995; Lerner, 2007). Nonetheless, both afford the opportunity to model relative influence between siblings attributable to environment and genetics, or at the very least, point towards avenues for closer gene–environment investigation (Pike, 2012b).

Sociology and psychoanalysis take issue with some of the principles which undergird a behavioural genetic perspective on sibling study (see Rose, 1995).

First and foremost, the favouring of biology's explanation of complex multifaceted social relationships traces back to ideas of biological parenting and common genes in the evolutionary psychological, neo-Darwinian sense (Edwards, Hadfield, Lucey, & Mauthner, 2006; Richards, 1996). Strathern (1992, as cited in Edwards *et al.*, 2006) contends, for example, that genetic links have come to be seen as an explication of that which is 'natural' and 'innate' in child-rearing, family functioning, and dynamics and so proffer a cohesive narrative to counter fears of 'traditional' and 'natural' family erosion. Behavioural genetics can be further accused of reductionistic conceptualization and theorizing of emotional ties between kin, where love and investment is reduced to the concept of genetic prosperity. For instance, siblings are theorized as competing against one another to secure parental attention and investment, and individuation is the process and strategy by which this advantage is maximized (Sulloway, 1996).

None of these debates are new, though the strength of the absoluteness of 'nature diametrically opposed to nature' assertions have lessened with the near universal acceptance of the diversity and complexity in individual-level development (Eaves & Eysenck, 1974; Lumsden & Wilson, 1981; Martin *et al.*, 1986). Vast and varied epigenetic and behavioural genetic evidence has emerged supporting biological systems and the environment's interlocking roles. This is not to say, however, that such inquiry has always rested on sound theoretical postulations or applications. As with any methodological strategy, behavioural genetics is not without its limitations, and the field should remain on guard against overextension of its models (Hatemi, Byrne, & McDermott, 2012).

Another issue affecting twin and adoption studies regards their wider application; generalization to the general populace is not directly possible. Twins are likely to be exposed to particular environmental circumstances unlike that of non-twinned individuals. One of the authors of this volume recalls her next-door neighbours: a pair of identical twins and their older brother. In almost every way the two twins were treated similarly and indeed turned out to be as similar as possible, from their change in hairstyle across time, down to their chosen profession and eventual city of residence. That they encountered considerably unique treatment from others as compared to their older brother is undisputed, and they will say just as much. A whole host of factors additionally systematically influence the production and likelihood of conceiving twins based on genetic propensity, age, number of past children, artificial insemination, and their related factors, in turn. Nonetheless, twins are arguably not that much different from the rest of the population based on some measures, although this branch of investigation requires greater review (e.g. Deary, Spinath, & Bates, 2006; Martin, Boomsma, & Machin, 1997).

New directions for growth

The diverse and encompassing nature of behavioural genetics, with its overlapping reach in biology, genetics, epigenetics, psychology, ethology, and statistics, has much to offer developmental science. The relationship to siblings in adolescence is twofold. First, studying twins, adoptive brothers and sisters, and siblings from the same family helps us understand the influence of genes, the environment, and their interrelationships in development. Second, sibling interactions and relationships are informed by genetically sensitive designs, extending our knowledge of the intimate relationship within and outside of the family sphere. On a larger scale, within- and between-family study of siblings forwards not only developmental research but may represent the bridge between the biological and social sciences (D'Onofrio, Lahey, Turkheimer, & Lichtenstein, 2013).

By studying siblings, responsible scholars are pushed to acknowledge and account for the developing individual, an active agent embedded within and interacting with their environment. Long gone are the days of absolute genetic determinism in the Goddardian-sense (Goddard, 1920), though many of the fundamental issues of behavioural genetics' nascency still face the developmental scientist of today (McGue, 2010). Through contributions that extend this strand of research, including expositions on the importance of nonshared familial and environmental influences in individual development (Plomin & Daniels, 1987) and Pike's collection of reports on unique peer and friendship effects, modern researchers are presented with suggestions and clues to new points of within-family inquiry. Embracing longitudinal child-centred approaches and multi-method testing in behavioural genetics – as in the case of the leading-edge examination of Reiss, Neiderhiser, Hetherington, and Plomin (2000) – imparts invaluable knowledge to understanding specific genetic and social environmental workings in adolescent development among individuals and between siblings.

References

Adams, G. R., & Berzonsky, M. D. (2003). *Blackwell handbook of adolescence*. Oxford, UK: Blackwell.

Anderson, E. R., Hetherington, E. M., Reiss, D., & Howe, G. (1994). Parents' nonshared treatment of siblings and the development of social competence during adolescence. *Journal of Family Psychology, 8*(3), 303–320.

Arnett, L. (2003). Coming of age in a multicultural world: Globalization and adolescent cultural identity formation. *Applied Developmental Science, 7*(3), 189–196.

Bandura, A. (1977). *Social learning theory*. Englewood Cliffs, NJ: Prentice Hall.

Bard, D. E., & Rodgers, J. L. (2003). Sibling influence on smoking behaviour: A within-family look at explanations for a birth order effect. *Journal of Applied Social Psychology, 33*(9), 1773–1795.

Bergen, S. E., Gardner, C. O., & Kendler, K. S. (2007). Age-related changes in heritability of behavioural phenotypes over adolescence and young adulthood: A meta-analysis. *Twin Research and Human Genetics, 10*(3), 423–433.

Billig, J. P., Hershberger, S. L., Iacono, W. G., & McGue, M. (1996). Life events and personality in late adolescence: Genetic and environmental relations. *Behaviour Genetics, 26*(6), 543–554.

Boeldt, D. L., Rhee, S. H., DiLalla, L. F., Mullineaux, P. Y., Schulz-Heik, R. J., Corley, R. P., Young, S., & Hewitt, J. K. (2012). The association between positive parenting and externalizing behaviour. *Infant and Child Development, 21*(1), 85–106.

Bouchard, T. J. (2004). Genetic influence on human psychological traits – A survey. *Current Directions in Psychological Science, 13*, 148–151.

Bouchard, T. J., Lykken, D. T., McGue, M., Segal, N. L., & Tellegen, A. (1990). Sources of human psychological differences: The Minnesota Study of twins reared apart. *Science, 250*, 223–228.

Bussell, D. A., Neiderhiser, J. M., Pike, A., Plomin, R., Simmens, S., Howe, G. W., Hetherington, E. M., Carroll, E., & Reiss, D. (1999). Adolescents' relationships to siblings and mothers: A multivariate genetic analysis. *Developmental Psychology, 35*(5), 1248–1259.

Buster, M. A., & Rodgers, J. L. (2000). Genetic and environmental influences on alcohol use: DF analysis of NLSY kinship data. *Journal of Biosocial Science, 32*, 177–189.

Cardno, A. G., & Gottesman, I. I. (2000). Twin studies of schizophrenia: From bow-and-arrow concordances to star wars Mx and functional genomics. *American Journal of Medical Genetics, 97*(1), 12–17.

Carey, G. (1986). Sibling imitation and contrast effects. *Behaviour Genetics, 16*, 319–341.

Charney, E. (2012). Behaviour genetics and post genomics. *Behavioural and Brain Sciences, 35*(5), 331–358.

Charney, E., & English, W. (2012). The voting gene. *Scientific American Magazine, 307*(5), p. 14.

Daniels, D. (1986). Differential experiences of siblings in the same family as predictors of adolescent sibling personality differences. *Journal of Personality and Social Psychology, 51*(2), 339–346.

Deary, I. J., Spinath, F. M., & Bates, T. C. (2006). Genetics of intelligence. *European Journal of Human Genetics, 14*(6), 690–700.

Deković, M., Buist, K. L., & Reitz, E. (2004). Stability and changes in problem behaviour during adolescence: Latent growth analysis. *Journal of Youth and Adolescence, 33*(1), 1–12.

DeThorne, L. S., & Hart, S. A. (2009). Use of the twin design to examine evocative gene-environment effects within a conversational context. *International Journal of Developmental Science, 3*(2), 175–194.

D'Onofrio, B. M., Lahey, B. B., Turkheimer, E., & Lichtenstein, P. (2013). Critical need for family-based, quasi-experimental designs in integrating genetic and social science research. *American Journal of Public Health, 103*, S46–S55.

Dunne, M. P., Martin, N. G., Statham, D. J., Slutske, W. S., Dinwiddie, S. H., Bucholz, K. K., Madden, P. A., & Heath, A. C. (1997). Genetic and environmental contributions to variance in age at first sexual intercourse. *Psychological Science, 8*, 1–6.

Eaves, L., & Eysenck, H. (1974). Genetics and the development of social attitudes. *Nature, 249*, 288–289

Eaves, L., Martin, N., Heath, A., Schieken, R., Meyer, J., Silberg, J., & Corey, L. (1997). Age changes in the causes of individual differences in conservatism. *Behaviour genetics, 27*(2), 121–124.

Edwards, R., Hadfield, L., Lucey, H., & Mauthner, M. (2006). *Sibling identity and relationships: Sisters and brothers.* Oxon: Routledge.

Ehringer, M. A., Rhee, S. H., Young, S., Corley, R., & Hewitt, J. K. (2006). Genetic and environmental contributions to common psychopathologies of childhood and adolescence: A study of twins and their siblings. *Journal of Abnormal Child Psychology, 34*(1), 1–17.

Elder, G. H. (1975). Age differentiation and the life course. *Annual Review of Sociology, 1*, 165–190.

Fossum, S., Morch, W. T., Handegård, B. H., & Drugli, M. B. (2007). Childhood disruptive behaviours and family functioning in clinically referred children: Are girls different from boys? *Scandinavian Journal of Psychology, 48*(5), 375–382.

Fowler, J. H., & Dawes, C. T. (2013). In defense of genopolitics. *American Political Science Review, 107*, 362–374.

Franić, S., Middeldorp, C. M., Dolan, C. V., Ligthart, L., & Boomsma, D. I. (2010). Childhood and adolescent anxiety and depression: Beyond heritability. *Journal of the American Academy of Child & Adolescent Psychiatry, 49*(8), 820–829.

Frick, P. J., & Jackson, Y. K. (1993). Family functioning and childhood antisocial behaviour: Yet another reinterpretation. *Journal of Clinical Child Psychology, 22*(4), 410–419.

Galton, F. (1875). History of twins, as a criterion of the relative powers of nature and nurture. In F. Galton (Ed.), *Inquiries into human faculty and its development* (pp. 155–173). London: Macmillan.

Gedda, L. (1961). *Twins in history and science* (Vol. 1). Springfield, MA: CC Thomas.

Gillespie, N. A., Zhu, G., Evans, D. M., Medland, S. E., Wright, M. J., & Martin, N. G. (2008). A genome-wide scan for Eysenckian personality dimensions in adolescent twin sibships: Psychoticism, extraversion, neuroticism, and lie. *Journal of Personality, 76*(6), 1415–1446.

Gjone, H., Stevenson, J., Sundet, J. M., & Eilertsen, D. E. (1996). Changes in heritability across increasing levels of behaviour problems in young twins. *Behaviour Genetics, 26*(4), 419–426.

Goddard, H. (1920). *Human efficiency and levels of intelligence*. Princeton, NJ: Princeton University Press.

Gottlieb, G. (1995). Some conceptual deficiencies in 'developmental' behaviour genetics. *Human Development, 38*, 131–141.

Hansell, N. K., Wright, M. J., Medland, S. E., Davenport, T. A., Wray, N. R., Martin, N. G., & Hickie, I. B. (2012). Genetic co-morbidity between neuroticism, anxiety/depression and somatic distress in a population sample of adolescent and young adult twins. *Psychological Medicine, 42*(6), 1249–1260.

Hatemi, P. K., Byrne, E., & McDermott, R. (2012). Introduction: What is a 'gene' and why does it matter for political science? *Journal of Theoretical Politics, 24*(3), 305–327.

Hatemi, P. K., Funk, C. L., Medland, S. E., Maes, H. M., Silberg, J. L., Martin, N. G., & Eaves, L. J. (2009). Genetic and environmental transmission of political attitudes over a life time. *Journal of Politics, 71*(3), 1141–1156.

Hatemi, P. K., Gillespie, N. A., Eaves, L. J., Maher, B. S., Webb, B. T., Heath, A. C., & Martin, N. G. (2011). A genome-wide analysis of liberal and conservative political attitudes. *Journal of Politics, 73*(1), 271–285.

Iacono, W. G., & McGue, M. (2002). Minnesota Twin Family Study. *Twin Research, 5*(5), 482–487.

Ingraham, L. J., & Kety, S. S. (2000). Adoption studies of schizophrenia. *American Journal of Medical Genetics, 97*(1), 18–22.

Jablonka, E., & Lamb, M. J. (2005). *Evolution in four dimensions: Genetic, epigenetic, behavioural, and symbolic variation in the history of life*. Cambridge, MA: MIT Press.

Jacobson, K. C., & Rowe, D. C. (1999). Genetic and environmental influences on the relationships between family connectedness, school connectedness, and adolescent depressed mood: Sex differences. *Developmental Psychology, 35*(4), 926–939.

Jenkins, J., Rasbash, J., Leckie, G., Gass, K., & Dunn, J. (2012). The role of maternal factors in sibling relationship quality: a multilevel study of multiple dyads per family. *Journal of Child Psychology and Psychiatry, 53*, 622–629.

Jessor, R., & Jessor, S. L. (1977). Problem behaviour and psychosocial development: A longitudinal study of youth. New York: Academic Press.

Kendall, P. C., & Comer, J. S. (2013). Decades not days: The research enterprise in clinical psychology. In J. Comer & K. P. Kendall (Eds.), *The Oxford handbook of research strategies for clinical psychology* (pp. 437–441). Oxford: Oxford University Press.

Koopmans, J. R., Slutske, W. S., Heath, A. C., Neale, M. C., & Boomsma, D. I. (1999). The genetics of smoking initiation and quantity smoked in Dutch adolescent and young adult twins. *Behaviour Genetics, 29*(6), 383–393.

Kretschmer, T., & Pike, A. (2010). Links between nonshared friendship experiences and adolescent siblings' differences in aspirations. *Journal of Adolescence, 33*(1), 101–110.

Lerner, R. M. (2007). Another nine-inch nail for behaviour genetics! *Human Development, 49*, 336–342.

Loehlin, J. C., & Nichols, R. C. (1976). *Heredity, environment, and personality.* Austin: University of Texas Press.

Lumsden, C. J., Wilson, E. O. (1981). *The coevolutionary process.* Cambridge, MA: Harvard University Press.

Martin, N. G., Boomsma, D., & Machin, G. (1997). A twin-pronged attack on complex traits. *Nature genetics, 17*(4), 387–392.

Martin, N. G., & Eaves, L. J. (1977). The genetical analysis of covariance structure. *Heredity, 38*(1), 79–95.

Martin, N. G., Eaves, L. J., Heath, A. C., Jardine, R., Feingold, L. M., & Eysenck, H. J. (1986). Transmission of social attitudes. *Proceedings of the National Academy of Sciences, 83*(12), 4364–4368.

Martin, N. G., Eaves, L. J., Kearsey, M. J., & Davies, P. (1978). The power of the classical twin study. *Heredity, 40*(1), 97–116.

McCartan, L. M. (2007). Inevitable, influential, or unnecessary? Exploring the utility of genetic explanation for delinquent behaviour. *Journal of Criminal Justice, 35*(2), 219–233.

McGue, M. (2010). The end of behavioural genetics? *Behaviour Genetics, 40*(3), 284–296.

McGue, M., Bacon, S., & Lykken, D. T. (1993). Personality stability and change in early adulthood: A behavioural genetic analysis. *Developmental Psychology, 29*(1), 96–109.

McHale, S. M., Updegraff, K. A., & Whiteman, S. D. (2012). Sibling relationships and influences in childhood and adolescence. *Journal of Marriage and Family, 74*(5), 913–930.

Miller, B. C. (2002). Family influences on adolescent sexual and contraceptive behaviour. *Journal of Sex Research, 39*(1), 22–26.

Miller, W. B., Pasta, D. J., MacMurray, J., Chiu, C., Wu, H., & Comings, D. E. (1999). Dopamine receptors are associated with age at first sexual intercourse. *Journal of Biosocial Science, 31*, 91–97.

Moffit, T. E. (1993). Adolescence-limited and life-course-persistent antisocial behaviour: A developmental taxonomy. *Psychological Review, 100*, 674–701.

Moore, D. (2006). A very little bit of knowledge: Re-evaluating the meaning of the heritability of IQ. *Human Development, 49*, 347–353.

Neale, M. C. (1999). Possible confounds and their resolution in multivariate genetic analyses: Comment on Bussell et al. (1999). *Developmental Psychology, 35*(5), 1260–1264.

Neiderhiser, J. M., Pike, A., Hetherington, E. M., & Reiss, D. (1998). Adolescent perceptions as mediators of parenting: Genetic and environmental contributions. *Developmental Psychology, 34*(6), 1459–1469.

O'Connor, T. G., Deater-Deckard, K., Fulker, D., Rutter, M., & Plomin, R. (1998). Genotype-environment correlations in late childhood and early adolescence: Antisocial behavioural problems and coercive parenting. *Developmental Psychology, 34*(5), 970–981.

Oliver, B. R., Pike, A., & Plomin, R. (2008). Nonshared environmental influences on teacher-reported behaviour problems: Monozygotic twin differences in perceptions of the classroom. *Journal of Child Psychology and Psychiatry, 49*(6), 646–653.

Panksepp, J., & Biven, L. (2012). A medition on the affective neuroscientific view of human and animalian MindBrains. In A. Fotopoulou, D. Pfaff, & A. Conway (Eds.), *In from the couch to the lab: Trends in psychodynamic neuroscience* (pp. 145–175). Oxford: Oxford University Press.

Pike, A. (2012a). Commentary: Are siblings birds of a feather? – Reflections on Jenkins *et al.* (2012). *Journal of Child Psychology and Psychiatry, 53*(6), 630–631.

Pike, A. (2012b). The importance of behavioural genetics for developmental science. *International Journal of Developmental Science, 6*(1–2), 13–15.

Pike, A., & Atzaba-Poria, N. (2003). Do sibling and friend relationships share the same temperamental origins? A twin study. *Journal of Child Psychology and Psychiatry, 44*, 598–611.

Pike, A., & Eley, T. C. (2009). Links between parenting and extra-familial relationships: Nature or nurture? *Journal of Adolescence, 32*(3), 519–533.

Pike, A., & Kretschmer, T. (2009). Shared versus nonshared effects: Parenting and children's adjustment. *European Journal of Developmental Science, 3*(2), 115–130.

Pike, A., McGuire, S., Hetherington, E. M., Reiss, D., & Plomin, R. (1996). Family environment and adolescent depressive symptoms and antisocial behaviour: A multivariate genetic analysis. *Developmental Psychology, 32*(4), 590–603.

Pike, A., & Plomin, R. (1996). Importance of nonshared environmental factors for childhood and adolescent psychopathology. *Journal of the American Academy of Child & Adolescent Psychiatry, 35*(5), 560–570.

Pike, A., & Plomin, R. (1997). A behavioural genetic perspective on close relationships. *International Journal of Behavioural Development, 21*(4), 647–668.

Plomin, R. (1989). Environment and genes: Determinants of behaviour. *American Psychologist, 44*(2), 105–111.

Plomin, R., & Daniels, D. (1987). Why are children in the same family so different from one another? *Behaviour and Brain Sciences, 10*, 1–60.

Plomin, R., Fulker, D. W., Corley, R., & DeFries, J. C. (1997). Nature, nurture, and cognitive development from 1 to 16 years: A parent-offspring adoption study. *Psychological Science, 8*, 442–447.

Plomin, R., Reiss, D., Hetherington, E. M., & Howe, G. W. (1994). Nature and nurture: Genetic contributions to measure of the family environment. *Developmental Psychology, 30*(1), 32–43.

Reiss, D., Neiderhiser, J., Hetherington, E. M., & Plomin, R. (2000). *The relationship code: Deciphering genetic and social patterns in adolescent development.* Cambridge, MA: Harvard University Press.

Rende, R. D., Plomin, R., Reiss, D., & Hetherington, E. M. (1993). Genetic and environmental influences on depressive symptomatology in adolescence: Individual differences and extreme scores. *Journal of Child Psychology and Psychiatry, 34*, 1387–1398.

Rende, R. D., Plomin, R., & Vandenberg, S. G. (1990). Who discovered the twin method? *Behaviour Genetics, 20*, 277–285.

Richards, M. (1996). Families, kinship and genetics. In T. Marteau & M. Richards (Eds.), *The troubled helix: Social and psychological implications of the new human genetics* (pp. 249–273). Cambridge: Cambridge University Press.

Richardson, K., & Norgate, S. (2006). A critical analysis of IQ studies of adopted children. *Human Development, 49*(6), 319–335.

Rodgers, J. L., & Bard, D. E. (2003). Behaviour genetics and adolescent development: A review of recent literature. In G. Adams & M. Berzonsky (Eds.), *Blackwell handbook of adolescence* (pp. 3–23). Oxford: Blackwell.

Rodgers, J. L., & Rowe, D. C. (1993). Social contagion and adolescent sexual behaviour: A developmental EMOSA model. *Psychological Review, 100*, 479–510.

Rose, R. J. (1995). Genes and human behaviour. In J. T. Spence, J. M. Darley, & D. J. Foss (Eds.), *Annual review of psychology* (Vol. 46, pp. 625–654). Palo Alto, CA: Annual Reviews.

Rose, R. J. (2007). Peers, parents, and processes of adolescent socialization: A twin-study perspective. In R. Engels, M. Kerr, & H. Stattin (Eds.), *Friends, lovers & groups: Key relationships in adolescence* (pp. 105–124). Chichester, UK: John Wiley & Sons Ltd.

Rose, R. J., Kaprio, J., Winter, T., Koskenvuo, M., & Viken, R. J. (1999). Familial and socioregional environmental effects on abstinence from alcohol at age sixteen. *Journal of Studies on Alcohol, 13*, 63–74.

Roth, W. E., & Finley, G. E. (1998). Adoption and antisocial personality: Genetic and environmental factors associated with antisocial outcomes. *Child and Adolescent Social Work Journal, 15*(2), 133–149.

Rowe, D. C., Woulbroun, E. J., & Gulley, B. L. (2013). Peers and friends as nonshared environmental influences. In E. Mavis Hetherington, D. Reiss, & R. Plomin (Eds.), *Separate social worlds of siblings: The impact of nonshared environment on development* (pp. 159–174). Hillsdale, NJ: Lawrence Erlbaum.

Scarr, S. (1992). Developmental theories for the 1990s: Development and individual differences. *Child Development, 63*(1), 1–19..

Scarr, S., & McCartney, K. (1983). How people make their own environments: A theory of genotype → environment effects. *Child Development, 54*, 424–435.

Shih, R. A., Belmonte, P. L., & Zandi, P. P. (2004). A review of the evidence from family, twin and adoption studies for a genetic contribution to adult psychiatric disorders. *International Review of Psychiatry, 16*(4), 260–283.

Siemens, H. W. (1924). *Die zwillingspathologie; ihre bedeutung, ihre methodik, ihre bisherigen ergebnisse.* Berlin: Springer.

Smoller, J. W., & Finn, C. T. (2003). Family, twin, and adoption studies of bipolar disorder. *American Journal of Medical Genetics Part C: Seminars in Medical Genetics, 123*, 48–58.

Strathern, M. (1992). *After nature: English kinship in the late twentieth century.* Cambridge: Cambridge University Press.

Sulloway, F. J. (1996). *Born to rebel: Birth order, family dynamics, and creative lives.* New York: Pantheon Books.

Tackett, J. L., Lahey, B. B., van Hulle, C., Waldman, I., Krueger, R. F., & Rathouz, P. J. (2013). Common genetic influences on negative emotionality and a general psychopathology factor in childhood and adolescence. *Journal of Abnormal Psychology, 122*(4), 1142–1153.

Turkheimer, E. (1998). Heritability and biological explanation. *Psychological Review, 105*, 782–791.

Turkheimer, E. (2000). Three laws of behaviour genetics and what they mean. *Current Directions in Psychological Science, 9*, 160–164.

Turkheimer, E., Haley, A., Waldron, M., Onofio, B, & Gottesman, I. I. (2003). Socioeconomic status modifies heritability of IQ in young children. *Psychological Science, 14*, 623–628.

Turkheimer, E., & Waldron, M. (2000). Nonshared environment: A theoretical, methodological, and quantitative review. *Psychological Bulletin, 126*, 78–108.

van den Oord, E. J. C. G., Boomsma, D. I., & Verhulst, F. C. (1994). A study of problem behaviours in 10- to 15-year-old biologically related and unrelated international adoptees. *Behaviour Genetics, 24*(3), 193–205.

van den Oord, E. J. C. G., & Rowe, D. C. (1997). Continuity and change in children's social maladjustment: A developmental behaviour genetic study. *Developmental Psychology, 33*(2), 319–332.

Viken, R. J., Kaprio, J., Koskenvuo, M., & Rose, R. J. (1999). Longitudinal analyses of the determinants of drinking and of drinking to intoxication in adolescent twins. *Behaviour Genetics, 29*, 455–461.

Weinberg, W. (1910). Weitere Beitrage zur Theorie der Vererbung. *Archiv für Rassen- und Gesellschafts-Biologie, 7*, 35–49.

Weisfeld, G. (1979). An ethological view of human adolescence. *Journal of Nervous and Mental Disease, 167*(1), 38–55.

Whiteman, S. D., Jensen, A. C., & Maggs, J. L. (2013). Similarities in adolescent siblings' substance use: testing competing pathways of influence. *Journal of Studies on Alcohol and Drugs, 74*(1), 104–113.

Whiteman, S. D., Jensen, A. C., & Maggs, J. L. (2014). Similarities and differences in Adolescent siblings' alcohol-related attitudes, use, and delinquency: Evidence for convergent and divergent influence processes. *Journal of Youth and Adolescence, 43*(5), 687–697.

Winerman, L. (2004). A second look at twin studies. *American Psychological Association Monitor, 35*(4), 46.

5

CROSS-CULTURAL AND INTERNATIONAL RESEARCH ON SIBLINGS IN ADOLESCENCE

Contents

Introducing cross-cultural and international research on siblings in adolescence

In this chapter, we provide a brief outline of cross–cultural views of development during adolescence, cultural and developmental systems theory approaches, and the foregoing's relevance for the sibling relationship. Throughout this chapter, we interweave significant cultural issues – both timely and timeless – that stress the importance of culturally specific understanding. Additionally, we highlight selected empirical and theoretical work on adolescent sibling relationships from a cultural perspective in order to illuminate proposed future directions and guide further international research.

Cultural beings and sensitive periods in cultural acquisition

Children are innate social creatures, hard-wired to acquire, create, and channel culture. (Greenfield, 1997; Trevarthen, 1980). Cultural acquisition and the attainment of other developmentally important faculties occur most readily during so-called sensitive periods, in which the maturing individual is particularly adept at gaining cultural skill sets. The inter-related, mutually supportive meanings of culture, on the one hand, and language, a core component of being socialized into a culture, on the other, both transpire during these sensitive periods. Sensitive periods include the early stage acquisition of language and culture (Cheung, Chudek, & Heine, 2011; Johnson & Newport, 1989; Kuhl, 2010). Language can be thought to be the communication component of culture and is paramount in ontogenetic processes in childhood and adolescence (e.g. Tomasello, Kruger, & Ratner, 1993). As Rita Mae Brown says, 'Language is the road map of a culture. It tells you where its people come from and where they are going'.

Research suggests that, like learning a language, sensitive periods for cultural acquisition roughly map onto one of the most important developmental openings: adolescence. Sensitive periods are windows of opportunity and times of prolific development. The sensitive stage preceding adolescence and its resolution holds disproportional weight and implications for later processes, and cultural differences appear to increase with age (e.g. Miller, 1984). At the extreme, those who do not acquire language abilities before or around the onset of puberty may never be able to fully develop this critical capacity, as in cases of extreme neglect and isolation (Grimshaw, Adelstein, Bryden, & MacKinnon, 1998; Newton, 2002), although there has been documented evidence to the contrary (see the case of Genie; Fromkin, Krashen, Curtiss, Rigler, & Rigler, 1974).

Conversely, multi-cultural people exposed to multiple cultural worldviews in their formative years and third culture kids (TCKs) who spend a portion of pre-adulthood in more than one culture may be able to navigate multiple cultural worlds and are comparatively adroit at switching and blending cultural schemas (e.g. Arnett Jensen, 2003; Heine & Hamamura, 2007; Tsai, Ying, & Lee, 2000; Wong & Hong, 2005). Multi-cultural individuals can illustrate 'adolescence as cultural gate holder' whereby exposure to another language or culture, before the end of adolescence, for instance, may enable individuals with integrated cultural identities to more readily traverse between cultural contexts (e.g. Arnett Jensen, 2003; Berry, 1997; Leung, Maddux, Galinsky, & Chiu, 2008; Maddux & Galinsky, 2009). With respect to sibling and other family relationships, positive familial bonds further promote socio-cultural adaptation via bolstered self-efficacy (Ittel & Sisler, 2012).

On a more general level, added support for the case of adolescence's crucial role in cultural development includes evidence that individuals who learn a second language after puberty often maintain an accent from their mother tongue, and those who learn a second culture might likewise maintain a holdover of certain aspects of culture (e.g. Cheung et al., 2011; McCauley & Henrich, 2006; Minoura, 1992;

Tsai *et al.*, 2000). Different biologically based maturational stage factors in ado-lescence drive these and other developmental processes and so exert influence on both the course and content of cultural learning such as cultural norms surrounding emotions and their expressions (Keller & Greenfield, 2000).

Given that adolescence is viewed as a prime period not only for cultural acquisition but also socio-emotional growth (Erikson, 1968), identity forma-tion (Kroger, 2004; Marcia, 1966, 1980; Marcia, Waterman, Matteson, Archer, & Orlofsky, 1993), and socio-political and ideology development (Duckitt, 2001; Merelman, 1972; Prewitt & Dawson, 1969) among other phenomena, it is important to understand the key socialization role siblings play in both universal and culturally specific processes. In referring back to social learning theory and Adlerian principles, those individuals held to be similar, of higher status, and who exhibit warmth within a relationship (e.g. parents, older siblings) are more likely to serve as models in the socialization process (Bandura, 1977; Whiteman, McHale, & Soli, 2011). Consequently, if mature individuals' (e.g. parents', older siblings') socio-culturally constructed behaviour represents an endpoint of cul-turally specific developmental pathways, their exchanges and mutual interac-tions assist in socializing an adolescent into a given culture or cultures (Keller & Greenfield, 2000; Rogoff, 2003).

Although notions that socialization agents, mainly adults, particularly parents, and increasingly siblings actively transmit cultural knowledge to children via instruction generally dominate the study of enculturation, background search turns up little ethnographic evidence (Lancy, 2010). For instance, Bruner (1966) and Rogoff's (1981) scanning of reel upon reel of native's firsthand observation and filmed footage of the Maya, !Kung, and Netsilik, respectively, turned up a near-complete lack of 'instructed learning'. Lancy (2010, in press) builds a strong case for children's active role in cultural learning. Children are active culture learners in and through play, interactions with peers, casual exchanges in the family set-ting like with similar-age siblings, and the practice of familial chores (Lancy, in press). From this perspective, cultural acquisition emerges less through purpose-ful instruction on the part of elders and more so from the characteristics, actions, and motivations of children themselves in their day-to-day environments (Goody, 2006). Social relational theory, a dialectical depiction of bidirectional processes in parent–child socialization, similarly sees children as active agents in acculturation and co-constructors of their internal cultural working models (e.g. Kuczynski & Parkin, 2007, 2009). Indeed, 'processes of contradiction, including conflict . . . are inherent within parent-child relationships' that are 'culturally embedded social relationships' and, importantly, 'set the stage for qualitative change' (Kuczynski, Navara, & Boiger, 2011, p. 174).

Unlike social relational theory, former models of top-down 'instructed learning' and socialization further subordinate the role of children, younger siblings, and the sibling relationship in cultural acquisition (Edwards, Hadfield, Lucey, & Mauthner, 2006; Kruger & Tomasello, 1996). This fits with the relative lack of attention paid to siblings across cultures and their involvement in different aspects of culture and its acquisition. More active constructions of children and adolescents' cultural agency are beneficial not only for framing enculturation through siblings but also guiding culture-specific knowledge of sibling relationships. To unpack the meaning of siblings within multiple contexts, we must understand universal and culturally detailed notions of adolescence and cultural influences in development. We therefore now turn to an exposition of contemporary cultural conceptions of the teenage years.

Adolescence and its cultural conceptions

Adolescence as a distinct period in the life course positioned between childhood and adulthood has existed for centuries in numerous societies (Schlegel & Barry, 1991). It appears the concept of adolescence is an existential universal, and thus, not a cultural invention, although both intra- and inter-cultural differences proliferate (Heine, 2011; Weisfeld, 1979). Modern conceptions of this period of transition – with its drawn-out preparation for adult life and institutional separation from it – map onto the rise of industrialism and the twentieth-century Zeitgeist (Arnett, 2004). Ethnographic accounts of adolescence from 175 pre-industrialized societies stressed that while most societies perceive adolescence as demarcating the stage between childhood and adulthood through specific physiological changes, accompanying role requirements, activities, practices, and individual processes, the features housed within these expectations are temporally (Schoon & Silbereisen, 2009) and culturally variable (Arnett, 2010; Schlegel & Barry, 1991). For instance, the tendency for different cultures to associate adolescence with expectations for occasional violent behaviour for boys and girls was highly variable even in comparing similarly structured agrarian and subsistence-oriented societies (13% and 3%, respectively). A further example includes the difference in perceptions of developmental course and values for Greek- and Anglo-Australians, with Greek-Australians considering initiative and independent behaviours, personal maturity, and interpersonal sensitivity to be appropriate at a later age, but Anglo-Australians viewing the opposite pattern for respect, self-control, and unsupervised activities (Rosenthal & Bornholt, 1988). These findings indicate that expectations around individual development express cultural values.

Western takes on youth

Prevailing cultural conceptualizations of adolescence in the West, on the other hand, emphasize the perceived tumultuousness of this period of youth (Arnett, 1999). The 'storm and stress' view of adolescence depicts young individuals as a whirlwind of chaos that poses a risk to themselves and others (Arnett, 2004). Under Western interpretations, challenge and conflict are integral components of 'growing up' and 'becoming an adult' (Skoe & von der Lippe, 1998). Moreover, this trend towards increasing problematic behaviour and difficulty that riddles some youths' experiences appears to be on the rise, at least in comparison to the first half of the century (Rutter & Smith, 1995), with greater likelihood of substance abuse, criminal activity, and parental divorce among the hazards presented to the adolescent. Most family and developmental research continues to adhere to the problem-based model, with few depictions of resilient adolescents and prosocial relations available – not to mention the sensationalistic media accounts of 'troubled' youth (Adorjan, 2010; Edwards *et al.*, 2006; Welch, Price, & Yankey, 2002).

For young people who have a greater role flexibility and opportunities than ever before, the aforementioned factors add to the uncertainty and complexities of growing up global. The dual impact of globalization and the 'second demographic transition' which incorporates declines in mortality and fertility in Western countries since the eighteenth century (Lesthaeghe, 2010) has vast repercussions for family formations and individual development. More and more, researchers take up issues related to mass migration, the meeting of different cultures, and impacts on family members of different migration status (e.g. first generation versus second generation) in their study of acculturative influences, necessary to address these demographic changes. For instance, Alonso-Arbiol, Abubakar, and Van de Vijver (2014) found both differences and commonalities in adolescent well-being considering parenting practices across migration and cultural backgrounds.

Some researchers have attributed these rapidly shifting influences and subsequent pressures on young people to the confluence of rising individualism and modernity in Western nations and their consequent spread across the world (Arnett, 1999, 2010; Dasen, 2000; Trommsdorff, 1995); and volatile markets and uncertainties in educational and vocational trajectories deepen the issue (Mills & Blossfeld, 2013). Furthermore, Hagan and colleagues contend that youth is itself a process of capitalization, with socialization into urbane, industrial market-based societies tied to the acquisition and accumulation of social, cultural, and economic forms of capital (Hagan, Boehnke, & Merkens, 2004). Through interactions with central socialization agents, including parents, teachers, and older siblings, adolescents gradually acquire various types of capital, while becoming more and more rooted into particular cultural contexts (Parsons & Bales, 1955).

Over and above the accumulation of various resources, mass-level societal shifts to market-based economic ideology arguably produce tangible change in social relationships (Hadjar, 2004). Indeed, an extensive theoretical base expounding the social and cultural mechanisms of market-oriented societies and their maintenance proliferates in both classical and modern literature. Simmel (1900/1978), Weber (1920/1958), and MacPherson (1962) assent that modern industrial societies are organized around dictates of success in terms of 'superior performance relative to others' and that this high level of competition is fundamentally linked to the logic of free-market capitalism (Hadjar, 2004). Competitive free-market value systems emphasize 'rational' relations *vis-à-vis* cost-benefit operations, de-emotionalization, competition, maximization of wealth, self-interest, and self-love, thought to derive in large part from Calvinist ideology and the Protestant work ethic (see Lenski, 1961; McClelland, 1961; Tawney, 1926/1962). MacPherson (1962) labelled these mechanisms 'possessive individualism', wherein societies marked by inequality, competition, and isolation lead to the centrality of an individual's striving for wealth and/or status that then impacts upon and permeates their social relationships. For adolescents, conflict and competition with siblings and peers over grades, toys, or other such status objects can be considered a natural component of being socialized into such societies (Hadjar, 2004; Hadjar, Baier, & Boehnke, 2008).

The trend towards increasing modernization and individualization across the globe has implications for social bonds between family members. Market-minded societies are linked to the loosening of close familial and social ties in exchange for more negotiated forms of social interaction (e.g. fleeting exchanges in trade-based societies; Greenfield, 2009). As ecologies swing towards large-scale societal (Gesellschaft) values during the process of industrialization (Tönnies, 1887/1957 in Greenfield, 2009), family relationships as chief social capital resources are negatively impacted. In turn, families influence the developing individual's accrual of culturally specific knowledge, obligations, expectancies, responsibilities, norms, and consents (Hagan et al., 2004). Indeed, Rice (2001) linked mass industrialization and urbanization processes in post–Second World War Japan to a number of consequences for the family, echoing an overall transfer towards transitory social exchanges with strangers versus lifelong social relations with interdependent kin (Greenfield, 2009).We elaborate on the observed impact of cultural shifts regarding the sibling relationship in a forthcoming section on Greenfield's theory of social change and human development.

Formalized education processes and their greater duration are additionally tied to socio-cultural and developmental change, as members of a society are prepared for integration into an increasingly diversified workforce (Arnett, 2004). The resulting prolonged nature of adolescence and its postponed recognition of adult status, aggregated with decreased regard for tradition and family loyalties, often leads to adolescent anxiety and tension (Fleming, 1948). Parents and elders are seen as authorities who must be resisted as youths grapple with the increased pressure to engage in the process of individuation, testing the precarious borders between parental authority and adolescent autonomy (Arnett, 1999). From this stance, the disturbances of Sturm and Drang (storm and stress) experienced in adolescence are logical by-products in the wider symptomatology of coming to age in contemporary individualistic post-industrialization contexts.

It would seem that the increased diversification of the workforce and the accompanying educational demands contribute to this lengthened social infancy and economic dependency (Arnett, 2004). As Fleming (1948) notes, the form that the adolescent phase assumes is variable between and within cultures, although pressures towards greater diversity in education, work, and life as a whole in modern industrialized nations have come to bear on adolescent girls and boys. Moreover, different developmental environments exhibit considerable variation in the amount of autonomy granted and claimed by adolescents; schools may demand more or less freedom and compliance than the family context, making boundary negotiation a constant challenge for youth. Youths from a migrant background may understandably find these potentially disparate requirements particularly troublesome as host society and family expectations often conflict (e.g. Buriel & De Ment, 1997; Juang & Cookston, 2009; Liebkind & Kosonen, 1998). It is this ever-negotiable acquiescence that may be a major contributor to the conflict and stress manifest in youths' relationships (e.g. sibling quarrels) and personal lives.

An alternative account of adolescence

While depictions of troubled youth are rife in popular media and research in the West, the universality of 'storm and stress' and related rivalry and conflict among siblings has been contested (Arnett, 1999). Margaret Mead (e.g. 1942, 1943) famously put forth an alternate cultural frame for this developmental phase. Mead contended that girls and boys of the Arapesh tribe do not present such individual-focused notions, and adolescence is consummated – often through a ceremony – by admission to the privileges of adult life. However, Mead's approach and findings have been questioned by the likes of Freeman (1983) who holds that her ethnographic approach was marred by false reports from informants.

Still, others argue that this pattern of earlier substantial inclusion and demands to make meaningful contributions to the social fabric of a community are typical for more subsistence-based societies with their reduced focus on leadership, competition, dominance, and private property, and therefore tend to equate adolescence less with instances of sibling rivalry and conflict and more with caregiving and cooperation (Maynard, 2004; Mead & Wolfenstein, 1955; Nuckolls, 1993; Weisner, 1993; Zukow, 1989). Nsamenang (1999) explains how Eurocentric views of child development that accentuate individualism and cognitive competence might discount 'cultures like the African that place primacy on interdependence and value cognition as a means to social development' (p. 160). Fundamental cultural differences in societal values, arrangements, and roles permeate daily family life and relationships and so impact development and socialization. As we shall see, adolescence holds factors both different and alike across cultures and so sways sibling relationships in similar and dissimilar ways.

Adolescence, changing cultures, and family relationships

The experience and expectations of adolescence varies according to culture and have varied over time. Adolescents' accounts and personal histories impact their personal development, and culture shapes their expectancies and attitudes towards their own and others' maturation. Yet although puberty and its accompanying physiological changes are the underlying *universal* drivers of adolescent biological change (Bastiana Archibald, Graber, & Brooks-Gunn, 2003), past explanations from a Western interpretive lens for adolescent turmoil resided solely in hormonal changes (Hall, 1916, cited in Heine, 2011). As previously mentioned, youth is associated with trouble in the majority of Western states, although only a small minority of youth are actually engaged in severe conflict (Fox, 1978). More precisely, violence on the part of young males is tied to adolescence, and the highest proportion of violent crime is related to being young and male, although culture certainly plays a crucial role here (e.g. Boden, Fergusson, & Horwood, 2010; Caspi et al., 2002; McAndrew, 2009).

Some have attributed this inclination towards heightened conflict as a function of the rise of individualism, although other factors are most certainly at play. The phenomenon of violence among adolescents is recognized as a critical social problem in Latin America, for example, and social conditions, namely, poverty, neighbourhood environment, and family dysfunction all contribute to the growth of youth violence (Welti, 2004). Macro-economics further governs such patterns, as violence can be traceable to macro-cultural influences such as the international illegal drug market (Andreas & Wallman, 2009). Furthermore, difficulty obtaining gainful employment and the pressure to provide for the family makes engaging in crime a more and more viable alternative. In this way, public policies that support families and individual development are required to foster positive adaptation and combat negative socio-cultural influence on multiple levels (e.g. Carrillo, Ripoll-Núñez, & Schvaneveldt, 2012).

As we outlined in Chapter 3 on sibling correlates, delinquent behaviour and substance use between siblings is very much a function of shared socio-environmental conditions and cultural expectations that help shape behaviour. Younger brothers may model their own substance use on that of older siblings, and in homes with an absentee parent or parental separation, the likelihood that both brothers hold permissive attitudes towards drug use increases (Brook & Brook, 1990; Green, 1979). However, aetiological factors may vary for different racial and ethnic groups. O'Donnell and Clayton (1979) found that family influences acted as buffers in white teenagers, while peer factors and early problem behaviour were more predictive for black teens. Clearly, there is a need to advance socio-culturally specific understanding of the moderators and mediators at work in the sibling relationship and individual behaviour; homogeneous examination of ethnic groups and ethnic minorities within and across nations can propel the much-needed non-Eurocentric knowledge.

All this is not to say that certain sibling phenomena 'belong' to one culture or another, simply that they may be more culturally salient (Arnett, 1999). As an illustration, within the Mundugumor tribe, rejection of children is common, as is intense hostility and conflict for power between siblings, between parents and children, and between spouses (e.g. Hsu, Watrous, & Lord, 1961; Sargent, 1949). Important cultural discrepancies must be noted as must certain socio-environmental contexts that mould family relationship dynamics. The New Zealand National Task Force on Adolescent Morbidity states that what matters the most for adolescent well-being is the environmental context, including socio-economic disadvantage and individual-, group-, and institutional-level discrimination, and therefore prescribes culturally specific and relevant wide-spanning measures (Gluckman & Hayne, 2011). Avenues for future research include the intersections between socio-economic disadvantage in various ethnic groups and how researchers can effectively target solutions in a culturally engaged way. We now move to analyzing the macro-system of the broader political, economic, and socio-cultural context through the previously mentioned ecological systems view, which will allow us to examine particular cultural forces at play in sibling and family dynamics (Bronfenbrenner, 1986).

Sibling relationships and cultural forces

What does culture and its requirements mean for siblings as they move through adolescence? Within the US, where most investigation has occurred, a lack of legal ties or prescribed sibling roles 'may mean that within-society subcultures and contexts are critical in shaping the sibling experience and its influence on child development' (McGuire & Shanahan, 2010). A few scattered investigations have explored important intra-cultural variation in terms of ethnicity or family structure and how they impact the sibling relationship. Those readers interested in ethnic minority sibling study within the US context will find McGuire and Shanahan's (2010) lucid yet comprehensive review of diverse family contexts and sibling experiences informative. The authors draw out the need to incorporate sibling research on Asian and other ethnic minority groups like Native Americans to add to our collective knowledge base of sibling experiences, acculturation, and family obligation.

Study on Mexican American families suggests that cultural factors are at work in regards to differential treatment effects, with more negative implications in individualistic contexts in contrast to collectivistic cultures (McHale, Updegraff, Shanahan, Crouter, & Killoren, 2005). Differential treatment by parents in individualistic eco-social contexts may have more of a negative outcome than in collectivistic cultures, which typically delineate family roles and expectations explicitly based upon gender and age (Nuckolls, 1993; Vespa, 2009; Weisner, 1993). Justification for alternate treatment might be established through these guiding norms and requirements, such that siblings perceive such treatment as fair. Moreover, the sibling relationship may then be less likely to be coloured by conflict. One's sense of family obligations, which reflect familism values, may additionally contribute to improved sibling relations among Mexican American adolescents, for example, and other communally oriented cultural groups (McHale et al., 2005; Nsamenang, 1999; Updegraff, McHale, Whiteman, Thayer, & Delgado, 2005).

Whether one looks at an ethnic minority group like African American families or a separate culture entirely like South America's Arawak in Guyana, it is important to trace out areas of convergence and divergence in comparison to other ethnic and cultural groups (Nsamenang, 2008). Cultural variability and similarity considers that wider socio-cultural factors may be more or less predominant based on the economic and social conditions experienced within a particular locale. McHale and colleagues' work provides an example of convergent findings: African American families and European American families with low to mid-range socio-economic status backgrounds both displayed analogous categories of sibling relationships regardless of ethnicity ('high-negativity', 'high-warmth', 'emotionally distant'). Furthermore, high sibling negativity was coupled with children depression and problem behaviour, and both groups' positive parent–child relationships were associated with sibling positivity (Kim, McHale, Crouter, & Osgood, 2007; McHale, Whiteman, Kim, & Crouter, 2007).

Specific divergent findings, however, include the concentration of family structure variables. African American and Mexican American sibling studies have both utilized two-parent and single-parent families, yet each group has revealed their own distinct patterns and histories. For instance, immigration and multi-generation households are critical in Mexican American sibling study, as is spirituality and racial identity in African American research. In a similar vein, Navara (2006) found patterns of cultural cocooning among Jamaican immigrant families in Canada where activities like church functions, cultural association events, household chores, and engaging with siblings, other family members, and schoolmates of similar ancestry assisted in enculturation. Further research suggests that African American sibling relationship quality varies in consideration of ethnic identity, discrimination experiences, and relationships (Brody, Stoneman, Smith, & Gibson, 1999; McHale et al., 2007). To our knowledge, researchers have undertaken neither a systematic study of 'whiteness' and sibling relationships nor comparable comparative studies of various ethnic groups. It is important to include a variety of ethnic heritages, in addition to Caucasian and mixed-race individuals, in order to clearly demarcate crossovers and separations in ethnic identity and cultural issues in sibling and family study (Root, 1998; Song, 2010).

Other distinct cultural findings highlight the caregiving responsibilities of older siblings and the hierarchical structure of sibling roles in non-Western societies, as well as cultural differences in sibling dynamics, including features already mentioned like rivalry and competition (Maynard, 2004; Nuckolls, 1993; Weisner, 1993; Zukow, 1989). As familism values generally loom larger in more collectivistic cultures, this fundamental cultural difference may contribute to the relative importance or, at least, the variable functions of siblings for youths in Asia and South America (e.g. Brown, Larson, & Saraswathi, 2002). Also, in Western societies, peers are believed to take on a primary socializing role in adolescence (for a review, see Brechwald & Prinstein, 2011), although this appears to occupy a minor role in South Asian and Arabic adolescent development, which may further implicate greater sibling effects and influence (Brown et al., 2002). These illustrative macro-cultural distinctions bring us to one of the most important features of cross-culturally sensitive sibling research: the application of a systems view of development.

Developmental systems theory in action

Fitting to a systems theory orientation, 'personal values are not cultural values writ small' (Kitayama, 2002, p. 93), just as cultural values are not individual beliefs writ large. Certain extant cultural values, say, embeddedness, harmony, and hierarchy of particular preference in some collectivistic cultures (Schwartz, 1992), are not significant because they are held by all members of the given culture; rather, these cultural values are meaningful because they have wrought and moulded existing cultural systems. Social institutions, cultural narratives, lay theories, daily practices, and activities are all inculcated by way of these systems (see Kitayama & Markus, 1999).

It stands to reason that members of a cultural group or society may exhibit greater or lesser affinities and preference for any given set of values or accompanying norms and mores. All the same, there will be substantial variation within this group as no cultural group is entirely homogeneous. In following, the cultural expression of family arrangements and patterns may appear quite different across settings such as the father acting as governing head in an authoritarian Japanese household with children's obedience expected above all else, and where the sibling relationship takes on a minor importance, in comparison to a traditional Muslim household tucked in the London boroughs and, let us suppose, a patriarchal nomadic clan located in the Mongolian Steppes, and yet may still possess a range of similarities. Systems theory helps us to access cultural universals as well as disentangle rich inter- and intra-cultural variations. This approach allows for the appreciation of individual experiences as shaped by larger macro-cultural forces (Scheithauer, Niebank, & Ittel, 2009) and is expedient to cross-cultural developmental research involving families.

Social change and human development

Patricia Greenfield's systemic theory of social change and human development offers one specific illustration of the systems science tradition in action. Greenfield's (2009) empirical and theoretical corpus puts forth a framework of psychological change in relation to socio-cultural change and is of significant importance for sibling research. Her body of work and extensive collection of data expound individual-level developmental change as intrinsically tied to wider societal shifts in socio-demographic ecologies and underscores the need to adopt a systems view in culturally sensitive adolescent development research.

During adolescence, young individuals detect and are socialized into cultural values, roles, and beliefs that guide future attitudes, behaviours, and the transition into the adult realm (Manago, 2010). Here, Greenfield's theory is a useful conceptual tool for understanding development. Its relevance lies in its immediate applications to cross-cultural investigations of sibling relationships, as it can illuminate how sibling relationships and shifts in the meaning and experiences connected to adolescence and familial life are connected to particular kinds of ecological affordances. And at the same time, this systemic view of development echoes the comprehensive perspective that considers adolescence as a sensitive period for socio-emotional and socio-cultural development and related adult role preparation.

As Greenfield and co-authors found in their longitudinal multi-generational examination of Mayan grandmothers, mothers, and daughters dating back over 40 years, familial structuring, expectations, and roles changed in accordance with the shift from Gemeinschaft (community/communal)-type arrangements to a Gesellschaft (society/individual) orientation (Greenfield, 2004; Greenfield, Maynard, & Childs, 2003; Maynard & Greenfield, 2008). Siblings were expected to continue to care for younger siblings, although the negotiation of these familial roles acted in accordance with movement towards greater economic activities of the society at large. Daughters in particular were seen as key socialization agents in transmitting cultural values and expectations to the rest of their siblings and became adept at interweaving and conjoining communitarian and Gesellschaft values (Maynard, 2013). Additionally, Toyote (2013) discovered that adolescents in low socio-economic status working Mayan migrant families combined traditional and non-traditional cultural practices as part of a greater trend to assure family and child well-being. These authors cite the ingenuity of the local communities and individual adolescents in melding both traditional and novel cultural ways to increase familial and social harmony among members.

Other investigators have studied the influence of societal turns towards urbanization and industrialization, reflecting Gemeinschaft to Gesellschaft orientational transition and how it comes to bear on adolescence and family structures. We now give focus to research that runs parallel to Greenfield's (2009) over-arching framework. Rogoff, Correa-Chavez, and Navichoc-Cotuc (2005) documented the historical change of children's learning environments over a 23-year span in a Mayan sample and showed that broad macro-cultural changes signposting the shift from subsistence and agrarian economies such as population increase, occupation diversification, and value of education were linked to social relational changes. For instance, informal education at home decreased in tandem with formal schooling's mounting importance, and so children were less likely to learn from the family via observational learning and modelling. Family size was reduced in accord with movement away from subsistence arrangements; siblings thus had fewer responsibilities tied to care for younger siblings with most of their time spent at school and with non-kin peers versus siblings. As sibling care is a major factor in the development of altruistic in contrast to egoistic behaviour (Whiting & Whiting, 1973), it stands to reason that increasing expectations for sibling conflict and rivalry in individualistic milieus is related to decreased sibling interaction in a caring context.

Considering another example of how socio-demographic change might impact sibling relationships in adolescence, one can examine the transformation in post–Second World War Japan. As per Rice (2001), Japan experienced a rapid swing to the industrial and urban, and so too, there was a documented change in the family's social relationships: mothers' subsistence roles were reduced, family size and extended family importance drastically so, and sibling caregiving lessened while individual maternal attention rose. Importantly, accompanying transitions towards pedagogic importance and maternal involvement led to more child-centred socialization processes. This change echoes Western Gesellschaft-focused traditions, where children are conceived as emotionally, culturally, and materially dependent on and shaped by their parents and nuclear family. Furthermore, Western psychological and psychoanalytic theories stress the parent–/mother–child bond as it purportedly constitutes the core formational relationship and so marginalizes the importance of sibling and other lateral relationships (Edwards *et al.*, 2006).

Emerging adults – especially women – raised under this new paradigm found roles to be less prescriptive and binding, as is typical for more individualistic versus collectivistic societies (Hofstede, 1980, 2001; Triandis, 1993). At the same time, an increased focus towards personal achievement and success and a reduction of social responsibilities like sibling care and care for elders were also predicted (Suzuki, 2000). These cases demonstrate significant alterations in socio-cultural conditions and contexts and shed light on notions of sibling rivalry, differential treatment, and sibling differentiation processes, confirming prior culturally comparative research (Maynard, 2004; Weisner, 1993; Zukow, 1989). This line of inquiry awaits empiric validation in terms of precisely how implicated socio-cultural differences and changes impact sibling bonds.

Teasing apart different cultural values, especially when disparate cultures inter-mix traditional values with increased modernization (e.g. Inglehart & Baker, 2000; Serpell, 1994), presents a challenge for future sibling research efforts. Nonetheless, the presented studies and their findings undertaken in diverse cultural settings appear to coalesce under a systemic approach in which human development is conceptualized as multi-levelled and nested. That is, Greenfield's framework of social change and human development and other systemic analyses offer us a way to probe the mechanisms at work in shaping sibling relationships; this deeper level understanding, however conceptually complicated, can be achieved by tracking socio-demographic, cultural, learning environment, and socio-cognitive developmental influences and their impact on adolescence (Whiteman *et al.*, 2011).

New directions

The previous examples illustrate what we propose is crucial for future research: complex intimate relationships like the sibling bond must be examined in multiple *dynamic* contexts in order to grasp the cultural universals as well as the specifics that dictate its expression. Again, the developmental systems perspective is apt, albeit challenging to enlist, for research of this nature. Few studies have taken on the challenge due to the perspective's relative newness and the difficulty of transitioning to systematic conceptualizations and surveys which have predominantly been mono-cultural and static. We take the opportunity to highlight some recent innovative sibling research projects carried out internationally in the appendix.

This chapter set out to provide an overview of cross-cultural features related to adolescence and sibling study. However, one of the field's primary limitations is the restricted focus on siblings in North America and Western Europe, which mirrors the most empirical investigations of developmental and family studies. Cross-cultural comparisons and the inclusion of siblings from under-represented groups, such as interethnic and multi-cultural families, are currently lacking yet crucial to further complete the portrait of sisters and brothers in adolescence. We suggest that advances in applied systems theory and within-family research designs gathered from longitudinal and cross-cultural samples are important starting points in building an environmentally grounded, culturally sensitive research base. From there, knowledge of sibling bonds in development can act as a valuable model for intimate relations across time and contexts. This vein of work is essential in light of increasing global mobility and our rapidly shifting environmental contexts.

References

Adorjan, M. C. (2010). Emotions contests and reflexivity in the news: Examining discourse on youth crime in Canada. *Journal of Contemporary Ethnography, 40*(2), 168–198.

Alonso-Arbiol, I., Abubakar, A., & Van de Vijver, F. J. (2014). Parenting practices and attachment as predictors of life satisfaction of mainstream Dutch and Moroccan-Dutch adolescents. In R. Dimitrova, M. Bender, & F. van de Vijver (Eds.), *Global perspectives on well-being in immigrant families* (pp. 291–309). New York: Springer.

Andreas, P., & Wallman, J. (2009). Illicit markets and violence: What is the relationship? *Crime, Law and Social Change, 52*(3), 225–229.

Arnett, J. J. (1999). Adolescent storm and stress, reconsidered. *American Psychologist, 54*, 317–326.

Arnett, J. J. (2004). Adolescents in western countries in the 21st century: Vast opportunities – for all? In B. Brown, R. Larson, & T. Saraswathi (Eds.), *The world's youth: Adolescence in eight regions of the globe* (pp. 307–343). Cambridge: Cambridge University Press.

Arnett, J. J. (2010). *Adolescence and emerging adulthood* (4th ed.). Englewood Cliffs, NJ: Prentice Hall.

Arnett Jensen, L. (2003). Coming of age in a multicultural world: Globalization and adolescent cultural identity formation. *Applied Developmental Science, 7*(3), 189–196.

Bandura, A. (1977). *Social learning theory*. Englewood Cliffs, NJ: Prentice Hall.

Bastiana Archibald, A., Graber, J. A., & Brooks-Gunn, J. (2003). Pubertal processes and physiological growth in adolescence. In G. R. Adams & M. D. Berzonsky (Eds.), *Blackwell handbook of adolescence* (pp. 24–47). Malden, MA: Blackwell.

Berry, J. (1997). Immigration, acculturation, and adaptation. *Applied Psychology, 46*(1), 5–68.

Boden, J. M., Fergusson, D. M., & Horwood, L. J. (2010). Risk factors for conduct disorder and oppositional/defiant disorder: Evidence from a New Zealand birth cohort. *Journal of the American Academy of Child & Adolescent Psychiatry, 49*, 1125–1133.

Brechwald, W. A., & Prinstein, M. J. (2011). Beyond homophily: A decade of advances in understanding peer influence processes. *Journal of Research on Adolescence, 21*, 166–179.

Brody, G. H., Stoneman, Z., Smith, T., & Gibson, N. M. (1999). Sibling relationships in rural African American families. *Journal of Marriage and the Family, 61*, 1046–1057.

Bronfenbrenner, U. (1986). Ecology of the family as a context for human development: Research perspectives. *Developmental Psychology, 22*(6), 723–742.

Brook, D., & Brook, J. (1990). The etiology and consequences of adolescent drug use. In R. Watson (Ed.), *Drug and alcohol abuse prevention*. Clifton, NJ: Humana Press.

Brown, B., Larson, R., & Saraswathi, T. S. (Eds.). (2002). *The world's youth: Adolescence in eight regions of the globe* (pp. 339–362). New York: Cambridge University Press.

Bruner, J. S. (1966). *Toward a theory of instruction*. Cambridge, MA: Harvard University Press.

Buriel, R., & De Ment, T. (1997). Immigration and sociocultural changes in Mexican, Chinese, and Vietnamese families. In A. Booth, A. Crouter, & N. Landale (Eds.), *Immigration and the family: Research and policy on US immigrants* (pp. 165–200). Mahwah, NJ: Lawrence Erlbaum.

Carrillo, S., Ripoll-Núñez, K., & Schvaneveldt, P. L. (2012). Family policy initiatives in Latin America: The case of Colombia and Ecuador. *Journal of Child and Family Studies, 21*(1), 75–87.

Caspi, A., McClay, J., Moffitt, T. E., Mill, J., Martin, J., Craig, I. W., *et al.* (2002). Role of genotype in the cycle of violence in maltreated children. *Science, 297*, 851–854.

Cheung, B. Y., Chudek, M., & Heine, S. J. (2011). Evidence for a sensitive period for acculturation younger immigrants report acculturating at a faster rate. *Psychological Science, 22*(2), 147–152.

Dasen, P. R. (2000). Rapid social change and the turmoil of adolescence: A cross-cultural perspective. *International Journal of Group Tensions, 29*, 17–49.

Duckitt, J. (2001). A dual-process cognitive-motivational theory of ideology and prejudice. In M. P. Zanna (Ed.), *Advances in experimental social psychology* (pp. 41–113). San Diego, CA: Academic Press.

Edwards, R., Hadfield, L., Lucey, H., & Mauthner, M. (2006). *Sibling identity and relationships: Sisters and brothers.* Oxon: Routledge.

Erikson, E. H. (1968). *Identity: Youth and crisis.* New York: W. W. Norton.

Fleming, C. M. (1948). *Adolescence: Its social psychology: With an introduction to recent findings from the fields of anthropology, physiology, medicine, psychometrics and sociometry* (Vol. 67). London: Taylor & Francis.

Fox, J. A. (1978). *Forecasting crime data: An econometric analysis.* Lexington, MA: Lexington Books.

Freeman, D. (1983). *Margaret Mead and Samoa: The making and unmaking of an anthropological myth.* Cambridge, MA: Harvard University Press.

Fromkin, V., Krashen, S., Curtiss, S., Rigler, D., & Rigler, M. (1974). The development of language in Genie: A case of language acquisition beyond the 'critical period'. *Brain and Language, 1*(1), 81–107.

Gluckman, P. D., & Hayne, H. (2011). *Improving the transition: Reducing social and psychological morbidity during adolescence.* New Zealand: Office of the Prime Minister's Science Advisory Committee.

Goody, E. N. (2006). Dynamics of the emergence of sociocultural institutional practices. In D. Olson & M. Cole (Eds.), *Technology, literacy and the evolution of society* (pp. 241–264). Mahwah, NJ: Erlbaum.

Green, J. (1979). Overview of adolescent drug use. In G. Beschner & A. Friedman (Eds.), *Youth drug abuse: Problems, issues, and treatment* (pp. 17–44). Lexington, KY: Lexington Books.

Greenfield, P. M. (1997). Culture as process: Empirical methods for cultural psychology. In J. W. Berry, Y. Poortinga, & J. Pandey (Eds.), *Handbook of cross-cultural psychology: Theory and methods* (Vol. 1, pp. 301–346). Boston, MA: Allyn & Bacon.

Greenfield, P. M. (2004). *Weaving generations together: Evolving creativity among the Mayas of Chiapas.* Santa Fe, NM: SAR Press.

Greenfield, P. M. (2009). Linking social change and developmental change: shifting pathways of human development. *Developmental Psychology, 45*(2), 401–418.

Greenfield, P. M., Maynard, A. E., & Childs, C. P. (2003). Historical change, cultural learning, and cognitive representation in Zinacantec Maya children. *Cognitive Development, 18*, 455–487.

Grimshaw, G., Adelstein, A., Bryden, M., & MacKinnon, G. (1998). First-language acquisition in adolescence: Evidence for a critical period for verbal language development. *Brain & Language, 63*, 237–255.

Hadjar, A. (2004). *Ellenbogenmentalität und Fremdenfeindlichkeit bei Jugendlichen. Die Rolle des Hierarchischen Selbstinteresses.* Wiesbaden: Verlag für Sozialwissenschaften.

Hadjar, A., Baier, D., & Boehnke, K. (2008). The socialization of hierarchic self-interest: Value socialization in the family. *Young, 16*(3), 279–301.

Hagan, J., Boehnke, K., & Merkens, H. (2004). Gender differences in capitalization processes and the delinquency of siblings in Toronto and Berlin. *British Journal of Criminology, 44*(5), 659–676.

Hall, G. S. (1916). *Adolescence*. New York: Appleton.

Heine, S. J. (2011). *Cultural psychology*. New York: W. W. Norton.

Heine, S. J., & Hamamura, T. (2007). In search of East Asian self-enhancement. *Personality and Social Psychology Review, 11*(1), 4–27.

Hofstede, G. (1980). *Culture's consequences: International differences in work-related values*. Beverly Hills, CA: Sage.

Hofstede, G. (2001). *Culture's consequences: Comparing values, behaviors, institutions, and organizations across nations*. Thousand Oaks, CA: Sage.

Hsu, F. L. K., Watrous, B. G., & Lord, E. M. (1961). Culture pattern and adolescent behavior. *International Journal of Social Psychiatry, 7*(1), 33–53.

Inglehart, R., & Baker, W. E. (2000). Modernization, cultural change, and the persistence of traditional values. *American Sociological Review, 65*, 19–51.

Ittel, A., & Sisler, A. (2012). Third culture kids: Adjusting to a changing world. *Diskurs Kindheits- und Jugendforschung, 7*(4), 487–492.

Johnson, J. S., & Newport, E. L. (1989). Critical period effects in second language learning: The influence of maturational state on the acquisition of English as a second language. *Cognitive Psychology, 21*(1), 60–99.

Juang, L. P., & Cookston, J. T. (2009). Acculturation, discrimination, and depressive symptoms among Chinese American adolescents: A longitudinal study. *Journal of Primary Prevention, 30*(3–4), 475–496.

Keller, H., & Greenfield, P. (2000). History and future of development in cross-cultural research. *Journal of Cross-Cultural Psychology, 31*, 52–62.

Kim, J. Y., McHale, S. M., Crouter, A. C., & Osgood, D. W. (2007). Longitudinal linkages between sibling relationships and adjustment from middle childhood through adolescence. *Developmental Psychology, 43*(4), 960–973.

Kitayama, S. (2002). Culture and basic psychological processes – Toward a system view of culture: Comment on Oyserman et al. (2002). *Psychological Bulletin, 128*, 89–96.

Kitayama, S., & Markus, H. R. (1999). Yin and yang of the Japanese self: The cultural psychology of personality coherence. In D. Cervone & Y. Shoda (Eds.), *The coherence of personality: Social cognitive bases of personality consistency, variability, and organization* (pp. 242–302). New York: Guilford Press.

Kroger, J. (2004). *Identity development during adolescence*. East Sussex: Routledge.

Kruger, A. C., & Tomasello, M. (1996). Cultural learning and learning culture. In D. Olson & N. Torrance (Eds.), *The handbook of education and human development* (pp. 369–387). Oxford: Blackwell.

Kuczynski, L., Navara, G., & Boiger, M. (2011). The social relational perspective on family acculturation. In S. S. Chuang & R. P. Moreno (Eds.), *On new shores: Understanding immigrant children in North America* (pp. 171–192). Lanham, MD: Lexington Books.

Kuczynski, L., & Parkin, C. M. (2007). Agency and bidirectionality in socialization: Interactions, transactions, and relational dialectics. In J. E. Grusec & P. Hastings (Eds.), *Handbook of socialization* (pp. 259–283). New York: Guilford Press.

Kuczynski, L., & Parkin, C. M. (2009). Pursuing a dialectical perspective on transaction: A social relational theory of micro family processes. In A. Sameroff (Ed.), *Transactional processes in development* (pp. 247–268). Washington, DC: APA Books.

Kuhl, P. K. (2010). Brain mechanisms in early language acquisition. *Neuron, 67*(5), 713–727.

Lancy, D. (2010). Learning 'from nobody': The limited role of teaching in folk models of children's development. *Childhood in the Past, 3*(1), 79–106.

Lancy, D. (in press). Ethnographic perspectives on culture acquisition. In C. Meehan & A. Crittenden (Eds.), *Origins and implications of the evolution of childhood*. Santa Fe, NM: SAR Press.

Lenski, G. (1961). *The religious factor*. Garden City, NY: Doubleday.

Lesthaeghe, R. (2010). The unfolding story of the second demographic transition. *Population and Development Review, 36*(2), 211–251.

Leung, A. K.-y., Maddux, W. W., Galinsky, A. D., & Chiu, C.-y. (2008). Multicultural experience enhances creativity: The when and how. *American Psychologist, 63*, 169–181. doi:10.1037/0003-066X.63.3.169

Liebkind, K., & Kosonen, L. (1998). Acculturation and adaptation: A case of Vietnamese children and adolescents in Finland. In J. E. Nurmi (Ed.), *Adolescents, cultures and conflicts: Growing up in contemporary Europe* (pp. 199–224). East Lansing, MI: Michigan State University Press.

MacPherson, C. B. (1962). *The political theory of possessive individualism: From Hobbes to Locke*. London: Oxford University Press.

Maddux, W. W., & Galinsky, A. D. (2009). Cultural borders and mental barriers: The relationship between living abroad and creativity. *Journal of Personality and Social Psychology, 96*, 1047–1061. doi:10.1037/a0014861

Manago, A. M. (2010). Studying Maya adolescents in a new high school in Zinacantan, Mexico. *CSW Update Newsletter, UCLA Center for the Study of Women*, pp. 6–10.

Marcia, J. E. (1966). Development and validation of ego-identity status. *Journal of Personality and Social Psychology, 3*(5), 551–558.

Marcia, J. E. (1980). Identity in adolescence. In J. Adelson (Ed.), *Handbook of adolescent psychology* (pp. 159–187). New York: Wiley.

Marcia, J. E., Waterman, A. S., Matteson, D. R., Archer, S. L., & Orlofsky, J. L. (Eds.). (1993). *Ego identity: A handbook of psychosocial research*. New York: Springer-Verlag.

Maynard, A. E. (2004). Sibling interactions. In U. Gielen & J. Roopnarine (Eds.), *Childhood and adolescence: Cross-cultural perspectives and applications* (pp. 229–252). Westport, CT: Praeger.

Maynard, A. E. (2013, June). Social change and the shift to formal education: Cognitive representation of three generations of children over 43 years in a Maya community. In A. Maynard (Chair), *Shifting sociodemographics, economics, and child development in the era of globalization*. Symposium conducted at the International Association of Cross-Cultural Psychology, University of California, Los Angeles.

Maynard, A. E., & Greenfield, P. M. (2008). Women's schooling and other ecocultural shifts: A longitudinal study of historical change among the Zinacantec Maya. *Mind, Culture, and Activity, 15*(2), 165–175.

McAndrew, F. T. (2009). The interacting roles of testosterone and challenges to status in human male aggression. *Aggression and Violent Behavior, 14*(5), 330–335.

McCauley, R. N., & Henrich, J. (2006). Susceptibility to the Müller-Lyer illusion, theory-neutral observation, and the diachronic penetrability of the visual input system. *Philosophical Psychology, 19*(1), 79–101.

McClelland, D. C. (1961). *The achieving society*. Princeton, NJ: D. Van Nostrand Company.

McGuire, S., & Shanahan, L. (2010). Sibling experiences in diverse family contexts. *Child Development Perspectives, 4*(2), 72–79.

McHale, S. M., Updegraff, K. A., Shanahan, L., Crouter, A. C., & Killoren, S. E. (2005). Siblings' differential treatment in Mexican American families. *Journal of Marriage and Family, 67*(5), 1259–1274.

McHale, S. M., Whiteman, S. D., Kim, J. Y., & Crouter, A. C. (2007). Characteristics and correlates of sibling relationships in two-parent African American families. *Journal of Family Psychology, 21*(2), 227–235.

Mead, M. (1942). *Growing up in New Guinea*. London: Penguin Books (First published New York: William Morrow, 1930).

Mead, M. (1943). *Coming of age in Samoa*. London: Penguin Books. (First published New York: William Morrow, 1928).

Mead, M., & Wolfenstein, M. (1955). *Childhood in contemporary cultures*. Chicago: University of Chicago.

Merelman, R. M. (1972). The adolescence of political socialization. *Sociology of Education, 45*, 134–166.

Miller, J. G. (1984). Culture and the development of everyday social explanation. *Journal of Personality and Social Psychology, 46*, 961–978.

Mills, M., & Blossfeld, H. P. (2013). The second demographic transition meets globalization: A comprehensive theory to understand changes in family formation in an era of rising uncertainty. In A. Evans & J. Baxter (Eds.), *Negotiating the life course* (pp. 9–33). Dordrecht, Netherlands: Springer.

Minoura, Y. (1992). A sensitive period for the incorporation of a cultural meaning system: A study of Japanese children growing up in the United States. *Ethos, 20*(3), 304–339.

Navara, G. S. (2006). Parent-child relationships in a cross-cultural context: Jamaican-Canadian families from the child's perspective (Unpublished doctoral dissertation). University of Guelph, ON, Canada.

Newton, M. (2002). *Savage girls and wild boys: A history of feral children*. New York: Picador.

Nsamenang, A. B. (1999). Eurocentric image of childhood in the context of the world's cultures. *Human Development, 42*, 159–168.

Nsamenang, A. B. (2008). Culture and human development. *International Journal of Psychology, 43*(2), 73–77.

Nuckolls, C. W. (1993). *Siblings in South Asia: Brothers and sisters in cultural context*. New York: Guilford Press.

O'Donnell, J., & Clayton, R. (1979). Determinants of early marijuana use. In G. Beschner & A. Friedman (Eds.), *Youth drug abuse: Problems, issues, and treatment* (pp. 63–110). Lexington, KY: Lexington Books.

Parsons, T., & Bales, R. (1955). *Family, socialization, and interaction process*. Glencoe, IL: Free Press.

Prewitt, K., & Dawson, R. (1969). *Political socialization*. Boston, MA: Little Brown & Company.

Rice, Y. N. (2001). Cultural values and socioeconomic conditions. In H. Shimuzu & R. A. LeVine (Eds.), *Japanese frames of mind: Cultural perspectives on human development* (pp. 85–110). Cambridge: Cambridge University Press.

Rogoff, B. (1981). Adults and peers as agents of socialization: A Highland Guatemalan profile. *Ethos, 9*, 18–36.

Rogoff, B. (2003). *The cultural nature of human development*. Oxford: Oxford University Press.

Rogoff, B., Correa-Chavez, M., & Navichoc-Cotuc, M. (2005). A cultural/historical view of schooling in human development. In D. Pillemer & S. H. White (Eds.), *Developmental psychology and social change* (pp. 225–263). New York: Cambridge University Press.

Root, M. P. (1998). Experiences and processes affecting racial identity development: Preliminary results from the Biracial Sibling Project. *Cultural Diversity and Mental Health, 4*(3), 237–247.

Rosenthal, D., & Bornholt, L. (1988). Expectations about development in Greek- and Anglo-Australian families. *Journal of Cross-Cultural Psychology, 19*(1), 19–34.

Rutter, M., & Smith, D. J. (Eds.). (1995). *Psychosocial disorders in young people: Time trends and their causes*. Chichester: Wiley.

Sargent, S. S. (Ed.). (1949). *Culture and personality*. New York: Viking Fund.

Scheithauer, H., Niebank, K., & Ittel, A. (2009). Developmental science: Integrating knowledge about dynamic processes in human development. In J. Valsiner, P. Molenaar, M. Lycra, & N. Chaudhary (Eds.), *Dynamic process methodology in the social and developmental sciences* (pp. 595–617). New York: Springer.

Schlegel, A., & Barry, H., III. (1991). *Adolescence: An anthropological inquiry.* New York: Free Press.

Schoon, I., & Silbereisen, R. K. (Eds.). (2009). *Transitions from school to work: Globalization, individualization, and patterns of diversity.* Cambridge: Cambridge University Press.

Schwartz, S. H. (1992). Universals in the content and structure of values: Theoretical advances and empirical tests in 20 countries. *Advances in Experimental Social Psychology, 25,* 1–65.

Serpell, R. (1994). An African social ontogeny: Review of A. Bame Nsamenang (1992): Human development in cultural context. *Cross-Cultural Psychology Bulletin, 28*(1), 17–21.

Simmel, G. (1900/1978). *The philosophy of money.* London: Routledge.

Skoe, E., & von der Lippe, A. (1998). *Personality development in adolescence: A cross national and life span perspective.* New York: Routledge.

Song, M. (2010). Does 'race' matter? A study of 'mixed race' siblings' identifications. *Sociological Review, 58*(2), 265–285.

Suzuki, L. K. (2000). The development and socialization of filial piety: A comparison of Asian Americans and Euro-Americans (Unpublished doctoral dissertation). University of California, Los Angeles.

Tawney, R. H. (1926/1962). *Religion and the rise of capitalism.* London: Murray.

Tomasello, M., Kruger, A. C., & Ratner, H. H. (1993). Cultural learning. *Behavioral and Brain Sciences, 16,* 495–511.

Tönnies, F. (1957). *Community and society (Gemeinschaft und Gesellschaft,* C. P. Loomis, Ed. & Trans.). East Lansing: Michigan State University Press. (Original work published in German, 1887)

Toyote, K. (2013, June). Child socialization in poor working Maya migrant families: Combining traditional and non-traditional cultural practices in order to assure family and child wellbeing. In A. Maynard (Chair), *Shifting sociodemographics, economics, and child development in the era of globalization.* Symposium conducted at the International Association of Cross-Cultural Psychology, University of California, Los Angeles.

Trevarthen, C. (1980). The foundations of intersubjectivity: Development of interpersonal and cooperative understanding in infants. In D. R. Olsen (Ed.), *The social foundations of language and thought* (pp. 316–342). New York: Wiley.

Triandis, H. C. (1993). Collectivism and individualism as cultural syndromes. *Cross-Cultural Research, 27,* 155–180.

Trommsdorff, G. (1995). Parent-adolescent relations in changing societies: A cross-cultural study. In P. Noack & M. Hofer (Eds.), *Psychological responses to social change: Human development in changing environments* (pp. 189–218). Berlin, Germany: De Gruyter.

Tsai, J. L., Ying, Y. W., & Lee, P. A. (2000). The Meaning of 'being Chinese' and 'being American' variation among Chinese American young adults. *Journal of Cross-Cultural Psychology, 31*(3), 302–332.

Updegraff, K. A., McHale, S. M., Whiteman, S. D., Thayer, S. M., & Delgado, M. Y. (2005). Adolescent sibling relationships in Mexican American families: Exploring the role of familism. *Journal of Family Psychology, 19*(4), 512–522.

Vespa, J. (2009). Gender ideology construction: A life course and intersectional approach. *Gender & Society, 23,* 363–387.

Weber, M. (1920/1958). *The protestant ethic and the spirit of capitalism.* New York: Charles Sribner' Sons.

Weisfeld, G. (1979). An ethological view of human adolescence. *Journal of Nervous and Mental Disease, 167*(1), 38–55.

Weisner, T. S. (1993). Overview: Sibling similarity and difference in different cultures. In C. Nuckolls (Ed.), *Siblings in South Asia: Brothers and sisters in cultural context* (pp. 1–17). New York: Guilford Press.

Welch, M., Price, E. A., & Yankey, N. (2002). Moral panic over youth violence: Wilding and the manufacture of menace in the media. *Youth & Society, 34*(1), 3–30.

Welti, C. (2004). Adolescents in Latin America: Facing the future with skepticism. In B. Brown, R. Larson, & T. Saraswathi (Eds.), *The world's youth: Adolescence in eight regions of the globe* (pp. 276–306). Cambridge: Cambridge University Press.

Whiteman, S. D., McHale, S. M., & Soli, A. (2011). Theoretical perspectives on sibling relationships. *Journal of Family Theory & Review, 3*(2), 124–139.

Whiting, J. W. M., & Whiting, B. B. (1973). Altruistic and egoistic behavior in six cultures. In L. Nader & T. W. Maretzki (Eds.), *Cultural illness and health: Essays in human adaptation* (pp. 56–66). Washington, DC: American Anthropological Association.

Wong, R. M., & Hong, Y. (2005). Dynamic influences of culture on cooperation in the Prisoner's dilemma. *Psychological Science, 16*, 429–434.

Zukow, P. G. (Ed.). (1989). *Sibling interaction across cultures: Theoretical and methodological issues.* New York: Springer-Verlag.

6

METHODS IN FAMILY AND SIBLING RESEARCH

Markus Hess

FREIE UNIVERSITÄT BERLIN

Contents

Introduction

The family represents a system in which individual development is embedded in the complex interactions between family members. Researchers must therefore bear in mind the multipartite nature of family data such as sibling pairs' dyadic ratings of family stress. Advances in the study of families and contemporaneous research on siblings necessitate concerted, empirically sound efforts to move beyond typically studied marital or mother–child relationships. Increasingly, additional family members like sons and daughters or grandparents and grandchildren are included in data collection for more complete depictions of family system and subsystem dynamics. This rich information is often hierarchical, and as such, analyses should take into account that data drawn from one family stem from different generations (parents and offspring) or display some form of interdependence such as the relationship between caretakers and caregivers. Without clear conceptions of the interactions and processes linking various familial components, cross-sectional and longitudinal surveying pose a challenge for research design and analysis. Moreover, investigators may be interested in individual data within one family or aggregated assessments of family functioning such as family climate, complicating the evaluation further. Last, investigations of the family can produce quantitative or qualitative data or a combination of both types of information through mixed methodology.

For these reasons, advanced family-based research calls for the adoption of sophisticated empirical methods. From a methodological standpoint, most research methods appropriate for family studies are equally suitable and complementary for the examination of various subsystems like that of the sibling relationship. As it stands, sibling study approaches have been generally constricted to basic quantitative measures, disregarding the richness and variety of this relationship. This chapter gives an overview of the different approaches for investigating family processes and focuses on quantitative methods, excluding however behavioural genetics which is depicted in Chapter 4. Qualitative methods are briefly discussed as a starting point for further quantitative exploration in addition to the blending of the two approaches, as demonstrated in mixed method studies, a more detailed discussion of which can be found in Chapter 7. We start by providing an overview of the most common methods for data collection in family research, which include standardized self and peer report measures, observational strategies, experimental settings, and diary approaches.

We then tackle the question of how to analyze family-related data. As Snijders and Kenny (1999) point out, data can be analyzed on the level of the whole family, the individual family member, as well as any dyad or other familial subgroup (e.g. siblings, female family members). In analytical terms, this perspective on family complexity often calls for multilevel approaches. Multilevel modelling is not only apposite for cross-sectional data but also for longitudinal data that are of special interest in family research (Lyons & Sayer, 2005). From among the many ways of dealing with longitudinal data, we provide an overview of basic longitudinal models, namely repeated measures analysis of variance (ANOVA), autoregressive models (ARMs) like cross-lagged panel designs and latent growth curve models

(LGCMs), and, based on a structural equation modelling (SEM) framework, a brief introduction to moderation and mediation analysis.

An additional issue typically raised in family research is the identification of different types of family structures. Addressing such concerns calls for person-centred approaches, as opposed to the variable-centred methods mentioned previously, which help to identify population subgroups based on certain theoretically derived parameters. Accordingly, we introduce latent class analysis (LCA) and cluster analysis as two person-centred approaches that assist in pinpointing typical family constellations; these groupings can then be analyzed concerning the given outcome variables.

Data collection in family research

In family and sibling research, as in other fields of psychology, researchers use a variety of methods to collect data. In the following section, we describe survey methods, observational techniques, and diary methods to give a brief impression of how they can be used in family and sibling research. We then discuss various methodologies by focusing on experimental quantitative designs and the issue of qualitative measures and address the growing call for mixed methods in family research (Weisner & Fiese, 2011).

Surveys

Perhaps the most frequently used assessment instrument in family studies is quantitative surveying using standardized questionnaires. A vast body of measures dealing with family functioning in paediatric contexts attests to the popularity of this approach (Alderfer *et al.*, 2008). Greenstein (2006) and others describe core aspects to consider in conducting a study based on standardized questionnaires (Price, 2013; Wilson Van Voorhis & Morgan, 2007). First, quantitative surveys should include a substantial number of participants to achieve the statistical power necessary to test certain assumptions. One advantage of a large sample size is that statistics based on a larger sample will tend to be closer to the population value (Price, 2013). Sample size concerns are also important because a large number of respondents helps statistically sound hypothesis testing by minimizing Type I (rejecting the null hypothesis when it is true) and Type II (not rejecting the null hypotheses when it is false) errors (Wilson Van Voorhis & Morgan, 2007). The most common significance level of statistical tests is $p < .05$ such that researchers can be 95 per cent confident that an observation indicates a nonrandom finding (Aron & Aron, 1999).

An additional statistical marker to test whether results are significant is statistical power. Statistical power refers to the degree of the overlap of two distributions: the lower the overlap, the higher the statistical power. In order to increase power researchers can either increase sample size or maximize effect size. Whereas increasing sample size is relatively easy to accomplish in theory, increasing effect size is a more complicated matter. As Wilson Van Voorhis and Morgan (2007) suggest, researchers can attempt to maximize the differences in levels of the independent variable, for example, when looking at the influence of socio-economic pressure on family processes one can aim to also include extreme levels of socio-economic background in the sample. However, these extremes are often not included in the data, so researchers should endeavour to measure the dependent variable as reliably as possible and to minimize measurement error (Wilson Van Voorhis & Morgan, 2007).

Greenstein (2006) suggests a second objective when planning a survey study: the correct construction of questionnaires. As an already well-established body of survey work exists in family research, the discussion of how to develop a scientific standardized empirical questionnaire goes beyond the scope of this chapter; we therefore refer interested readers to Price (2013). The third aspect of survey research to consider is that results are generally coded by numerical values (e.g. applying Likert-Scales) and are then analyzed using statistical software like IBM SPSS, R, Mplus, Stata, or HLM amongst others.

Sampling strategies and sample structure – above and beyond the mere number of participants – also have a substantial influence on the interpretation of survey results. In short, sampling strategies can be grouped into the categories of probability sampling, where researchers can give information about the probability that each member of a population will be selected for the sample, and nonprobability sampling, where researchers have no information about this probability (Price, 2013). A huge amount of psychological research is based on nonprobability sampling where so-called convenience samples are used. A convenience sample can be characterized as a sample of persons who are available at a certain time point and who consent to participate in the survey. To achieve a probability sample one has to have profound knowledge about the population in accordance with the research questions. Once an according sampling frame (list of all possible members of the interesting population) is determined, one can choose participants based on several strategies: simple random sampling (all members of the population have an equal chance of being drawn), stratified random sampling (the number of members in the sample is based on certain information about the population, e.g. number of divorced mothers or families with certain migrant backgrounds), and cluster sampling (prior to selecting individuals, clusters are chosen, e.g. towns with a certain population size from which the individual sample will be drawn).

Among sampling biases, particular attention should be paid to the nonresponse bias and to whether survey respondents systematically differ from the persons who actively or passively declined to participate in the survey, as systematic non-participation of portions of the selected sample threatens the validity of the survey results (Price, 2013).

Observation

One common procedure in the collection of data on family processes is systematic observation. According to Kerig (2001), family observations provide deep insight into the dynamics within families and shed light on the reciprocal and transactional nature of family interactions. Moreover, observational techniques often, albeit not always, avoid the biases associated with self-report measures used in survey research like social desirability or self-serving biases, especially when observations are structured in ways that participants are not immediately aware of the observation. Naturally, in accordance with the guidelines of ethical research, scientific observations require compulsory informed consent by participants.

Observations can take place in the laboratory or in the field. Ostrov and Hart (2013) give an overview of best practices in observational methods which can be applied to family research. To begin, a clear definition of the behaviours under investigation is necessary. The behaviours should be discrete and coding should be mutually exclusive to ensure that no one behaviour occupies dual categories, thereby rendering the data superfluous. The observational procedure should be standardized and applicable in the context under observation. As new coding schemes are developed, they should be pilot tested and subsequent observations should be independent (e.g. research observers may not exchange information regarding their observations). Although advocates of observational techniques often highlight their objectivity compared with self-reports, observations too are at the risk of subjectivity even in the presence of highly consistent coding manuals. Indeed, to a certain degree, behaviour selection and subsequent coding remains the choice of the individual investigator (Kerig, 2001). An important, although not always feasible, requirement calls for the 'blinding' of observers to the study's hypotheses as well as the construct behind the observation so as to best avoid selective observation biases. However, frequently, the categories themselves indicate the underlying hypotheses. In addition, coders should be trained to use the observation manual and to detect the relevant behaviour under investigation. When enlisting more than one observer, a sufficient level of inter-observer reliability prior to the actual study should be achieved and controlled for using Cohen's Kappa as a measure of inter-rater reliability. These and other actions, such as standardizing observation and coding or avoiding contact with the subjects/objects under observation, work to prevent biases which could distort results. Observational studies require a great deal of resources, including personnel, developing coding schemes, creating appropriate settings in laboratory or family homes, and coding the material in a scientifically sound manner. Technologies, as in application-based empirical tracking and tests, offer the researcher a valuable tool in their toolbox of possible methodologies (Ostrov & Hart, 2013).

We now introduce a selection of the many observational systems applicable to family system examination. The first observation procedure developed by Robinson and Eyberg (1981), the Dyadic Parent–Child Interaction Coding System (DPICS), is for use in observation of families with children with behavioural conduct problems. It has been used in diverse settings, for instance, with 2- to 7-year-old children in two 5-minute sequences in a laboratory setting. The two sessions were organized whereby in one session (the child-directed interaction, CDI) the parents were told to follow the child's play instructions, whilst in the other session (the parent-directed interaction, PDI) the parents took the lead and the children followed the rules given by the parents. Meanwhile, the observers coded utterances and behaviours in a separate room. In a further study, Webster-Stratton (1985) compared different settings (laboratory vs. natural family context) and correlated the results observed in these different settings. Within this research, structured clinical settings were the most demanding for parents; thus these contexts may be particularly useful in eliciting rich interaction sequences in a short period of investigation. However, depending on the research aims, observing 'naturalistic' behaviour within the home setting or unstructured settings in the laboratory may prove more useful.

The Marschak Interaction Method (MIM; McKay, Pickens, & Stewart, 1996) depicts another observation system that specifically tackles behaviour measurement when parents are under stress. A structured situation is created whereby the parent and child dyad gather around a table and the participating parent is instructed to fulfil several tasks with the child (e.g. telling a story, drawing a picture). Each task lasts about 3 minutes, with the whole session lasting approximately half an hour. Although the coding rationale is not highly elaborate, it nonetheless gives a representative depiction of the interaction quality during the fulfilment of the presented tasks.

Another observational method, the Iowa Family Interaction Rating System (IFIRS; Melby & Conger, 2001), offers insight beyond micro-processes within family interactions through the analysis of relatively stable processes within families on general systematic levels. Results provide a window into global family interaction and behaviour styles, as the IFIRS is not overly concerned with the detailed description of special situations. An observer training is necessary to deploy the IFIRS, and observers need to be experienced with observational practices with nearly 60 behavioural scales for assessing specific family members. These scales can be divided into subcategories, with the numbers of scales used depending on the task applied in the family setting. For a more detailed description of observational methods in family research, we encourage readers to consult Kerig and Lindahl (2001) and Willihnganz (2002).

Diary methods

Up until now, the majority of studies in the field of family research have been based on ratings derived from memory representing a summary of past or actual events that may at times be biased according to rater effects. However, in family research, as in other contexts like the classroom or workplace, researchers might be interested in the actual event taking place in real life, as these effects offer deeper understanding into the dynamics of family functioning in particular and social functioning in general.

Diary methods, which aim to capture events shortly after their happening, represent a useful approach to collect day-to-day experience-based data (for a general overview see Bolger, Davis, & Rafaeli, 2003). Of the numerous ways to use diaries as a research tool, experience sampling, daily diaries, interaction records, momentary sampling, and real-time data capture all amass rich information on participants' lives (Laurenceau & Bolger, 2005). Different techniques are applied in diary research such as classical paper-and-pencil diary studies (e.g. Reis & Wheeler, 1991; Wheeler & Nezlek, 1977) as well as more modern designs applying electronic devices like Personal Digital Assistants (PDA) (for a discussion on advantages and disadvantages of diary applications see Green, Rafaeli, Bolger, Shrout, & Reis, 2006). Mobile phones are increasingly employed as a means for collecting diary data due to their ubiquity and ease of use (Rönkä, Malinen, Kinnunen, Tolvanen, & Lämsä, 2010).

The assessment of daily-life activities typically employed in diary family work (e.g. standardized diaries that target gender typing within families) include thoughts, feelings, and behaviours which are recorded several times a day based on a fixed schedule or when triggered by specific events like a marital conflict (Laurenceau & Bolger, 2005). Participants may also be asked to rate their mood when signalled by an electronic device or may receive a call from researchers on an agreed time every day. In the case of behavioural monitoring, participants might keep track of marital, parent–child, or sibling conflicts. Some diary studies require assessments several times a day, while others require only one rating per day, but trace experiences over a course of several weeks. Calls from researchers can foster diary commitment and thus reduce drop-out and missing data points, resources permitting.

Laurenceau and Bolger (2005) sum up the five leading advantages of diary methods. First, diary methods allow for a generalization of results beyond artificial laboratory set-ups to natural real life settings, such as sibling conflict situations. Second, by conducting diary-based research, one gets closer to the micro-level processes by adding detailed information to the macro-level and global factor findings (e.g. school environment or a general measure of relationship satisfaction) examined by way of cross-sectional or longitudinal surveying. Third, diaries provide information about situational and contextual factors contributing to family functioning such as which situations typically cause stressful conversation between marital partners (Halford, Gravestock, Lowe, & Scheldt, 1992). Fourth, diary methods produce helpful data on within-subject change by measuring behaviour, cognition, or emotions over extended periods of time. Note that subjects in this case can be individuals, dyads, or larger groups like entire family units. Fifth, diary data may complement more traditional methods like observation or self-report by drawing out rich, real-time responses.

Three main techniques are used in diary research that differ according to the diary prompt or trigger. In interval-contingent recording, entries are made at regular, predetermined intervals, for example, each day at noon; in signal-contingent recording, participants are asked to report experiences in alignment with protocol or schedules laid out by the researcher team; and in event-contingent recording, participants make their entries whenever certain a priori determined events occur, such as siblings' tracking their conflicts in the home environment (Laurenceau & Bolger, 2005). Concerning analytic strategies for diary data, Laurenceau and Bolger (2005) additionally recommend adopting multilevel modelling, which we describe towards the end of the chapter.

Experimental settings

In general, experiments attempt to uncover the influence of an independent variable on a dependent variable of interest based on theoretical assumptions. The independent variable must be under control and manipulated on at least two levels. It can be conducted in the laboratory (with the advantage of better controllability) or in the field (with the advantage of ecological validity) (Goodwin, 2010). According to Goodwin (2010), independent variables can be divided into three subcategories, namely situational, task, and instructional variables. Situational variables are based on variations in the environment, for example, private versus public conflict situations. Task variables deal with variations in the problems the participants are to solve, for example, inferring emotions versus intentions from conflict situations. Finally, instructional variables deal with the manipulation in the instruction given to the participants regarding certain tasks, for example, inferring emotional states during conflicts by paying attention to gestures versus wording. In some experiments, as in controlled trials, an experimental, intervention or treatment group, who receives a certain treatment, is compared to a control group who does not receive such a treatment. When all other conditions are held constant and the two groups are comparable on relevant characteristics, changes between the groups after treatment can be causally attributed to the effect of the treatment. An additional issue in experimental research states that the effect be exclusively attributable to the controlled manipulation; therefore researchers have developed a plethora of techniques to control for so-called extraneous or confounding variables (directly related to the study variables) which threaten the validity of the results (Goodwin, 2010).

Without going into great detail, additional aspects to consider in experimental research are mentioned here; for a more detailed discussion, see Goodwin (2010). Concerning the measurement of the dependent variable, one has to be cautious in terms of the sensitivity to change: dependent variables should not be prone to random variation. Independent variables can be either actively manipulated, for instance, showing participants different videotaped conflict resolution styles, or assessed independently, including ex post facto, natural group, or subject variables. Other issues which should be addressed concern the selection and assignment (e.g. randomized vs. not-randomized) of the study samples and dealing with sample problems such as attrition in repeated measures designs. As a final aspect mentioned here, one has to decide whether to use a between-subjects design or a within-subject design. In a between-subject design, not all subjects are measured on all levels of the independent, most obviously the case when the independent variable is a subject variable. In a within-subject design, all participants are assessed at all levels of the independent variable, with the advantage of fewer participants required. However, in choosing a within-subjects design, one has to control for the danger of order effects, apparent when all participants go through the different conditions of the experiment in the same order.

Experimental settings in family study

Although experimental settings are not common in family research (Greenstein, 2006), their usefulness has been acknowledged by past family researchers. As Cummings (1995) points out, family research has come to a level where researchers are increasingly interested in the causal interrelation of family variables. For example, high levels of parental well-being might lead to compliant and agreeable child behaviour, but on the other hand, compliant and agreeable child behaviour might promote parental well-being. However, until now, classic experiments located in a controlled laboratory setting with systematic manipulation of independent variables are scarce. Feeney and Noller (2013) list different types of experimental studies which have been conducted in the context of family.

The first type described by Feeney and Noller (2013) is the analogue studies in which researchers attempt to imitate real life situations in laboratory settings. For instance, in the past studies, videotapes of inter adult conflicts were presented to children to examine how children react to different conflict situations (Cummings, Simpson, & Wilson, 1993; El-Sheikh, Cummings, & Reiter, 1996). By using video material, children were not exposed to real conflicts, making it possible to manipulate certain conditions like conflict resolution by simultaneously holding constant all other parts of the situation. A similar design was used by Noller, Atkin, Feeney, and Peterson (2006) with an audiotaped conflict. The second type was called 'response to hypothetical situations', where participants were asked to imagine certain situations, such as, 'imagine your sibling just ate your dessert without asking', usually in written form. The participants were then advised to rate their actions, feelings, and so on, when confronted with such a situation. Examples of this type can be found in studies conducted by Beach *et al.* (1998) or Mikulincer and Shaver (2007) in the field of attachment. As a third form of experimental design, Feeney and Noller (2013) describe standard content methodology and cite research conducted by Noller (1984, 2001), who tested differential perception of non-verbal cues within couples with different levels of interpersonal stress levels.

As a final remark on conducting experiments in family research, Cummings (1995) discusses some cautions and the advantage of this research design in family research. For example, discretion related to questions of ethics, as research often deals with sensitive topics (e.g. marital conflict), and of feasibility or objectivity as laboratory settings in general may not elicit naturally occurring behaviour. Thus, experiments in family research, as in other domains, are best suited for precisely defined hypotheses concerning a few relevant variables in which it is necessary to hold surrounding conditions constant and where the third variables are controlled.

Quantitative data analysis in family research

The next section refers to some of the requirements of data analysis researchers face when conducting family research in general and sibling research in particular.

Setting the stage

To maximize the benefit of data analysis, statistical methods should be tailored to the data structure. Family research poses particular challenges: data are often hierarchical, meaning that individual data are embedded in larger contexts, namely dyads or families, which calls for sophisticated methods briefly discussed in the following section.

As in other areas of social sciences, within family research, the statistical analysis of data based on observed variables using ANOVA, regression models or path analysis are supplemented or even replaced by methods of SEM. The growing popularity of SEM is due to one major reason: in traditional regression analysis, as in path analysis, models assume that there is no measurement error, which is often not the case in reality. SEM (a combination of path analysis and factor analysis) protects against biased parameter estimations from previous measurement error calculations that threaten the validity of results (Eid, Gollwitzer, & Schmidt, 2013).

As SEM is relevant for nearly all methods described in the following sections of this chapter, we will now present a brief introduction of its basic principles. A SEM is divided into two sub models: a measurement model and a structural model. The measurement model refers to factor analysis, where observed or so-called manifest variables are summed up into a latent variable, which is not directly observed; in general, to build a fitting measurement model, at least two observed indicators are required. As in path analysis, the latent variables are then related to one another based on theoretical assumptions within the structural model component (Eid *et al.*, 2013). The latent variables are assumed to be continuous in nature; however, there are cases in which latent variables are ordinal or lower in data level (e.g. Muthén, 2002). In a structural model, one can now address all the questions to be answered using regression or a more general path analysis, thus including moderation (also known as interactions) and mediation (for a description of these terms, see below). A more detailed introduction in SEM can be found, for example, at Ullman and Bentler (2003) and Kline (2011).

Moderation and mediation

As knowledge about socialization within families has grown over the past decades, researchers often conclude that the simple distinction between independent and dependent variables does not suffice to adequately describe the complexity under investigation. As an answer to this challenge, empirical investigations often address the issue of how the third variables influence the relationships between other variables. The two possibilities of how a third variable influences the relation between two other variables are moderation and mediation, a distinction described and discussed in a classic paper by Baron and Kenny (1986). Baron and Kenny (1986) offer a basic definition of a moderator: '[. . .] a moderator is a qualitative (e.g. sex, race, class) or quantitative (e.g. level of reward) variable that affects the direction and/or strength of the relation between an independent or predictor variable and a dependent or criterion variable' (p. 1174). In the framework of ANOVA, a moderator effect can also adopt the term 'interaction'. The statistical method to choose to analyze moderation depends on the measurement level of the variables involved (Aiken & West, 1991; Baron & Kenny, 1986; Cohen, Cohen, West, & Aiken, 2003). Whisman and McClelland (2005) analyzed moderator effects in family research. Based on their theoretical assumptions, they conjectured that stress produced by life events (e.g. socio-economic pressure) may lead to depression but that this relation might be weakened by family support. In statistical terms, a moderator analysis in this case with continuous predictor and continuous criterion variables can be conducted by using a regression model where depression is regressed on family stress, measure of life events, and the product term of the two. In this regression model, the significance of a product term indicates an interaction or moderation effect. In their comments on common misleading practices in moderator analysis, Whisman and McClelland (2005) caution against the use of median splits in interaction analysis, a method often used to conduct a simple two-way ANOVA. Some of the biases of using this practice are that median splits are based on the frequency distribution of the present sample, so results may lack comparability with other samples. Moreover, it has been shown that splitting continuous data according to their median will reduce the statistical power of the analysis and may even produce false effects (Whisman & McClelland, 2005).

As in other fields of quantitative research, one issue concerning moderator analysis revolves around optimal sample size in order to detect effects or, in other words, statistical power. Different recommendations about optimal sample sizes to achieve sufficient statistical power in moderation analysis can be found in Cohen (1988), Whisman and McClelland (2005), as well as in Shieh (2009). Estimates are often optimistic since they assume that variables are measured without error, which is often not the case in reality. Unfortunately, this increases the necessary sample size. As a rule of thumb, approximately 200 participants are needed to detect a medium effect, whereas 1,000 participants are necessary to detect small effects. Thus, the apparent lack of results involving interaction analyses in family research may be in part due to low sample sizes. One additional concern is related to the distribution of ratings on the respected scale; a sufficient number of sample participants should obtain extreme values on both the ends of the distribution. Otherwise, in the case of a distribution where certain parts of the range are severely oversampled, it would be difficult to detect an interaction effect. In family studies in particular, extreme values are often underrepresented. A final aspect to consider here is the existence of outliers in the data set, since interactions in data analyses could potentially be spurious in the sense that only a few outliers may be responsible for a significant interaction effect (Judd & McClelland, 1989).

Mediation is a more complicated matter to grasp conceptually and to apply on a theoretically sound basis. Baron and Kenny (1986) describe mediation as a situation where 'in general, a given variable may be said to function as a mediator to the extent that it accounts for the relation between the predictor and the criterion' (p. 1176). The criterion is regressed on the predictor and the mediator, and, in addition, the mediator is regressed on the predictor. A full mediation is achieved when the predictor explains a significant amount of variance in the mediator and the mediator explains a significant amount of variance in the outcome. Moreover, a previous significant path between the predictor and the outcome should be reduced to non-significance after controlling for the aforementioned paths including the mediating variable. However, a partial mediation can exist irrespective of the path of significance between the predictor and the outcome unless the indirect path proves to be significant (Little, 2013). As a common test of significance of mediation, the 'Sobel-test', is a typically utilized procedure introduced by Sobel (1982). Mediation is based on assumptions of causality and is thus important for longitudinal designs (Little, 2013) such as in half-longitudinal and full-longitudinal mediation. The former describes a design with two measurement points, in which the value of the outcome and the mediator at second measurement time are controlled for the initial values to model change on these variables. Accordingly, for a full-longitudinal mediation model, at least three measurement points are necessary. As in other longitudinal models, optimal time intervals between assessments are required for mediation detection. For a more detailed description of how to specify mediation models, interested readers are referred to Little (2013), who extends a five-step procedure proposed by Cole and Maxwell (2003). The analysis of mediation is also possible with cross-sectional data, but as mediation in a strict sense refers to 'explained change', mediation with cross-sectional data can only be a proxy for expected mediation, describing merely an indirect effect and not necessarily mediation (Little, 2013). Additionally, moderation and mediation can be tested using a traditional approach with observed variables or a SEM approach with a measurement and a structural model as described above, whereas mediation is tested within a path analytic framework.

Mediation and moderation can also be combined as in mediated moderations or moderated mediation in order to adequately reflect social reality within interactional contexts (Hayes, 2009; Muller, Judd, & Yzerbyt, 2005). In short, a moderated mediation assumes that the impact of the mediating variable depends on the values of a given moderator. A mediated moderation is similar in nature to moderated mediation and occurs when an overall moderation effect of a moderating variable in the relation of a predictor and an outcome exists but the effect of the mediator would be different in alternate combinations of the predictor and the moderator. It seeks to explain the moderation by adding a mediation variable.

Dyadic data analysis

One of the most common data structures in family research is dyadic data, for example, mother–father data, parent–child data, or sibling data. Dyadic partner data involve interdependence with the research focus often revolving around how the individuals under investigation influence one another based on variables measured at the dyadic level (Gonzalez & Griffin, 2012). In fact, one of the most noteworthy fields to explore in family research is the manner in which family members interact;

for example, the interplay between parental perceptions and child characteristics facilitating or hindering effective parenting (e.g. Jouriles *et al.*, 1991; McBride, Schoppe, & Rane, 2002; Sturge-Apple, Davies, & Cummings, 2006) or different opinions about child rearing influencing marital and sibling relationship quality (e.g. Goldberg & Easterbrooks, 1984; Yu & Gamble, 2008). Kenny (2011) pointed out that although most researchers are aware of the dependent and bidirectional nature of dyadic assessments, differential management strategies prevaricate on how to handle such data. One strategy to avoid interdependence, for instance, suggests collecting data from only one participant. Another strategy is to analyze data from individuals independently so as to artificially create independence. Although statistically speaking such a procedure produces sound results concerning significance testing, this strategy nonetheless neglects pivotal multi-informant relational information, and the analysis will inevitably lose power (Kenny, 2011). Moreover, in analyzing dyadic social partner data separately, correspondence in between related participants will not be taken into account.

Kenny (2011) gives several examples of how to handle dyadic or in other words relational data properly. A design in which the predictor is dyadic, for example, parenting overload is rated by both parents, and the outcome is not dyadic, for example, school readiness of one child allows for data to be handled using SEM, where the two predictors are correlated to account for the dependent structure of the data, a path is drawn from the predictors to the outcome. Assuming a certain data structure, the occurrence of missing data is usually addressed by using full information maximum likelihood (FIML) estimation. In addition, the assumption of similar influence of both parents on child school readiness can be tested in a nested model comparison. In a nested model comparison, one can compare different competing hypotheses by either artificially fixing relevant parameters to certain values or to be equal within one basic model and to evaluate the statistical fit of the separate 'nested' models. In the aforementioned example, one can fix the paths from both parents to the child to be equal and compare whether this model fits the data as well as a model without these limitations. If the limitations do not worsen the model fit, then averaging the multi-perspective ratings is a good option.

Another dyadic data structure arises with a single predictor and a dyadic outcome. Imagine a situation where you have an assessment of the child's temperament and you are interested in its influence on parents' level of distress. In this case, a multilevel approach is appropriate to analyze the data using any statistical program outfitted for multilevel modelling. A more detailed description of multilevel approaches in family research follows.

The third possibility of dyadic data is a structure where both the predictor and the outcome are measured in a bipartite manner. As an example, imagine you want to test the influence of marital quality rated by both partners on the assessment of co-parenting rated again by both partners (Barzel & Reid, 2011, cited from Kenny, 2011). Here Kenny, Kashy, and Cook (2006) as well as Gonzalez and Griffin (2012) depict an actor–partner model (APM) or an actor–partner interdependence model (APIM). Figure 6.1 gives a graphical impression of the APM.

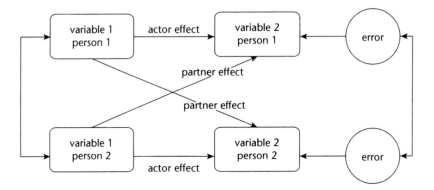

FIGURE 6.1 Graphical depiction of a basic actor–partner interdependence model (APIM)

According to Tambling, Johnson, and Johnson (2011), the APIM is especially suitable for smaller samples typical, for example, in counselling research on romantic partnerships. In addition, this model can be applied to small-scale sibling investigations. An important point to consider when utilizing an APIM is the distinguishing of social partners within the dyad. This may be relatively easy in case of heterosexual romantic partners, where one partner is male and the other one female, or in sibling dyads, where siblings are of different gender or of different age. Tambling *et al.* (2011), however, introduce situations where distinguishing features are absent or where such characteristics are rather artificial and offer no real source of variance, as in same-sex roommate analysis. In this case, evaluation of data will turn out to be much more complex (descriptions of apposite analysis strategies can be found in Kenny *et al.* (2006)).

Another important prerequisite for applying the APIM requires that the outcome variable and at least one predictor be measured using the same instrument for both partners. Outcomes can be continuous or categorical in nature. Matters become more complicated, however, in the case of categorical outcomes (Kenny *et al.*, 2006). Predictor variables can be classified according to the following features (Tambling *et al.*, 2011): between dyad predictors, where the values for both partners are the same but can differ compared to other dyads (e.g. living together within the same household); within-dyad predictors, where the values within one dyad differ but on average all dyads have the same values (e.g. in case of heterosexual partners where gender is dummy coded [females assigned a value of 1 and males a value of 0]); and mixed predictors, which can vary within and between dyads (this being the case for the majority of variables measured by traditional quantitative self-report instruments). An APIM can be organized cross-sectionally or longitudinally, consisting of two assessments of the same variables divided across two time points or a predictor and outcome variable measured either cross-sectionally or longitudinally.

Finally, one can apportion the APIM into actor effects and partner effects. For the former, the outcome or the second measurement is regressed on the predictor or initial measurement within the same person. Accordingly, the partner effect is identified by a regression between partners in a dyadic model. It is important to note that both effects are calculated simultaneously meaning that partner influence is controlled for actor influence and vice versa (Cook & Kenny, 2005). In addition, independent variables and residuals or error terms of the dependent variables are correlated to include further measures of control within the analysis. Statistically, an APIM can be analyzed using ordinary regression analysis, SEM, and multilevel modelling. One final note on the analysis of APIM addresses the issue of the relation between the partners in a dyad. Common statistical approaches suit situations where the partners within a dyad are distinguishable (e.g. parent–child, older vs. younger sibling); a data structure where dyads are not distinguishable calls for more sophisticated analyses (Kenny, Kashy, & Cook, 2006).

Longitudinal approaches

As in other areas of socialization research in family and sibling studies, researchers are often interested in capturing the dynamic processes responsible for adaptive or maladaptive functioning of individuals or groups. This calls for appropriate methodological approaches in quantitative research in order to model these processes. DeHaan, Hawley, and Deal (2013) describe such a method applied to illustrate the processes of family resilience. One core assumption of resilience research holds that resilience is most adequately explored using a developmental perspective and through observation of the family over an extended period of time (e.g. Walsh, 2003). Several methodological approaches have been applied, albeit with concerns regarding their effectiveness. A helpful introduction into how to analyze change can be found in Geiser (2010), depicting strategies of handling longitudinal data based on SEM, namely latent-state model (LSM), latent-state-trait model (LSTM), ARM, latent-change model, and LGCM. A detailed discussion of these models is beyond the scope of the present chapter; therefore each model is only briefly summarized (for more details, see Geiser, 2010 or Little, 2013). The first two approaches deal with situation-specific differences in variables measured longitudinally, whereas the latter three models try to find changes in trait-like variables over time.

Latent-state and latent-state-trait models

To give a short impression of a possible situation in family research where LSM or LSTM would be the method of choice, imagine you have measured the degree of parenting self-efficacy several times over the course of 3 years using a sample of fathers and you now wish to determine whether the construct of 'parenting self-efficacy' can be described as a situation-dependent state or rather a trait-like concept. As a first step, one might apply an LSM, where no distinction between situation specific and stable parts of variance is made. In such a case, the result of the analysis will be a first judgement of the degree of stability of the construct.

Similar to a confirmatory factor analysis, the construct of 'parenting self-efficacy' is first modelled separately for each occasion using a SEM approach, then the latent variables of 'parenting self-efficacy' are correlated with each other. These correlations are an important part of the analysis since they determine the level of stability of the construct: high correlations imply a high stability. However, this limited statistical strategy serves best as a starting point for further more complex analyses. The correlation between time points may be substantial, but in most instances one will aim to separate the share of variance representing the trait and the variance representing the state component of the construct from each other. Here, LSTM is the most suitable to analyze the data. Within such a model, a latent trait factor is added to the latent-state variables of parenting self-efficacy previously analyzed using an LSM. This latent trait factor replaces the correlations between the latent-state factors. In the case of parenting self-efficacy, this trait factor could be labelled 'general self-efficacy'. In a subsequent calculation, described in detail in Geiser (2010), one can assess the level of variance attributed to the trait factor.

Whereas these types of analysis assume a trait-like structure of certain variables and only seek to separate this trait factor from state components of variance, the second component of possible longitudinal analyses addresses actual change in variables measured, such as how marital satisfaction changes over time within a long-term relationship. One common method used in longitudinal research is the cross-lagged panel design that in some respect resembles the APIM discussed previously and may be employed with at least two measurement points.

Cross-lagged panel designs

Current perspectives on children's development highlight the bidirectional influence between children, their relationship partners, and social contexts like the family (e.g. Sameroff, 2009; Yates, Obradović, & Egeland, 2010; Yeh & Lempers, 2004). Beyond theoretical considerations, researchers are interested in ways of empirically testing these assumptions and quantifying the magnitude of influence outside of laboratory experimental settings through field studies that often use traditional quantitative survey instruments. One popular analytical method to achieve this goal is the cross-lagged panel design (Christ & Schlüter, 2012; Delsing, Oud, & De Bruyn, 2005; Geiser, 2010). Cross-lagged panel designs are based on more general so-called ARMs developed to analyze panel data (Jöreskog, 1979). Despite the need to exercise caution (Rogosa, 1980), cross-lagged panel designs enable statements of causality to be made regarding two or more variables using a longitudinal approach in field studies with an absence of a systematic variation of factors only possible in experimental designs. As the term 'panel design' implies, computation of a cross-lagged panel analysis necessitates simultaneous repeated measurements of the variables of interest, which are then linked according to Figure 6.2.

The arrows between variables and across time points represent the mutual influence, which can be unidirectional, when only one cross-lagged path is significant, or bidirectional, when both cross-lagged paths are significant. Cross-lagged effects are controlled for autoregressive effects so that cross-lagged effects can be interpreted

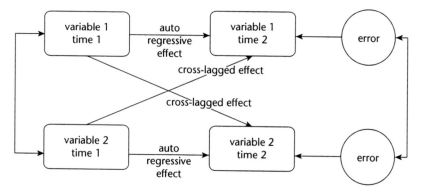

FIGURE 6.2 The basic structure of a manifest two-variable, two time points cross-lagged panel design

as responsible for change, a key advantage of the design. One critical aspect regarding cross-lagged analysis is the choice of time intervals between measurements (Delsing *et al.*, 2005). One must select intervals so that change occurs (versus, say, a stable characteristic like aggression) but at the same time changes should not be missed in passing (as in more unstable constructs like emotions). Cross-lagged panel designs can be applied using manifest (or in other words directly observed) variables. However, several conditions favour a structural equation approach with so-called latent variables – variables that are not directly observed but inferred from observed variables. In short, by using a latent structure of the variables, one can test measurement in variance, a central issue of delineating effects due to change of measurement from effects due to a real change in the target variable. In addition, latent cross-lagged models take into account the error variance, and therefore results are unbiased in this respect.

Delsing *et al.* (2005) discuss the challenge that researchers face in applying cross-lagged panel analyses when unable to delineate between time-lagged and instantaneous effect. They compared models with different time intervals between measures and included a continuous effect by applying an approximate discrete model (ADM) procedure developed by Bergstrom (1984). The author found with their data sample of family climate and childlike problem behaviour with 288 Dutch families that time intervals impart a strong influence on the magnitude of the cross-lagged and autoregressive paths, which can be reduced using the constraints implemented by the ADM.

Latent growth curve modelling

One of the most popular alternatives to ARM is LGCM. LGCM slightly differs from ARM in that it focuses on intra-individual change over time and tries to answer questions about different change trajectories of different individuals (Little, 2013). On a basic level, growth curves have three features in common: (1) the same construct of interest is observed several times, (2) the same assessment instruments are used, and

(3) the timing of the assessments is known (McArdle & Nesselroade, 2003). Growth Curve Analysis in general refers to the analysis of growth patterns and the making of inferences about the structure of change (Baltes & Nesselroade, 1979). McArdle and Nesselroade (2003, p. 448) postulate five objectives of longitudinal research and LGCM: the analysis (1) of intra-individual change, (2) of inter-individual differences in intra-individual change, (3) of interrelationships in change, (4) of causes (determinants) of intra-individual change, and (5) of causes (determinants) of inter-individual differences in intra-individual change. Growth Curve Analysis has a long history (McArdle & Nesselroade, 2003), and recent statistical modelling addresses such issues as different times between intervals, nonrandom sample attrition, unequal amounts of participants per group, or alternate measures used at different times (McArdle & Nesselroade, 2003). A LGCM requires that a continuous dependent variable be assessed across at least three measurement points, assessment units be labelled the same way, and that the same construct is measured. A third precondition for conducting LGCM holds that all participants are measured at the same intervals. The intervals between measurement points however can vary (Kline, 2011). As Kline (2011) describes, LGCM is in general conducted in a two-step fashion. In the first step, only the change is depicted in the model, whereas in the second step, variables that are hypothesized to be responsible for change are incorporated into the model.

An important step in LGCM involves the specification of parameters, which can be readily completed in statistical software packages. In general, two latent growth parameters are estimated: the initial status (IS) or intercept and the linear change (LC) or slope. In order to be able to interpret these latent growth parameters, several other paths within the model should be fixed when the LGCM is formulated. Basically, the latent growth parameters are related to the measurement points such that the paths from the intercept variable to the measurement point are all fixed to a value of one, in general, whereas the paths from the slope variable to the measured variables over time represent the time lag between the measurement points, and there are several alternatives to model change (Little, 2013). LGCM can be combined with other LGCM to see if changes are interrelated or one can add covariates to check for their influence on intercepts or change. A number of applications are described in Little (2013).

An example for the application of an LGCM in sibling research can be found in a study conducted by Buist (2010). She interrelated three LGCMs with three measurement points each to analyze the mutual influence of levels and changes of sibling relationships and delinquency with 249 sibling pairs with a mean age of about 12 years. Main findings suggested that problematic sibling relationships go along with higher rates of delinquent behaviour of older but not younger siblings and that the level of delinquent behaviour and changes in delinquent behaviour are related in sibling dyads.

Repeated measures ANOVA

Repeated measures designs can be found in various areas of psychology and in family research in particular. Repeated measures designs address issues like process research, conflict research, developmental studies, outcome research, profile analysis, single-subject studies, and research on treatment effects (Ellis, 1999). Although not all research questions and data structure suit the statistical procedure of an ANOVA, it is a widespread method to deal with data measured at multiple time points.

The basic concept behind conventional ANOVA involves comparing more than two means and checking if three or more groups have scored the same on a certain variable (Field, 2009). Experimental studies constitute the typical context enlisting ANOVAs. However, classical ANOVA deals with independent groups, and in longitudinal data sets or certain experimental settings, researchers are confronted with repeated measures and therefore dependent data. In this case, classical ANOVA is not applicable. Instead, such data structures call for repeated measures ANOVA or mixed ANOVA, two procedures proven to be relevant for family research especially in the context of evaluating treatment effects in controlled trials.

A repeated measures ANOVA in experimental settings is conducted when all study participants perform all tasks in the study. Despite several advantages of this method, one main analytical disadvantage described by Field (2009) regards the lack of independence of data, a basic assumption related to accuracy of the F-statistic computed in an ANOVA. To face this challenge, the concept of sphericity (equal level of dependence in experimental conditions) is introduced into repeated measures ANOVA and should be tested prior to interpreting results, which is accomplished by common statistical program packages such as SPSS. So-called mixed designs are more complex in that both independent (or between-subject data) and dependent (or within-subject data) are present. Such a data structure calls for mixed ANOVA (Field, 2009). A typical study where mixed ANOVA deals with evaluating the effectiveness of a certain treatment, for instance, a controlled trial intervention group (receiving the treatment) will be compared to a control group (not receiving the treatment) on usually three different occasions: prior to treatment (pre), directly after treatment (post), and a certain time after treatment (follow-up). The research design can be described as a 2 (intervention vs. control, between-subject variable) × 3 (pre vs. post vs. follow-up, within-subject variable) design calling for mixed ANOVA. A detailed description of various repeated measures designs and some applications for ANOVA can be found in Ellis (1999).

We now briefly introduce two example studies where a repeated measures ANOVA was used to analyze data in a sibling context. The first study attends to children with a chronically ill or disabled sibling facing serious challenges in their own development, among them the extra challenge of acting as a caregiver or differential treatment from other family members. This research conducted by Lobato and Kao (2002) deals with the effectiveness of a sibling/parent intervention aiming at improving sibling knowledge, sibling adjustment to chronic illness and disability, and finally children's sense of connectedness to similar families. The sample consisted of 54 siblings and 47 parents, and relevant variables were assessed at three time points (prior to group sessions, directly after group session commencement, and 3 months post intervention). The intervention consisted of six 90-minute sessions and lasted 6–8 weeks. All families completed treatment, such that there was no control group. In this case, repeated measures ANOVA was applied to test for treatment effects. As expected, after treatment, siblings reported more disorder knowledge and showed an increased sense of connectedness as well as a decreased level of behavioural problems.

McHale, Updegraff, Helms-Erikson, and Crouter (2001) conducted the/a second example study that investigated the influence of siblings on gender role development within families. A conservative design testing the relevance of the social learning process between siblings was chosen. The sample consisted of 198 families (father, mother, two siblings); different rating scales on all targeted variables were used, and longitudinal data were collected over a period of 3 years via home and telephone interviews. Collected data were analyzed using mixed ANOVAs (as described above) as per follows: to obtain information about patterns of developmental change, the authors conducted a 2 (family size: 2 children vs. larger families) × 4 (gender constellation: girl–girl, girl–boy, boy–girl, boy–boy) × 2 (sibling: firstborn vs. second-born) × 3 (time) mixed ANOVAs (with sibling and time as within-groups factors) with gender role attitudes as one of the dependent variables. General developmental changes were of interest as were interaction terms available from the mixed ANOVA results. Results showed that siblings influence each other concerning gender role development. However, whereas influence can be explained by applying social learning theory for second-borns, firstborn siblings' influence is less evident, and firstborns may become more differentiated in their gender roles than second-borns (so-called de-identification). These examples are just two of the various possibilities of repeated and mixed ANOVAs in family and sibling research. However, as longitudinal research is conceptually very rich and diverse, it calls for a multitude of analytical strategies depending on research questions and data structure. Therefore, the following sections introduce additional means of dealing with longitudinal data.

Multilevel approaches

Family researchers seek to understand how socialization processes within the family shape individual development of family members. This conceptualization considers the individual as embedded within the family and influenced by family processes. It can be assumed that members within a context are more similar than members between certain contexts (Jenkins et al. 2009). Thus, when it comes to explain certain variance in a variable, for example, aggression in adolescence, one must delineate the part of variance which depends on individual factors and the part of variance which depends on features of the family. In statistical terms, the assumption of independence of error terms – which is a prerequisite for using traditional regression analysis strategies – is not true for nested data like family-based data. Rather, it can be assumed that error variance concerning specific variables is correlated, as for example in different family members' ratings of sibling relationships. When using traditional regression analysis where error terms are used for calculating tests for statistical significance, the estimated parameters will be biased and therefore results may not be interpretable. More generally, the individual is often embedded in social groups like families, school classes, peer groups, colleagues, and so on, and in ordinary multivariate approaches like multiple regression, these parts of variances (individual and group) are not separated. In order to take into account such a (hierarchical) data structure apparent within many samples, multi-level modelling approaches were developed for the social sciences. These analytical approaches take into account the different levels of sources for variance within data (e.g. individual level as level 1 and family level as level 2 units). In this section, an overview of handling family data using a multilevel approach will be presented. When reviewing the research on interdependent or nested data structure, different terms for the same method of analysis are used. In sum, multilevel modelling or hierarchical modelling can be used interchangeably, and both represent an analysis method called linear mixed modelling (LMM) (Garson, 2013).

Jenkins et al. (2009) analyzed two different family data sets describing common features of family data and their analysis via multilevel modelling. Their first data set consisted of multiple children within one family with one measure per child. The second data structure consisted of multiple children within one family and each assessed by multiple raters. This structure is especially common in family research since often there are ratings of both parents concerning their children. The data are therefore not only nested but also cross-classified (Jenkins et al. 2009). A cross-classified data structure implies that the multilevel data are not necessarily hierarchical in nature, but instead that ratings are nested within different level 2 units like different contexts (e.g. classrooms and peer groups at the same time) or different raters (e.g. ratings from children and parents in one family) (Goldstein, 2011; Jenkins et al., 2009).

How does multilevel modelling operate in a family context? In a multilevel analysis, the whole variance of a specific variable is partitioned into a between- and a within-family component. The within-family segment represents the variance attributed to unique features of the family member, for example, one sibling in relation to other siblings. The between-family component of variance represents the common portion shared by the family members in relation to other families, for example, a sibling in family A versus a sibling in family B. As in multiple regression, multilevel model predictors can be included in the model and in multilevel model-ling at the individual (within) and group (between) level.

One example depicting the advantages of multilevel modelling is seen in the work of Jenkins and colleagues (2009) who discuss the differential modes of influence of parenting on child outcomes like aggression. Multilevel modelling helps delineate the impact of parenting practices directed towards a child and the impact of general parenting practices within the family, which can be directed to other individuals such as siblings within the family. On a practical note, in a multilevel model, one can include the family average for negative parenting on the between as well as the child-specific deviation from the family average on the within-family level.

For cross-classified multilevel data in family research, Jenkins et al. (2009) give an example of how to handle multi-informant (in this case the source of cross-classification) data within a family setting. Here, cross-classification stems from the separate ratings of child characteristics provided separately by both parents. The authors analyze the data, so that they can judge the between- and within-family parts of variance that can be attributed to fathers and mothers and compare these effects. For instance, Jenkins *et al.* (2009) show that in considering within-family variance, mothers rate their children more differently than fathers regarding emotional problems.

A few more examples illustrate that multilevel modelling has been used in family research to address several issues. Hussey and Guo (2003) applied multilevel scaffolding to account for the fact that in longitudinal studies the different measures over time are nested within individuals. In so doing, it is possible to detect individual trajectories at level 1 and to regress these individual growth parameters on time-fixed individual parameters at level 2. In this study, a longitudinal trajectory of childlike psychiatric symptoms on different dimensions (e.g. externalizing behaviour, anxiety) measured with the Devereux Scales of Mental Disorders (DSMD) was analyzed at level 1 and age and gender added at level 2. Results revealed no effect of level 2 units on the shape of the trajectories on all dimensions of the DSMD (Hussey & Guo, 2003). In another investigation, Hoffmann (2002) used a multilevel approach to explore the role of family composition and individual factors like school dropout in combination with community aspects like level of urbanization, poverty, percentage of woman headed households, as well as percentage of unemployed men in explaining adolescent drug abuse. Results revealed that community level variables explained only a small portion of variance above and beyond individual and family level variables.

In their 2005 article, Lyons and Sayer focus on dyadic multilevel modelling with longitudinal data; dyadic data are common in family research. Using this method allows for the study of individual parameters like health, subjective well-being, depression, and so on, within dyadic relationships like the father–son dyad or the sibling dyad whilst controlling for the interdependent nature of dyadic ratings. In addition, characteristics describing the dyad such as marital satisfaction or differences in parenting styles can be entered into the analyses of individual outcome variables. One important point to consider in relation to common multilevel data analysis refers to the interchangeability of the level 1 units. For example, when pupils are examined within their school classes, all individuals within one class are interchangeable. This is often not the case when dyadic family data are analyzed (Lyons & Sayer, 2005). Obviously, partners are often not interchangeable, but are characterized by status differences like in parent–child or sibling (older vs. younger sibling) dyads. In multilevel modelling of this kind, it is then necessary to create a dummy variable representing the difference between the dyadic level 1 units (e.g. dummy coding like father = 1; son = 2) and to consider this dummy variable during the analysis. For a more detailed description of the statistical procedure, readers are referred to Lyons and Sayer (2005).

Within their model of social relations, Snijders and Kenny (1999) introduce another application of multilevel modelling. This approach takes into account family dynamics in which a certain characteristic found within families may be manifested at the family level, the individual level, or a specific dyadic level within the family. For example, hostility can be an attribute of the whole family climate, but can also be attributed to certain individuals within the family like an elder sibling as well as certain dyads like the sibling pair. A model able to delineate these different aspects is the Social Relations Model (SRM) (Kashy & Kenny, 1990). In contrast to the APIM, where Snijders and Kenny (1999) speak of actor and partner effects, the meaning of these terms in the context of an SRM is somewhat different. In an SRM, the actor is the one who is rating another person within the family, the social partner. Similar to the APIM, in an SRM, the basic level of analysis is the dyad. The model itself is rather simple. It consists of the actor effect that reflects how one generally rates others within the family, the partner effect that refers to how one person is seen by other family members, and the residual that represents the interaction between actor and partner. Multilevel modelling is again an apt statistical method to analyze such data structures, where individuals (actor and partner) are nested within dyad pairs and nested within the group (family). The complex structure of the data with the interrelation of actors and partners as two individual levels represents special extensions to standard multilevel models (Bryk & Raudenbush, 1992) necessary for allowing crossed random effects like the one already described by cross-classification (Snijders & Kenny, 1999). An analysis example is given in Snijders and Kenny (1999), but a detailed description of the procedure exceeds the scope of the present chapter.

Analyzing types of families

Cluster analysis

Instead of using variable-centred approaches to investigate family processes, one can adopt increasingly popular person-centred approaches to analyze families. Family research often addresses the question of how to classify types of families on diverse relevant dimensions and how to link these types of families with risk or protective factors. The present section concentrates on one prevalent technique used to detect types of groups: cluster analysis. Whereas cluster analysis only suits special data structures, the following section discusses an additional person–centred technique, namely LCA.

Cluster analysis is infrequently used in family research (Mandara, 2003), although it appears useful to combine a selection of variables in order to find specific types of families based on similarities and combination of similarities according to these variables. In cluster analysis, units (e.g. individuals, families) are grouped together so that both the similarity within groups and the difference between groups are maximized by combining variables of interest (Henry, Tolan, & Groman-Smith, 2005). When applying cluster analysis, it is important to bear in mind that clusters can be found in almost all data sets; thus prior to running cluster analyses, a solid theoretical background is necessary to produce interpretable final cluster solutions as well as to choose the appropriate statistical method for clustering the data. Apart from decisions about the relevant variables concerning families, researchers have to be particularly cognizant of the issue of different informants within one family. For example, one has to consider the possible results when using averaged or individual data prior to clustering data on marital quality, parent–child relationships, or general family climate (Henry et al., 2005).

Another important step prior to running a clustering algorithm is to be certain that all variables are standardized to have an equal scaling, as cases of differential scaling (e.g. 3- vs. 5-point Likert-Scales) variables with a greater scale ranges will have stronger weights in the clustering process. Milligan and Cooper (1988) suggest dividing the variable score by its range to leave differences in variance intact. One possible additional step before performing the cluster analysis is to visually examine the distribution of the variables. Combining the variables and visualizing them in a scatter plot where all data points are displayed can help to detect types of data clusters grouped together. In regards to at least two or three dimensions, this is a helpful way to analyze the data structure on an explorative basis.

Following these preliminary steps, one is now ready to choose the appropriate method of clustering. In family-based research, hierarchical and non-hierarchical methods are the most commonly used (Henry et al. 2005). To explain the concept behind the clustering methods, consider the concept of attachment (Bowlby, 1969/1982). According to the strange situation test (Ainsworth et al., 1978), every child can be assigned a certain type of attachment pattern. Theoretically, a non-hierarchical structure underlying this structure exists, and hierarchical and non-hierarchical clustering strategies would be appropriate. However, if one additionally distinguishes between secure and insecure attachment patterns as a whole, and one subsumes avoidant and ambivalent attachment patterns under the label of insecure attachment, a hierarchical clustering would better serve the data and the theoretical assumptions.

When a hierarchical cluster solution corresponds with theoretical assumptions then researches can choose between different clustering methods. Common between all methods is the principle of joining, which refers to the grouping of the most similar observations concerning the chosen variables or dimensions. After accomplishing these clusters, similar clusters are grouped together and so on until finally one cluster remains. As one can imagine, the decision about the number of clusters to interpret largely depends on the theoretical presumptions and the knowledge, experience, or competence of the researcher and may represent a rather subjective choice. Moreover, prior to analysis, the researcher has to decide about the distance metric (the unit which expresses the difference of observations in the multidimensional space) and the linkage (which represents a decision about how to form clusters) (Henry et al., 2005).

Latent class analysis

LCA resembles Cluster Analytic strategies in that the primary aim involves classifying individuals according to their characteristics on different measured variables (e.g. solving a problem or ratings of sibling relationship quality on a 4-point Likert-Scale). The relation of measured variables is expressed by latent classes that are inferred from the measured data (Lanza, Flaherty, & Collins, 2003). Individuals of one latent class provide the same answers to questions and scored the same way on tests. As in exploratory factor analysis, LCA aims to successfully reduce data into meaningful components (Geiser, 2010). In Cluster Analysis, these classes are called clusters and are characterized by the best possible similarity of ratings within a cluster and the highest possible dissimilarity between clusters. The basic strategy of an LCA is highly similar, and under certain conditions, LCA and Cluster Analysis are closely connected, specifically in the case of multivariate mixture estimation (Titterington, Smith, & Makov, 1985). LCA serves as a statistical tool to detect subpopulations in the whole population based on certain attributes, for example, detecting family types based on levels of co-parenting and parenting practices. In contrast to Cluster Analysis, it uses a latent structure, meaning that the latent variable that describes the different classes is not directly observed but inferred from the observed variables. The categories of the latent variables are termed classes and are equivalent to the clusters in Cluster Analysis. Although originally developed for categorical observed data (Lanza et al., 2003), more recent approaches of LCA allows for nominal, ordinal, continuous, and count data on the observed variables (Eshghi, Haughton, Legrand, Skaletsky, & Woolford, 2011). Advantages of latent approaches include the use of multiple indicators for the latent classes, multiple indicators assist in describing an underlying latent structure provide information about measurement error, and finally LCA can be used for confirmatory purposes since values for model fit are computed and can be compared according to theoretical assumptions made prior to analyzing the data (Lanza et al., 2003). As Lanza et al. (2003, p. 666) sum up, 'in latent class models, the data are used to estimate the number of classes in the population, the relative size of each class, and the probability of a particular response to each item, given class membership'. Examples and extensions of core LCA analysis are given in Lanza et al. (2003).

Mixed methods

To take into account the complex nature of family processes, research methods must incorporate different levels of data collection. Unfortunately, both family study, generally, and sibling scholarship, specifically, are lacking in this regard. Still, one promising approach is to combine qualitative and quantitative measures. This mixed methods methodology (Weisner & Fiese, 2011) uses modern strategies to collate and synthesize data from qualitative and quantitative sources to yield maximum insight into family and sibling-specific processes. Such a paradigmatic lens complements hard statistical data with rich, detailed, and often multiperspectival accounts, allowing for great insight through methods' triangulation. Unfortunately, such approaches have been criticized as of late with claims of mixed methods representing 'empty promises' among other points of contention (e.g. Creswell, 2011). One can side with these critiques whilst taking on the implied areas to guide and improve practical research.

Mixed methodology holds potential within the field of sibling study. The impact of recent societal developments, such as the growing labour participation of female family members, the international mobility of entire families or select members to the rise of technology-mediated interactions, call for qualitative methods to be able to describe the relevant phenomena and to obtain appreciation of how family interaction and functioning are impacted by such pivotal changes. For instance, siblings may now provide one another significant social and emotional support via communicative channels such as online video chat platforms, potentially buffering the impact of uprooting for school or economic purposes (Ittel & Sisler, 2012). In combination with qualitative data, qualitative approaches assist in furthering our understanding of complex family processes. We describe mixed methodology more in depth in the final chapter. Nonetheless, the knowledge gleaned thus far on siblings and siblings in adolescence, in particular, remains in the initial phases as researchers sharpen their pre-existing empirical tools and seek to add new ones to their methodological toolkit.

References

Aiken, L. S., & West, S. G. (1991). *Multiple regression: Testing and interpreting interactions.* Newbury Park, CA: Sage.

Ainsworth, M. D. S., Blehar, M. C., Waters, E., & Wall, S. (1978). *Patterns of attachment: A psychological study of the strange situation.* Oxford: Lawrence Erlbaum Associates.

Alderfer, M. A., Fiese, B. H., Gold, J. I., Cutuli, J. J., Holmbeck, G. N., Goldbeck, L., et al. (2008). Evidence-based assessment in pediatric psychology: Family measures. *Journal of Pediatric Psychology, 33*, 1046–1061.

Aron, A., & Aron, E. N. (1999). *Statistics for psychology* (2nd ed.). Upper Saddle River, NJ: Prentice Hall.

Baltes, P. B., & Nesselroade, J. R. (1979). History and rationale of longitudinal research. In J. R. Nesselroade & P. B. Baltes (Eds.), *Longitudinal research in the study of behaviour and development* (pp. 1–39). New York, NY: Academic Press.

Baron, R. M., & Kenny, D. A. (1986). The moderator-mediator variable distinction in social psychological research: Conceptual, strategic and statistical considerations. *Journal of Personality and Social Psychology, 51*, 1173–1182.

Barzel, M., & Reid, G. J. (2011). Coparenting in relation to children's psychosocial and diabetes-specific adjustment. *Journal of Pediatric Psychology, 36*, 618–629.

Beach, S. R. H., Tesser, A., Fincham, F. D., Jones, D. J., Johnson, D., & Whitaker, D. J. (1998). Pleasure and pain in doing well together: An investigation of performance related affect in close relationships. *Journal of Personality and Social Psychology, 74*, 923–938.

Bergstrom, A. R., (1984). Continuous time stochastic models and issues of aggregation over time. In Z. Griliches & M. D. Intriligator (Eds.), *Handbook of econometrics* (Vol. 2, pp. 1145–1212). Amsterdam: North-Holland.

Bolger, N., Davis, A., & Rafaeli, E. (2003). Diary methods: Capturing live as it is lived. *Annual Review of Psychology, 54*, 579–616.

Bowlby, J. (1969/1982). *Attachment and loss: Attachment* (Vol. I). New York, NY: Basic Books.

Bryk, A. S., & Raudenbush, S. W. (1992). *Hierarchical linear models in social and behavioural research: Applications and data analysis methods* (1st ed.). Newbury Park, CA: Sage.

Buist, K. L. (2010). Sibling relationship quality and adolescent delinquency: A latent growth curve approach. *Journal of Family Psychology, 24*, 400–410.

Christ, O., & Schlüter, E. (2012). *StrukturgleichungsmodellemitMplus – EinepraktischeEinführung* [Structural equation modelling with Mplus – An applied introduction]. München: Oldenbourg.

Cohen, J. (1988). *Statistical power analysis for the behavioural sciences* (2nd ed.). Mahwah, NJ: Lawrence Erlbaum Associates.

Cohen, J., Cohen, P., West, S. G., & Aiken, L. S. (2003). *Applied multiple regression/correlation analysis for the behavioural sciences* (3rd ed.). Hillsdale: Erlbaum.

Cole, D. A., & Maxwell, S. E. (2003). Testing meditational models with longitudinal data: Questions and tips in the use of structural equation modelling. *Journal of Abnormal Psychology, 112*, 558–577.

Cook, W. L., & Kenny, D. A. (2005). The actor-partner interdependence model: A model of bidirectional effects in developmental studies. *International Journal of Behavioural Development, 29*, 101–109.

Creswell, J. W. (2011). Controversies in mixed methods research. In N. K. Denzin & Y. S. Lincoln (Eds.), *The Sage handbook of qualitative research* (Vol. 4, pp. 269–284). Thousand Oaks, CA: Sage.

Cummings, E. M. (1995). Usefulness of experiments for the study of the family. *Journal of Family Psychology, 9*, 175–185.

Cummings, E. M., Simpson, K. S., & Wilson, A. (1993). Children's responses to interadult anger as a function of information about resolution. *Developmental Psychology, 29*, 978–985.

DeHaan, L. G., Hawley, D. R., & Deal, J. E. (2013). Operationalizing family resilience as process: Proposed methodological strategies. In D. Becvar (Ed.), *Handbook of family resilience* (pp. 17–30). New York, NY: Springer.

Delsing, M. J. M. H., Oud, J. H. L., & De Bruyn, E. E. J. (2005). Assessment of bidirectional influences between family relationships and adolescent problem behaviour: Discrete vs. continuous time analysis. *European Journal of Psychological Assessment, 21*, 226–231.

Eid, M., Gollwitzer, M., & Schmitt, M. (2013). *Statistik und Forschungsmethoden* (3. Aufl.) [Statistics and research methods (3rd ed.)]. Weinheim: Beltz.

Ellis, M. V. (1999). Repeated measures designs. *The Counseling Psychologist, 27*, 552–578.

El-Sheikh, M., Cummings, E. M., & Reiter, S. (1996). Preschoolers' responses to ongoing interadult conflict: The role of prior exposure to resolved versus unresolved arguments. *Journal of Abnormal Child Psychology, 24*, 665–679.

Eshghi, A., Haughton, D. M., Legrand, P., Skaletsky, M., & Woolford, S. W. (2011). Identifying groups: A comparison of methodologies. *Journal of Data Science, 9*, 271–291.

Feeney, J. A., & Noller, P. (2013). Perspectives on studying family communication: Multiple methods and multiple sources. In A. L. Vangelisti (Ed.), *The Routledge handbook of family communication* (2nd ed., pp. 29–45). New York, NY: Routledge.

Field, A. (2009). *Discovering statistics using SPSS* (3rd ed.). London: Sage.

Garson, G. D. (2013). *Hierarchical linear modelling: Guide and applications*. Thousand Oaks, CA: Sage.

Geiser, C. (2010). *Datenanalyse mit Mplus: Eine anwendungsorientierte Einführung* [Data analysis with Mplus: An application-oriented introduction]. Wiesbaden, Germany: VS-Verlag.

Goldberg, W. A., & Easterbrooks, M. (1984). Role of marital quality in toddler development. *Developmental Psychology, 20*, 504–514.

Goldstein, H. (2011). *Multilevel statistical models* (4th ed.). London: Arnold.

Gonzalez, R., & Griffin, D. (2012). Dyadic data analysis. In H. Cooper, P. M. Camic, D. L. Long, A. T. Panter, D. Rindskopf, & K. J. Sher, (Eds.), *APA handbook of research methods in psychology: Data analysis and research publication* (Vol. 3, pp. 439–450). Washington, DC: American Psychological Association.

Goodwin, J. C. (2010). *Research in psychology: Methods and design* (6th ed.). Toronto: John Wiley & Sons.

Green, A. S., Rafaeli, E., Bolger, N., Shrout, P. E., & Reis, H. T. (2006). Paper or plastic? Data equivalence in paper and electronic diaries. *Psychological Methods, 11*, 87–105.

Greenstein, T. N. (2006). *Methods of family research* (2nd ed.). Thousand Oaks, CA: Sage.

Halford, W. K., Gravestock, F. M., Lowe, R., & Scheldt, S. (1992). Toward a behavioural ecology of stressful marital interactions. *Behavioural Assessment, 14*, 199–217.

Hayes, A. F. (2009). Beyond Baron and Kenny: Statistical mediation analysis in the new millennium. *Communication Monographs, 76*, 408–420.

Henry, D. B., Tolan, P. H., & Gorman-Smith, D. (2005). Clustering methods in family psychology research. *Journal of Family Psychology, 19*, 121–132.

Hoffmann, J. (2002). The community context of family structure and adolescent drug use. *Journal of Marriage and Family, 64*, 314–330.

Hussey, D. L., & Guo, S. (2003). Measuring behaviour change in young children receiving intensive school-based mental health services. *Journal of Community Psychology, 31*, 629–639.

Ittel, A., & Sisler, A. (2012). Third culture kids: Adjusting to a changing world. *DiskursKindheits- und Jugendforschung Heft, 4*, 487–492.

Jenkins, J. M., Cheung, C., Frampton, K., Rasbash, J., Boyle, M. H., & Georgiades, K. (2009). The use of multilevel modelling for the investigation of family process. *European Journal of Developmental Science, 3*, 131–149.

Jöreskog, K. G. (1979). Basic ideas of factor and component analysis. In K. G. Jöreskog & D. Sörbom (Eds.), *Advances in factor analysis and structural equation models* (pp. 5–20). Cambridge, MA: Abt Books.

Jouriles, E. N., Murphy, C. M., Farris, A. M., Smith, D. A., Richters, J. E., & Waters, E. (1991). Marital adjustment, parental disagreements about child rearing, and behaviour problems in boys: Increasing the specificity of the marital assessment. *Child Development, 62*, 1424–1433.

Judd, C. M., & McClelland, G. H. (1989). *Data analysis: A model comparison approach.* New York, NY: Harcourt Brace Jovanovich.

Kashy, D. A., & Kenny, D. A. (1990). Analysis of family research designs: A model of interdependence. *Communications Research, 17*, 462–482.

Kenny, D. A. (2011). Commentary: Dyadic analyses of family data. *Journal of Pediatric Psychology, 36*, 630–633.

Kenny, D. A., Kashy, D. A., & Cook, W. L. (2006). *Dyadic data analysis.* New York, NY: Guilford Press.

Kerig, P. K. (2001). Introduction and overview: Conceptual issues in family observational research. In P. K. Kerig, & K. M. Lindahl (Eds.), *Family observational coding systems: Resources for systemic research* (pp. 1–22). Mahwah, NJ: Lawrence Erlbaum Associates.

Kerig, P., & Lindahl, K. (2001). *Family observational coding systems: Resources for systemic research.* Mahwah, NJ: Lawrence Erlbaum Associates.

Kline, R. B. (2011). *Principles and practice of structural equation modelling* (3rd ed.). New York, NY: Guilford Press.

Lanza, S. T., Flaherty, B. P., & Collins, L. M. (2003). Latent class and latent transition analysis. In J. A. Schinka & W. F. Velicer (Eds.), *Handbook of Psychology: Research methods in Psychology* (Vol. 2, pp. 663–685). New York, NY: John Wiley & Sons.

Laurenceau, J-P., & Bolger, N. (2005). Using diary methods to study marital and family processes: Special issue on methodology in family science. *Journal of Family Psychology, 19*, 86–97.

Little, T. D. (2013). *Longitudinal structural equation modelling.* New York, NY: Guilford Press.

Lobato, D., & Kao, B. (2002). Integrated parent-sibling group intervention to improve sibling knowledge and adjustment to chronic illness and disability. *Journal of Pediatric Psychology, 27,* 711–716.

Lyons, K., & Sayer, A. G. (2005). Longitudinal dyad models in family research. *Journal of Marriage and Family, 67,* 1048–1060.

Mandara, J. (2003). The typological approach in child and family psychology: A review of theory, methods and research. *Clinical Child & Family Psychology Review, 6,* 129–146.

McArdle, J. J., & Nesselroade, J. R. (2003). Growth curve analysis in contemporary psychological research. In J. Schinka & W. Velicer (Eds.), *Comprehensive handbook of psychology: Research methods in psychology* (Vol. 2, pp. 447–480). New York, NY: Wiley.

McBride, B. A., Schoppe, S. J., & Rane, T. R. (2002). Child characteristics, parenting stress, and parental involvement: Fathers versus mothers. *Journal of Marriage and Family, 64,* 998–1011.

McHale, S. M., Updegraff, K. A., Helms-Erikson, H., & Crouter, A. C. (2001). Sibling influences on gender development in middle childhood and early adolescence: A longitudinal study. *Developmental Psychology, 37,* 115–125.

McKay, J. M., Pickens, J., & Stewart, A. (1996). Inventoried and observed stress in parent-child interactions. *Current Psychology: Developmental, Learning, Personality, Social, 15,* 223–234

Melby, J. N., & Conger, R. D. (2001). The Iowa Family Interaction Rating Scales: Instrument summary. In P. Kerig, & K. Kindahl (Eds.), *Family observational coding systems: Resources for systemic research* (pp. 33–56). Mahwah, NJ: Lawrence Erlbaum Associates.

Mikulincer, M., & Shaver, P. R. (2007). Boosting attachment security to promote mental health, prosocial values, and inter-group tolerance. *Psychological Inquiry, 18,* 139–156.

Milligan, G., & Cooper, M. (1988). A study of standardization of variables in cluster analysis. *Journal of Classification, 5,* 181–204.

Muller, D., Judd, C. M., & Yzerbyt, V. Y. (2005). When moderation is mediated and mediation is moderated. *Journal of Personality and Social Psychology, 89,* 852–863.

Muthén, B. (2002). Beyond SEM: General latent variable modelling. *Behaviourmetrika, 29,* 81–117.

Noller, P. (1984). *Nonverbal communication and marital interaction.* Oxford: Pergamon.

Noller, P. (2001). Using standard content methodology to assess nonverbal sensitivity in dyads. In J. A. Hall & F. Bernieri (Eds.), *Interpersonal sensitivity: Theory and measurement* (pp. 243–264). Mahwah, NJ: Lawrence Erlbaum Associates.

Noller, P., Atkin, S., Feeney, J., & Peterson, C. (2006). Family conflict and adolescents. In L. Turner, & R. West (Eds.), *The family communication sourcebook* (pp. 165–183). Thousand Oaks, CA: Sage.

Ostrov, J. M., & Hart, E. J. (2013). Observational methods. In T. D. Little (Ed.), *The Oxford handbook of quantitative methods in psychology* (Vol. 1, pp. 285–303). Oxford: Oxford University Press.

Price, P. C. (2013). *Research methods in psychology: Core concepts and skills.* Retrieved from http://solr.bccampus.ca:8001/bcc/file/ef1500d5-fc15-4a36-8d1c-283bf01de2f2/1/research-methods-in-psychology-1st-cdn-ed.pdf

Reis, H. T., & Wheeler, L. (1991). Studying social interaction with the Rochester Interaction Record. In M. P. Zanna (Ed.), *Advances in experimental social psychology* (Vol. 24, pp. 270–318). San Diego, CA: Academic Press.

Robinson, E., & Eyberg, S. M. (1981). The dyadic parent-child interaction coding system: Standardization and validation. *Journal of Consulting and Clinical Psychology, 49,* 245–250.

Rogosa, D. R. (1980). A critique of cross-lagged correlation. *Psychological Bulletin, 88,* 245–258.

Rönkä, A., Malinen, K., Kinnunen, U., Tolvanen, A., & Lämsä, T. (2010). Capturing daily family dynamics via text messages: Development of a mobile diary. *Community, Work and Family, 13*, 5–21.

Sameroff, A. E. (2009). *The transactional model of development: How children and contexts shape each other.* Washington, DC: American Psychological Association.

Shieh, G. (2009). Detecting interaction effects in moderated multiple regression with continuous variables: Power and sample size considerations. *Organizational Research Methods, 12*, 510–528.

Snijders, T. A. B., & Kenny, D. A. (1999). The social relations model for family data: A multilevel approach. *Personal Relationships, 6*, 471–486.

Sobel, M. E. (1982). Asymptotic intervals for indirect effects in structural equations models. In S. Leinhart (Ed.), *Sociological methodology* (pp. 290–312). San Francisco, CA: Jossey-Bass.

Sturge-Apple, M. L., Davies, P. T., & Cummings, E. M. (2006). Hostility and withdrawal in marital conflict: Effects on parental emotional unavailability and inconsistent discipline. *Journal of Family Psychology, 20*, 227–238.

Tambling, R. B., Johnson, S. K., & Johnson, L. N. (2011). Analysing dyadic data from small samples: A pooled regression actor-partner interdependence model approach. *Counseling Outcome Research and Evaluation, 2*, 101–114.

Titterington, D. M., Smith, A. F. M., & Makov, U. E. (1985). *Statistical analysis of finite mixture distributions.* New York, NY: John Wiley & Sons.

Ullman, J. B., & Bentler, P. M. (2003). Structural equation modelling. In J. A. Schinka & W. F. Velicer, (Eds.). *Handbook of psychology: Research methods in psychology* (Vol. 2, pp. 607–634). New York, NY: John Wiley & Sons.

Walsh, F. (2003). Family resilience: A framework for clinical practice. *Family Process, 42*, 1–19.

Webster-Stratton, C. (1985). Comparisons of behaviour transactions between conduct disordered children and their mothers in the clinic and at home. *Journal of Abnormal Child Psychology, 13*, 169–184.

Weisner, T. S., & Fiese, B. H. (2011). Introduction to special section of the Journal of Family Psychology, advances in mixed-methods in family psychology: Integrative and applied solutions for family science. *Journal of Family Psychology, 25*, 795–798.

Wheeler, L., & Nezlek, J. (1977). Sex differences in social participation. *Journal of Personality and Social Psychology, 35*, 742–754.

Whisman, M. A., & McClelland, G. H. (2005). Designing, testing, and interpreting interactions and moderator effects in family research. *Journal of Family Psychology, 19*, 111–120.

Willihnganz, H. (2002). *Parent-child interaction observation systems: A review of methods of psychological research* (Working Paper No. 7). UCLA Sloan Center on Everyday Lives of Families.

Wilson Van Voorhis, C. R. W., & Morgan, B. L. (2007). Understanding power and rules of thumb for determining sample sizes. *Tutorials in Quantitative Methods for Psychology, 3*, 43–50.

Yates, T. M., Obradović, J., & Egeland, B. (2010). Transactional relations across contextual strain, parenting quality, and early childhood regulation and adaptation in a high-risk sample. *Development and Psychopathology, 22*, 539–555.

Yeh, H. C., & Lempers, J. D. (2004). Perceived sibling relationships and adolescent development. *Journal of Youth and Adolescence, 33*, 133–147.

Yu, J. J., & Gamble, W. C. (2008). Pathways of influence: Marital relationships and their association with parenting styles and sibling relationship quality. *Journal of Child and Family Studies, 17*, 757–778.

7

FINDINGS AND FUTURES IN SIBLING RESEARCH

Introduction

In this final chapter, we sketch out a research programme for the contextualized study of siblings and their families, discussing different comprehensive developmental models that inform social relationships, pointing to areas in need of further research, and detailing perspectives and approaches concerning future work. An overview of systems science and its offshoots, developmental systems perspective (DSP), family systems, and ecological systems theory will be put forth and situated as to their applications in sibling investigations. In addition, we include core theses and key insights gleaned from previous chapters to anchor proposals for future multiangled research programmes. In so doing, this chapter serves to both appraise and organize past work, guiding future research. Such efforts should be undertaken with the hope of furthering not only efficient and innovative work on siblings, families, and close relationship across the lifespan, but inform best practice and public policy initiatives in tandem. The Appendix additionally spotlights promising projects which illustrate innovative sibling science.

In this volume, we sought to bring together recent research from a number of sub-disciplines that consider adolescent sibling relationships and their development within and outside of the family context. As others have alluded to before us, scholarship on the sibling bond lacks an organizing structure, and adolescent research, more generally, confronts a similar dilemma (Adams & Berzonsky, 2003; Caspi, 2011). To make valuable albeit scattered work from numerous fields accessible and applicable is too large an undertaking for any one theoretical perspective, and so we do not purport to proffer a golden standard on which subsequent research should solely rely.

Rather, we wish that the overview offered assists in capturing the many-sided nature of the intimate sibling tie within and across dynamic contexts during the developmentally intense phase of adolescence. The resulting conceptual template coalesces a few examples of front-line research concerning processes that are influential in the development of the sibling bond over the span of adolescence, and incorporates methodologies and techniques designed for multiple types of data. For those curious as to what possible quantitative methods entail, Chapter 6 delineates some of these statistical and methodological strategies, such as path analysis and multilevel modelling, best applied to the suggestions we present here. In this way, we hope to encourage scalable process-level sibling and family research.

Family and social changes

It may strike the modern reader as remarkable that back in 1800, the average woman gave birth to eight children; today, two or fewer births per woman is considered normal (Arnett, 2003). In this light, understanding how changes in family structure accompany considerable demographic shifts is central to successfully contextualizing development against wider societal-level change. This notion cuts back to the position of classic sociology of the family that changes in the family cannot be understood apart from changes in wider economic and social structures (e.g. Burgess, 1926; Davis, 1941; Ogburn, 1932; Parsons, 1944). As the personal became increasingly relegated to the family sphere, and public displays of opinion at the workplace were in essence proscribed, families were granted what can be considered as undue amounts of pressure regarding personal fulfilment, warmth, comfort, intimacy, and retreat. In keeping with this idea, the concomitant effects of greater expectation and responsibility placed on relatively smaller so-called nuclear families, familial relationships are arguably more central in individual development over the life course (Bengtson, 2001). A host of demographic shifts, contained under the umbrella terms of the 'Second Demographic Transition' and globalization, including increased life expectancy, mobility, contraceptive use, and family structure diversity have likely contributed to this phenomenon, all of which impact the meaning of siblinghood (Mills & Blossfeld, 2013; Popenoe, 1993; Stacey, 1996).

Within the scope of individuals' ever-lengthening lifespan, sibling relationships might be the most enduring intimate bond (Bank & Kahn, 1982). More than that, they are heavily affect-laden and ubiquitous (Dunn, 2005); siblings spend more time with one another than parents by middle childhood (McHale & Crouter, 1996). Beyond direct effects of the sibling bond on the family, siblings' ties can have indirect and wide-reaching sway, imparting great influence on each other's cognitive, social, and health development as they age (Brody, 2004; Cicirelli, 1995). The mounting significance of brothers and sisters in individuals' lives is clear not only across time (Oliva & Arranz, 2005; Parke, 2004), but particularly during the developmentally meaningful and rich teenage years that are second only to that of infancy (Lerner & Villarruel, 1994; Petersen, 1988).

The specifics, however, of the ways in which adolescence comes to bear on sibling relationships and vice versa demand the examination of often disparate strands of research, and an eventual synthesis of a proposed research programme by which to frame the results and guide future work. This aids us in forwarding our developmental knowledge, encouraging contextualized application in order to benefit adolescent brothers and sisters and involved others' lives from multiple viewpoints.

Developmental systems perspective in action

As we have previously mentioned, DSPs draw from, among others, the related disciplines of sociology, psychology, anthropology, behavioural genetics, as well as the biological and educational sciences, and align closely to that of the family-ecological systems, itself housed under the unifying meta-theoretical framework of developmental systems theories (DSTs) (see, for instance, Gottlieb, 2007; Granic & Hollenstein, 2003; Petermann, Niebank, & Scheithauer, 2004; Scheithauer, Niebank, & Gottlieb, 2007; Scheithauer, Niebank, & Ittel, 2009). Additionally, it borrows extensively from seminal work on the ecological theory of development proffered by Bronfenbrenner (1979, 1986, 1992). Like the excellent contribution of Granic, Dishion, and Hollenstein (2003) in their furtherance of adolescent–parent relationship knowledge through systems perspective and its principles, we too encourage the adoption of DST and its tenets as a heuristic tool for making sense of and organizing empirical data during the field's nascency. Moreover, evaluation of translational and applied findings from systems-based research will assist in gaining significant inroads into public policy measures informed by best practice (Ripoll-Núñez & Carrillo, 2014).

A brief reiteration of systems theory is in order. The systems approach represents a meta-theoretical framework for studying stability and change, born from the study of complex and nonlinear systems in physics and maths. Major features of systems theory, the foremost of which is the view of self-organizing interdependent systems and their interface, can create dynamic representations that inform individual and social development (Witherington, 2007). The advantage of the

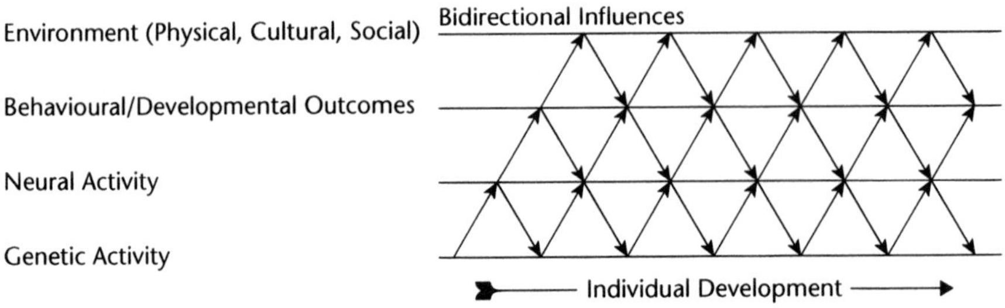

Environment (Physical, Cultural, Social)

Behavioural/Developmental Outcomes

Neural Activity

Genetic Activity

Bidirectional Influences

Individual Development

FIGURE 7.1 Developmental systems perspective of development depicting complete bi-directional interaction between and within multiple levels of influence

Source: Based on Gottlieb (1992/2002, p. 186; modified by Scheithauer, Niebank, & Ittel, 2009, p. 603; with permission from IOS Press).

systems approach to development is that as no normative stage plan is laid out, each individual's development is approached as a unique case. The self-organizing properties of various systems interacting in tandem to exert a balancing influence on the greater system or organism as a whole are thought to be superior in capturing maturation than traditional static stage theories (Lavalli, Pantoja, Hsu, Messinger, & Fogel, 2005). Stage theory depictions have largely fallen to the wayside in developmental science in favour of dynamic approaches, although the gap between theory and praxis continues to be under addressed (e.g. Schermerhorn & Cummings, 2008) (Figure 7.1).

Adopting systems theory as an explanatory model for development has not come without its share of controversy (Cox & Paley, 1997; Reis, Collins, & Berscheid, 2000). Criticism launched against systems theory or family systems theory in particular may relate to the difficulty in enlisting such a complex model for respectively complex processes of ontogenesis. Still, other scholars believe that DSP principles offer 'the conceptual toolkit necessary for considering the complexity surrounding normative adolescent development' (Granic, Dishion, & Hollenstein, 2003, p. 63). Developmental scientists have applied the tenets of systems theory like feedback, interdependent time scales, and nonlinear change in the conceptualization of multistability to advance traditional models of ontogenesis (e.g. Fogel, 1993; Ford & Lerner, 1992; Lewis, 1997; Lewis & Granic, 2000; Thelen & Smith, 1994). For specific examples of how DSP principles work within a psychosocial framework of adolescent development, we refer the reader to Granic, Dishion, and Hollenstein's (2003) timely summarizing table (pp. 68–69).

A viable proposal for the comprehensive study of the intimate sibling relationship over adolescence first requires the consideration and incorporation of (all) the domains of influence at work. In our proposal for a novel research programme, we do not attempt to re-invent the wheel and so call upon foregoing researchers who have also endeavoured to capture the multifaceted and manifold forces implicated in adolescent development. Granic, Dishion, and Hollenstein (2003) have similarly based their organizing framework for discussing normative adolescence and the role of the family on developmental scientists like Bronfenbrenner (1986, 1989, 1992; Bronfenbrenner & Morris, 1998) and Hinde (1989). These systems theories envision and depict the developing individual as embedded within concentric realms at varying levels of influence through dynamic bi-directional interactions and processes with their surroundings.

According to ecological theories of development, of which Urie Bronfenbrenner's stands out among the best regarded (Bronfenbrenner, 1979, 1986, 1989, 1992; Bronfenbrenner & Evans, 2000; Bronfenbrenner & Morris, 1998), four domains (time, person, process, and context) interact to bring about multifaceted dynamics, relational patterns, and outcomes in adolescence. Beyond these four dimensions, biological change in adolescence is deemed a 'prime mover' with its accompanying physiological shifts in physical growth, hormone levels, brain development, and associated emotional and cognitive development; all of these factors assist in bringing forth transitions in transactional microsocial processes and social environments. The implications such alterations in the microsocial and ecosocial environment have for the adolescent can be made evident through longitudinal surveying of developmental outcomes. In this way, adolescents' developmental courses and their constituent qualitative and quantitative changes can be tracked. As Sameroff and MacKenzie (2003) state:

> Children affect their environments and environments affect children. In addition, environmental settings affect and are affected by one another. Moreover these effects change over time in response to normative and non-normative events. To get evidence of the multidirectional chaining of such influences will require longitudinal research that pays equal attention to the details of each individual and setting. (p. 636)

The role of place in development

To return to adolescent development contextualized, it is taken as manifest that patterns of behaviour and processes of interaction initiated during this period set the maturational stage; they hold great later-age sway (Conger & Petersen, 1984; Heaven, 1994). If one is to adopt an ecological perspective of individual development, all change and growth occurs in juxtaposition to, and embedded within, coordinating and contrasting layers of influence, a tenant which echoes with transactional developmental models (Sameroff & MacKenzie, 2003; Schermerhorn & Cummings, 2008). Indeed, contextualized space, or place, is of great importance in the life experience of an individual as they offer affordances for events or important moments (Bukowski & Lisboa, 2007; Lewin, 1939). Development needs to be understood according to the context in which it occurs as it shapes and directs individuals. Unfortunately, the influence of place has not been so firmly grasped.

Multiple researchers take the stance that the void between domain-specific study and meta-theoretical posturing on properties of the environment–person interaction needs to be filled (e.g. Bukowski & Lisboa, 2007; Granic, Dishion, &

Hollenstein, 2003; Sameroff, 2009). Research programmes that seek to explain the nature of certain settings by individual interactions identify and describe basic features and processes of environments of interest, work out ways of measuring individual differences between contexts, and develop and assess influence processes (Bukowski & Lisboa, 2007). Applied and empirical developmental work has lagged behind theory in this regard, feasibly due to the practical challenges of studying dynamic development, and the limitations of theories and methods typically employed (Schermerhorn & Cummings, 2008). We believe that deployment of the DSP model can assist.

DSP and development contextualized

Ecological theory aims to combine the principles of DSP and the privileging of place by emphasizing the essential processes that define interaction between person and context, without favouring one to the detriment of the other. During the life course, a person's interactions with overlapping environments become more complex, and the number of environments that a child participates in on a daily basis becomes greater, especially across adolescence (Lewin, 1939; Maughan, 2011). Furthermore, instead of expecting directional effects, ecological theory, along with dialectical social relational theory (see Kuczynski and colleagues, e.g. Kuczynski & Parkin, 2009; Kuczynski, Pitman, & Mitchell, 2009), assumes bi-directionality whereby individuals, groups, and cultures influence each other in a reciprocal manner (Bukowski & Lisboa, 2007).

One example of place research includes Kerr, Stattin, and Kiesner's (2007) innovative assessment of everyone and everyplace in an adolescent's life space in their study of peer relations, which moves beyond the assessment of typically studied contexts. Some intriguing results from this study include the following: (1) older peers who were not classmates exerted influence in antisocial behaviour development, (2) the strong pull of conjoint effects (e.g. overlapping social circles within and outside of school), (3) some girls displayed more overlap than boys, with early-to-mature girls displaying more delinquent and antisocial behaviour as well as more older peers, and (4) the over-arching power of continuity in experiences across peer contexts. A recent longitudinal study tracking the relationship between differential peer experiences, sibling conflict, and relationship quality in adolescents adds to the conversation on place and highlights the importance of considering spheres of overlapping influence (Greer, Campione-Barr, Debrown, & Maupin, 2014). Considering high levels of differential peer group involvement, youngest siblings reported greater sibling conflict while oldest siblings indicated higher levels of relationship positivity, and second-oldests had the most negative relationship experiences. Oscillations across adolescence and variations between siblings based on birth order reiterate the importance of recognizing multiple domains and contexts.

These findings illuminate effects beyond traditional approaches of purely familial or classroom-based studies. One of the resounding advantages of this embedded approach is the stress on the social in maturational processes, and the view that relationships need to be conceived as contexts for development in their own right. Family research and sibling interaction study would do well to adopt the scope of this type of contextualized work, as individual siblings interact with one another and multiple other agents in varying conditions.

These contexts for development can be readily constrained by multiple micro-social processes, especially familial influence. Transactional family dynamics helps us to conceptualize the multitudinous ways family members impact each other via within-family mutual influence processes (Schermerhorn, Chow, & Cummings, 2010; Schermerhorn & Cummings, 2008). Parents, for instance, choose to move children from one school to another or encourage a younger sibling to accompany an older sibling to an extracurricular activity and further manage children's social relationships with an eye toward the future (Parke & Buriel, 2006). Similarly, Granic and colleagues' work depict examples of the combinatorial influence of microsocial processes and ecological adaptations during adolescence on later outcomes (Granic, Dishion, & Hollenstein, 2003).

Some researchers contend that positive familial contexts and within-family dynamics are related to positive outcomes (e.g. Hill, 1987; Hill & Holmbeck, 1986; Holmbeck, 1996; Holmbeck, Paikoff, & Brooks-Gunn, 1995; Steinberg, 1990), while negative matrices and patterns of interaction in families can compound subsequent relational problems in children (e.g. Meunier, Wade, & Jenkins, 2012). Others, on the other hand, view conflict and ambiguity as dialectical driving forces for qualitative change and optimal development, at least to a degree (Kramer, 2010; Kuczynski & Parkin, 2007, 2009; Kuczynski et al., 2009). What remains to be examined is the way in which these contexts operate, that is, which dynamics and processes are at play and in what way do they interact and adapt in relation to more distal surrounding structures in an adolescent's ecological milieu.

Exemplary research: Ecological and family systems theory applied

Developmentalists who have adopted DSP principles and ecological system theory perspectives, either explicitly or implicitly, have produced fruitful, promissory work. These studies typically account for ecological factors through statistical methods like multilevel modelling and sibling studies where analysis both between and within families is enabled; here, multiple layers running from proximal to distal are thought to mediate and moderate family influence processes (Pike, 2012). Intrinsic to the sibling study approach, unique non-shared environmental variance and its importance in individual adolescent development have been pointed out by many researchers of late, as we profiled in Chapter 4 (e.g. review by Turkheimer & Waldron, 2000). The difficulty in studies of this nature is not only theoretical but also logistical in that considerably large sample sizes and multiple-informant measures are required for the ideal multilevel model to be applied to conceptual DSP frameworks.

One such investigation that used ecological systems theory principles by way of a multilevel modelling approach and siblings design was Meunier *et al.*'s (2012) recent look at differential parenting and children's socio-emotional outcomes. The researchers were able to inspect the moderating role of contextual risk factors including maternal characteristics (e.g. education, parenting, depression, history of abuse, and teenage parenthood), parental and family characteristics (single-parent, step-parent families, and marital conflict), and home and community characteristics (household disorganization, neighbourhood quality, collective efficacy, and personal safety). Their results point to the great weight of context, particularly in regard to differential negativity. Stronger links between differential parenting and child outcomes were found for greater levels of contextual risk, with the less favoured child faring poorly. This holistic depiction of the various levels of influence and their interactive routes within and between families provides a fine example of systems-based sibling inquiry.

From a study of a more psychopathological and behavioural genetic tenor comes results that underscore the importance of shared influences beyond the majority of heritable variance in substance abuse. A recent Swedish twin and sibling study (Kendler, Maes, Sundquist, Ohlsson, & Sundquist, 2013) drawing on data from a nation-wide registry shows the need for in-depth within-family study for particular phenomena, as findings ran in contrast to previous mentions of the role of unique non-shared environmental influence, that is, child-specific effects, in outcomes like socio-emotional well-being (e.g. Kowal, Kramer, Krull, & Crick, 2002). The study at hand found that a substantial proportion of the shared environmental effect on drug abuse stemmed from community-wide rather than family-level influence, including neighbourhood social deprivation. The blending of a systems theory approach to family research in which social mechanisms like buffering influences or patterns of coercion could inform and flesh-out exactly how particular siblings or groups of siblings manage to escape the trappings of community-level environmental effects. Again, conceptualizing these environmental factors as moderators or mediators of family-level processes like parenting style might be an avenue for future research that aims towards effective interventional efforts.

Longitudinal analyses allow for the depiction of changes in relationship processes and outcomes by highlighting the importance of life history, experience, and time processes at play in the chronological dimensions of ecological systems theory and development. Although understandably limited due to difficulties in scalability, examinations in this manner are incredibly valuable for informing bi-directional influence in sibling relationships in adolescence, for instance (Conger & Little, 2010).

Researchers have attempted such longitudinal analyses, including Buist, Reitz, and Dekovic's (2008) examination of attachment quality and relationship dynamics in adolescent siblings and their parents. Their findings underscored the relative stability of attachment processes alongside the importance of adolescents' individual internal working models as well as relationship-specific qualities. Another longitudinal study undertaken by Solmeyer, McHale, and Crouter (2013) looked at the sibling bond, assessing the associations between sibling intimacy and conflict and adolescents' reports of risky behaviour. Multivariate multilevel models allowed these investigators to see whether the sibling relationship quality–risky behaviour link was moderated by birth order, sex, or dyad sex constellation. Upon controlling for parent–youth conflict, the findings showed within-person covariation between sibling conflict and risky behaviour for all youths except firstborns with younger brothers. Furthermore, for brother–brother dyads, sibling intimacy was positively related to risky behaviour. The authors posit that the sibling relationship can be considered as a context for adolescents' individual development, which varies according to the differential influence of dyadic characteristics such as birth order, sex, and dyad sex constellation.

Finally, Granic and associates have conducted adolescent and family systems research directly using a DSP (e.g. Granic & Hollenstein, 2003; Granic, Hollenstein, Dishion, & Patterson, 2003; Hollenstein, 2007). These researchers highlight the change in structure of family interactions in one such study of adolescent boys and the parental dyad. Longitudinal observations enabled analysis through state space grids, a novel method for dynamic systems study. These studies illuminate the complexities of sibling relationships and the need to further mine this rich area of study.

'Global Youth Culture' and the need for narrative accounts of siblinghood

Adolescence is now an influential and prolonged period in the life course. Its increased duration is directed by a lowered age of puberty due to improved health and the later-age individuals are societally accepted as adults (Gluckman & Hayne, 2011). Schlegel (2000) speaks of the attendant rise of global youth culture, at least within the middle class, in which youth tend to wear the same clothing and hairstyles, listen to similar music, and adopt similar slang expressions. Some of these are brought about by shared culture enabled through technological advances (e.g. the Internet), uniting individuals never before able to communicate with such ease and immediacy (Arnett, 2003). All the same, the concept of adolescence is vastly different the world over and signals the influence of both global and localized processes (Heine, 2011). Young people in China who drop out of school to become entrepreneurs in the rising market economy (e.g. Stevenson & Zusho, 2002) have entirely different demands and requirements to meet their survival and thriving than those of youth in Egypt who generally experience limited contact between opposite sexes even in the school setting, where further education does not necessarily relate to gender egalitarianism (Mensch, Ibrahim, Lee, & El-Gibaly, 2003). In Southeast Asia, youth marriage continues to be the norm, and childbearing is expected shortly thereafter, with females entering into marriage at an average of 15.6 years based on 2001 national census data. These cultural variations thus challenge notions of protracted and prolonged adolescence (Adhikari, 2003; Coltabiano & Castiglioni, 2008).

The form adolescence and the experience of youth assume is remarkably distinctive and diverse, varying within and between different settings and cultures.

Certainly, central biological, cognitive, and psychological imperatives of human development and maturation exist, as do common challenges of life in the twenty-first century. These issues are then adapted and shaped to the needs of each society, and are often transformed and given special meaning inside distinctive cultural systems. Recognition of the tentative configuration of youth today does not preclude the preeminence of the biological in sensitive periods of human development, as in infancy or adolescence (Brown & Larson, 2002). Indeed, certain physiological near-universal imperatives drive maturational processes, all the while being influenced and imparting influence in turn on the individual's environment (Weisfeld, 1979). That brothers and sisters come of age in changing familial circumstances and dynamic sociocultural worlds is evident, yet the processes of these developmental pathways are less understood, and not so easily depicted.

Given these disparate and rapidly shifting accounts in conjunction with varied findings from sibling and adolescent research, within and between contexts, it would be perspicacious of the field to acknowledge the value of qualitative study anchored in the anthropological and sociological traditions. Indeed, the rich information proffered by sibling's first-hand accounts of their experiences for their own development is all too often overlooked in favour of tidy cost and time-effective statistical analyses. Edwards and colleagues adopted a qualitative strategy in their thoughtful glimpse into the sibling bond through intensive interviews covering a range of topics (Edwards, Hadfield, Lucey, & Mauthner, 2006). Importantly, they were able to interweave direct first-person accounts with theoretical and empirical work, and subsequently shed light on areas of divergence and overlap as well as those previously hidden from view. For example, this descriptive method gave voice to individuals typically thrown out of traditional family studies such as adopted, half, and foster siblings, and delved into issues of ethnicity, gender, class, and their intersectionality. In the same vein, Avidan Milevsky (2011) in his qualitative investigations and text on siblings in childhood and adolescence vividly illustrates with narrative accounts the relational impacts brothers and sisters have on one another. Multiple informants and diverse sampling help to propel these pioneering studies that honour participants' intersubjectivities.

One particular investigation illustrative of different perspectives within and across families and culture was undertaken by Cooper, Baker, Polichar, and Welsh (1993), and assessed issues involving familistic values and communication in Mexican, Chinese, Vietnamese, and Filipino descent adolescents. Their findings intimate both intergenerational continuity and change, with the suggestion that in cultures where relationships with parents are more formal, adolescents' relationships with siblings and peers may play especially important roles. Furthermore, Mexican, Chinese, Vietnamese, and Filipino descent adolescents all endorsed values of mutual support among siblings, while family responsibility for care varied by ethnicity and by generational grouping. Broader investigation of cultural contingencies and disparities warrants attention because not all ethnic groups, collectivistic or otherwise, view familism values identically, either between or within the cultural group itself.

Future research demands the injection of unheard voices into spots of silence; here, DST allows for the blending of methodologies as in mixed-methods research to bridge the gap between theory and real-world accounts. Prospective systems-based study could utilize a novel mixed-methods approach, guided by post-positivist theory to evaluate individuals' perspectives through both quantitative and qualitative components (Todd, Nerlich, McKeown, & Clarke, 2004). Triangulation of data and methods, whereby more than one type of data (statistical and descriptive) and their accompanying methodologies (qualitative and quantitative) are enlisted in the research process, offers a more comprehensive understanding of a specific construct in context, such as sibling rivalry in a common peer group (Mathison, 1988). Integrative designs are advantageous, in that they combine the strength of confirmatory results from quantitative multivariate analyses with the 'deep structure' explanatory accounts of underlying mechanisms. Both research programmes, quantitative and qualitative, inform one another while providing vital distinctive material; for instance, a detailed descriptive qualitative report of experiences and perceptions of individuals themselves compliments quantitative data that describe and compare individuals and subgroups of individuals over time, but would risk external validity in isolation. The highly social element of life events and their appraisals can be best captured through this design (Castro, Kellison, Boyd, & Kopak, 2010). Together, the results of a mixed-methods investigation open up individual and social levels of analysis that are potentially inaccessible by strict quantitative measures, such as untapped cultural themes.

Just how could researchers incorporate mixed methods in their sibling study designs? A number of scholars like Johnson and Onwuegbuzie (2004) have written on apposite plans of attack within the educational sciences. It is at the *person* dimension in Bronfenbrenner's ecological theory that person-centred accounts can, for instance, be matched against statistical data or be made into quantified variables for incorporation into quantitative analyses. A mixed-methods approach could assess, for example, differential meanings or themes that emerge from 'traditional' family arrangements versus 'non-traditional' families like children from multigenerational, single-parent, and 'blended' households; children of same-sex and mixed-ethnicity couples, or siblings from adoptive or assisted reproductive technology backgrounds. The intersection of the dual phenomena of the 'second demographic transition' and globalization necessitates such innovative methods to study and understand changing family formations and life courses (see Mills & Blossfeld, 2013).

In fact, McGuire and Shanahan (2010) have written an appeal for inquiry of this nature in their article which enlists an ecological framework for reviewing the complexity of sibling experiences in diverse and changing family contexts. These authors make claim to the criticality of considering macro-contextual forces that impact micro-level sibling processes and show that sibling relationships offer an untapped resource for grasping the interconnections between development, family, and cultural contexts. By privileging the diversity of lived-sibling experiences in ever-changing societies and related changes in familial structuring, associations between a child's development, family context, and culture can be enlightened.

This triangulation of data leads to a cross-examination of various groupings of results, adding contextualizing aspects to typically stationary quantitative tests of sibling- and family-related theory. To these ends, we encourage collaboration between sociologists, anthropologists, psychologists, and other developmentalists, in order to cross-fertilize one another's research for the betterment of siblings, families, and individuals' development.

Interventional initiatives

The majority of the intervention and prevention efforts for sibling relationships have been geared towards decreasing conflict. As we have seen, this falls in alignment with much problem-directed sibling study to date (e.g. Edwards & Gillies, 2004; Kramer, 2004). Like McHale, Updegraff, and Whiteman (2012) summarize in their review, interventions can be broken into three areas, encompassing (1) at-risk youth and their siblings, (2) programmes to specifically change aspects of the sibling relationship through family-wide or subsystem-specific focus on behaviours and cognitions, and (3) family programmes and their spillover effects for siblings.

Due to the ubiquity of sibling conflict, programmes under the second category have attempted to train parents to assist in reducing sibling struggles in order to improve the relationship (e.g. Kramer, 2004; Siddiqui & Ross, 2004; Smith & Ross, 2007). Most of these interventions were designed for and carried out with children as opposed to adolescents. Nevertheless, innovative sibling-specific interventions have proven to be highly effective in promoting positive aspects and decreasing negative outcomes in families. For instance, the afterschool programme, Siblings Are Special (SAS), produced highly beneficial results for not only sibling relationships and outcomes, but also mothers' depression levels and the development of appropriate strategies for parenting siblings (Feinberg, Solmeyer, Hostetler, et al., 2012; Feinberg, Solmeyer, & McHale, 2012). Moreover, these effects were not contingent upon conditions like sibling gender, age, family characteristics, or base-risk levels. Another innovative interventional programme devised by Kramer (2004), 'Fun with Sisters and Brothers', supports siblings' relationships by using skills and qualities gleaned from a foregoing review, including play, conversation, mutual enjoyment, valuing help and support, learning to respect opinions and interests, emotional regulation, managing faulty attributions, conflict management, and parental discussion around the impact of differential treatment (Kramer, 2010). Results involving 4- to 8-year-olds reported that participating children required less parental direction to control negative emotions and abstained from focusing negative actions towards others following participation (Kennedy & Kramer, 2008). Again, the majority of these efforts have been with middle-socioeconomic, city dwelling, Caucasian North American or British families (Dunn, 2011). However, one prevention and intervention effort geared toward bolstering positive family-wide effects in African American families has proved largely effective in positive adjustment for youth and has furthered understanding of family influence processes (Brody, Kogan, Chen, & Murry, 2008). Subsequent work should follow these models, using homogeneous and heterogeneous samples of ethnic minorities and cross-cultural samples measured longitudinally – which enables causal understanding – for maximal effect.

Future research directions and demands

Sibling relationships are akin to familial and intimate relationships in the main: their fluctuations depend on spatial and temporal contexts, and, importantly, associated dynamics operate at multiple levels of influence (Whiteman, McHale, & Soli, 2011). To address adolescent sibling ties from an as complete as possible intra- and inter-individual vantage point, a comprehensive research programme must attempt to encapsulate the multifaceted nature of adolescence and, by extension, both entrenched and emergent relationship properties. The very multidimensionality of this bond, at this sensitive period, necessitates a fundamentally flexible framework. Understandably, no one theoretical standpoint can fulfil these demands. Nonetheless, the principles some developmentalists have borrowed from systems theory perspective seem best suited to take the study of adolescent sibling relationships to task. Longitudinal, within-family systems, culturally specific work is further possible within ecological and systems theory's consideration of chronological, microsocial, and sociocultural parameters.

In order to advance the current state of research, a blending of the sub-disciplines in a transdisciplinary integrative approach is required. That is not to say that any and all perspectives should be thrown together within any one empirical undertaking; complementary approaches should be identified and grouped to aid in streamlining previous and subsequent efforts. For instance, new developments in cultural psychology, sociology, and anthropological science may be put against standing knowledge of psychoanalytic sibling and family dynamics typically gleaned through homogeneous Western-dominated samples. In this way, new lines of inquiry will fill-in gaps and clarify murky areas like the cultural generalizability of notions of sibling rivalry.

Complementary to these theoretical depictions, within-family research designs, mixed methodologies, and multilevelled statistical strategies offer a fruitful way to tap into family system processes and contextualized influences. Behavioural genetics tells us as much, in highlighting the often overlooked importance of non-shared variance between siblings and its meaning in development (for a review, see Turkheimer & Waldron, 2000). Although working with a multilayered model and adopting what may appear to be loose principles poses logistical challenges, development itself is characterized by non-linearity and dynamic change and shifts. Just as Plomin and Daniels (1987) wrote, nearly three decades ago, one is unlikely to find basic systematic linear associations between specific experiences and developmental outcomes; the researcher must embrace this complexity, and certainly many have accordingly responded with original studies and interventions. Only through such innovative means can we adequately address the needs and uniqueness of siblings during an at-times turbulent developmental phase in an increasingly complex ecosocial space.

The agenda for future research we depict here sets the stage for discoveries that will not only extend our understanding of sibling's development in distinct contexts during adolescence and beyond, but will lead to advances in prevention and intervention for families and perhaps, communities as a whole. Efforts that aspire to improve the lives of children and their families must pay heed to increasing transdisciplinary international and longitudinal research demands to fit with multiperspectival accounts of individuals and their experiences. Ideally, matching public policy measures to tackle both microsocial influences and powerful macrosocial factors will be informed by best-practice translational research (Carrillo, Ripoll-Núñez, & Schvaneveldt, 2012); such policy implementation should run parallel to scientific advances (Ripoll-Núñez & Carrillo, 2014). With comprehensive and thoughtful empirical undertakings, the multiplicities of siblings and their bonds can be best addressed. Our brothers and sisters deserve as much.

References

Adams, G. R., & Berzonsky, M. D. (2003). *Blackwell handbook of adolescence*. Oxford: Blackwell.

Adhikari, R. K. (2003). *Early marriage and childbearing: Risks and consequences*. In S. Bott, S. Jejeebhoy, I. Shah, & C. Puri (Eds.), *Towards adulthood: Exploring the sexual and reproductive health of adolescents in South Asia* (pp. 62–66). Geneva: World Health Organization. (WHO Sexuality).

Arnett, L. (2003). Coming of age in a multicultural world: Globalization and adolescent cultural identity formation. *Applied Developmental Science, 7*(3), 189–196.

Bank, S. P., & Kahn, M. D. (1982). *The sibling bond*. New York: Basic Books.

Bengtson, V. L. (2001). Beyond the nuclear family: The increasing importance of multigenerational bonds. *Journal of Marriage and Family, 63*(1), 1–16.

Brody, G. H. (2004). Siblings' direct and indirect contributions to child development. *Current Directions in Psychological Science, 13*, 124–126.

Brody, G. H., Kogan, S. M., Chen, Y. F., & Murry, V. M. (2008). Long-term effects of the strong African American families program on youths' conduct problems. *Journal of Adolescent Health, 43*(5), 474–481.

Bronfenbrenner, U. (1979). *The ecology of human development: Experiments by nature and design*. Cambridge: Harvard University Press.

Bronfenbrenner, U. (1986). Ecology of the family as a context for human development: Research perspectives. *Developmental Psychology, 22*(6), 723–742.

Bronfenbrenner, U. (1989). Ecological systems theory. In R. Vasta (Ed.), *Annals of child development: Six theories of child development: Revised formulations and current issues* (Vol. 6, pp. 187–249). Greenwich, CT: JAI Press.

Bronfenbrenner, U. (1992). Ecological systems theory. In R. Vasta (Ed.), *Six theories of child development: Revised formulations and current issues* (pp. 187–249). London: Jessica Kingsley.

Bronfenbrenner, U., & Evans, G. W. (2000). Developmental science in the 21st century: Emerging questions, theoretical models, research designs and empirical findings. *Social Development, 9*(1), 115–125.

Bronfenbrenner, U., & Morris, P. (1998). The ecology of developmental processes. In R. M. Lerner (Ed.), *Handbook of child psychology. Theoretical models of human development* (5th ed., Vol. 1, pp. 993–1028). New York: Wiley.

Brown, B. B., & Larson, R. W. (2002). The kaleidoscope of adolescence: Experiences of the world's youth at the beginning of the 21st century. In B. B. Brown, R. W. Larson, & T. S. Saraswathi (Eds.), *The world's youth: Adolesence in eight regions of the Globe* (pp. 1–20). New York: Cambridge University Press.

Buist, K. L., Reitz, E., & Deković, M. (2008). Attachment stability and change during adolescence: A longitudinal application of the social relations model. *Journal of Social and Personal Relationships, 25*(3), 429–444.

Bukowski, W., & Lisboa, C. (2007). Understanding the place of place in developmental psychology. In C. Rutger, E. Engels, & M. Kerr (Eds.), *Friends, lovers and groups: Key relationships in adolescence* (pp. 167–173). West Sussex: John Wiley & Sons.

Burgess, E. W. (1926). The family as a unity of interacting personalities. *The Family, 7*, 3–9.

Carrillo, S., Ripoll-Núñez, K., & Schvaneveldt, P. L. (2012). Family policy initiatives in Latin America: The case of Colombia and Ecuador. *Journal of Child and Family Studies, 21*(1), 75–87.

Caspi, J. (2011). Future directions for sibling research, practice, and theory. In J. Caspi (Ed.), *Sibling development: Implications for mental health practitioners* (pp. 377–390). New York: Springer.

Castro, F. G., Kellison, J. G., Boyd, S. J., & Kopak, A. (2010). A methodology for conducting integrative mixed methods research and data analyses. *Journal of Mixed Methods Research, 4*(4), 342–360.

Cicirelli, V. G. (1995). *Sibling relationships across the life span*. New York: Plenum.

Coltabiano, M., & Castiglioni, M. (2008). Changing family formation in Nepal: Marriage, cohabitation and first sexual intercourse. *International Family Planning Perspectives, 34*(1), 30–39.

Conger, J., & Petersen, A. (1984). *Adolescence and youth: Psychological development in a changing world* (3rd ed.). New York: Harper & Row.

Conger, K. J., & Little, W. M. (2010). Sibling relationships during the transition to adulthood. *Child Development Perspectives, 4*(2), 87–94.

Cooper, C. R., Baker, H., Polichar, D., & Welsh, M. (1993). Values and communication of Chinese, Filipino, European, Mexican, and Vietnamese American adolescents with their families and friends. *New Directions for Child and Adolescent Development, 62*, 73–89.

Cox, M. J., & Paley, B. (1997). Families as systems. *Annual Review of Psychology, 48*(1), 243–267.

Creswell, J. W. (2013). *Research design: Qualitative, quantitative, and mixed methods approaches* (2nd ed.). London: Sage.

Davis, K. (1941). Family structure and functions. *American Sociological Review, 8*, 311–320.

Dunn, J. (2005). Commentary: Siblings in their families. *Journal of Family Psychology: JFP: Journal of the Division of Family Psychology of the American Psychological Association (Division 43), 19*(4), 654–657.

Dunn, J. (2011). Sibling influences. In D. Skuse, H. Bruce, L. Dowdney, & D. Mrazek (Eds.), *Child psychology and psychiatry: Frameworks for practice* (2nd ed., pp. 8–12). West Sussex: John Wiley & Sons.

Edwards, R., & Gillies, V. (2004). Support in parenting: Values and consensus concerning who to turn to. *Journal of Social Policy, 33*(4), 627–647.

Edwards, R., Hadfield, L., Lucey, H., & Mauthner, M. (2006). *Sibling identity and relationships: Sisters and brothers*. Oxon: Routledge.

Feinberg, M. E., Solmeyer, A. R., Hostetler, M. L., Sakuma, K. L., Jones, D., & McHale, S. M. (2012). Siblings are special: Initial test of a new approach for preventing youth behavior problems. *Journal of Adolescent Health, 53*(2), 166–173.

Feinberg, M. E., Solmeyer, A. R., & McHale, S. M. (2012). The third rail of family systems: Sibling relationships, mental and behavioral health, and preventive intervention in childhood and adolescence. *Clinical Child and Family Psychology Review, 15*(1), 43–57.

Fogel, A. (1993). *Developing through relationships: Origins of communication, self, and culture.* Chicago: University of Chicago.

Ford, D. H., & Lerner, R. M. (1992). *Developmental systems theory: An integrative approach.* Newbury Park, CA: Sage.

Gluckman, P. D., & Hayne, H. (2011). *Improving the transition: Reducing social and psychological morbidity during adolescence.* New Zealand: Office of the Prime Minister's Science Advisory Committee.

Gottlieb, G. (2002). *Individual development and evolution.* Mahwah, NJ: Erlbaum. (Original work published 1992, by New York: Oxford University Press)

Gottlieb, M. S. (2007). The developmental point of view: Anything can change everything; permission to doubt dogma, the Gilbert Gottlieb legacy. *European Journal of Developmental Science, 1*, 200–207.

Granic, I., Dishion, T., & Hollenstein, T. (2003). The family ecology of adolescence: A dynamic systems perspective on normative development. In G. Adams & M. Berzonsky (Eds.), *Blackwell handbook of adolescence* (pp. 60–91). Oxford: Blackwell.

Granic, I., & Hollenstein, T. (2003). Dynamic systems methods for models of developmental psychopathology. *Development and Psychopathology, 15*(3), 641–669.

Granic, I., Hollenstein, T., Dishion, T. J., & Patterson, G. R. (2003). Longitudinal analysis of flexibility and reorganization in early adolescence: A dynamic systems study of family interactions. *Developmental Psychology, 39*(3), 606–617.

Greer, K. B., Campione-Barr, N., Debrown, B., & Maupin, C. (2014). Do differences make the heart grow fonder? Associations between differential peer experiences on adolescent sibling conflict and relationship quality. *Journal of Genetic Psychology, 175*(1), 16–34.

Heaven, P. (1994). *Contemporary adolescence: A social psychological approach.* Melbourne: Macmillan.

Heine, S. J. (2011). *Cultural psychology* (3rd ed.). New York: W. W. Norton.

Hill, J. P. (1987). Research on adolescents and their families: Past and prospect. In C. E. Irwin Jr. (Ed.), *Adolescent social behavior and health* (New Directions for Child Development No. 37, pp. 13–31). San Francisco, CA: Jossey-Bass.

Hill, J. P., & Holmbeck, G. N. (1986). Attachment and autonomy during adolescence. In G. J. Whitehurst (Ed.), *Annals of child development* (Vol. 3, pp. 145–189). Greenwich, CT: JAI Press.

Hinde, R. A. (1989). Ethological and relationship approaches. In R. Vasta (Ed.), *Annals of child development: Six theories of child development: Revised formulations and current issues* (Vol. 6, pp. 251–285). London: JAI Press.

Hollenstein, T. (2007). State space grids: Analyzing dynamics across development. *International Journal of Behavioral Development, 31*(4), 384–396.

Holmbeck, G. N. (1996). A model of family relational transformations during the transition to adolescence: Parent–adolescent conflict and adaptation. In J. A. Garber, J. Brooks-Gunn, & A. C. Petersen (Eds.), *Transitions through adolescence: Interpersonal domains and contexts* (pp. 167–199). Mahwah, NJ: Erlbaum.

Holmbeck, G. N., Paikoff, R. L., & Brooks-Gunn, J. (1995). Parenting adolescents. In M. Bornstein (Ed.), *Handbook of parenting: Children and parenting* (Vol. 1, pp. 91–118). Mahwah, NJ: Erlbaum.

Johnson, R., & Onwuegbuzie, A. (2004). Mixed methods research: A research paradigm whose time has come. *Educational Researcher, 33*, 14–26.

Kendler, K. S., Maes, H. H., Sundquist, K., Ohlsson, H., & Sundquist, J. (2013). Genetic and family and community environmental effects on drug abuse in adolescence: A Swedish National Twin and Sibling Study. *American Journal of Psychiatry, 171*(2), 209–217.

Kennedy, D. E., & Kramer, L. (2008). Improving emotion regulation and sibling relationship quality: The more fun with sisters and brothers program. *Family Relations, 57*(5), 567–578.

Kerr, M., Stattin, H., & Kiesner, J. (2007). Peers and problem behavior: Have we missed something. In C. Rutger, E. Engels, & M. Kerr (Eds.), *Friends, lovers and groups: Key relationships in adolescence* (pp. 125–153). West Sussex: John Wiley & Sons.

Kowal, A., Kramer, L., Krull, J. L., & Crick, N. R. (2002). Children's perceptions of the fairness of parental preferential treatment and their socioemotional well-being. *Journal of Family Psychology, 16*(3), 297–306.

Kramer, L. (2004). Experimental interventions in sibling relations. In R. D. Conger, F. O. Lorenz, & K. A. S. Wickrama (Eds.), *Continuity and change in family relations: Theory, methods and empirical findings* (pp. 345–380). Mahwah, NJ: Erlbaum.

Kramer, L. (2010). The essential ingredients of successful sibling relations: An emerging framework for advancing theory and practice. *Child Development Perspectives, 4*, 80–86.

Kuczynski, L., & Parkin, C. M. (2007). Agency and bidirectionality in socialization: Interactions, transactions, and relational dialectics. In J. E. Grusec & P. Hastings (Eds.), *Handbook of socialization* (pp. 259–283). New York: Guilford Press.

Kuczynski, L., & Parkin, C. M. (2009). Pursuing a dialectical perspective on transaction: A social relational theory of micro family processes. In A. Sameroff (Ed.), *Transactional processes in development* (pp. 247–268). Washington, DC: APA Books.

Kuczynski, L. Pitman, R., & Mitchell, M. B. (2009). Dialectics and transactional models: Conceptualizing antecedents, processes, and consequences of change in parent-child relationships. In L. Mancini & K. Roberto (Eds.), *Pathways of development: Explorations of change* (pp. 151–170). Lexington, MA: Lexington Books.

Lavalli, M., Pantoja, A. P. F., Hsu, H.-C., Messinger, D., & Fogel, A. (2005). Using microgenetic designs to study change process. In D. M. Teti (Ed.), *Handbook of research methods in developmental science* (pp. 41–65). Malden, MA: Blackwell.

Lerner, R. M., & Villarruel, F. A. (1994). Adolescence. In T. Husen & T. N. Postlethwaite (Eds.), *The international encyclopedia of education* (2nd ed., pp. 83–89). Oxford: Pergamon.

Lewin, K. (1939). The field theory approach to adolescence. *American Journal of Sociology, 44*, 868–897.

Lewis, M. D. (1997). Personality self-organization: Cascading constraints on cognition-emotion interaction. In A. Fogel, P. Lyra, & J. Valsiner (Eds.), *Dynamics and indeterminism in developmental and social processes* (pp. 193–216). Mahwah, NJ: Erlbaum.

Lewis, M. D., & Granic, I. (Eds.). (2000). *Emotion, development and self-organization: Dynamic systems approaches to emotional development.* New York: Cambridge University Press.

Mathison, S. (1988). Why triangulate? *Educational Researcher, 17*(2), 13–17.

Maughan, B. (2011). Family and systemic influences. In D. Skuse, H. Bruce, L. Dowdney, & D. Mrazek (Eds.), *Child psychology and psychiatry: Frameworks for practice* (2nd ed., pp. 3–7). West Sussex: John Wiley & Sons.

McGuire, S., & Shanahan, L. (2010). Sibling experiences in diverse family contexts. *Child Development Perspectives, 4*(2), 72–79.

McHale, S. M., & Crouter, A. C. (1996). The family contexts of children's sibling relationships. In G. H. Brody (Ed.), *Sibling relationships: Their causes and consequences* (pp. 173–195). Westport, CT: Ablex.

McHale, S. M., Updegraff, K. A., & Whiteman, S. D. (2012). Sibling relationships and influences in childhood and adolescence. *Journal of Marriage and Family, 74*(5), 913–930.

Mensch, B. S., Ibrahim, B. L., Lee, S. M., & El-Gibaly, O. (2003). Gender-role attitudes among Egyptian adolescents. *Studies in Family Planning, 34*(1), 8–18.

Meunier, J. C., Wade, M., & Jenkins, J. M. (2012). Mothers' differential parenting and children's behavioural outcomes: Exploring the moderating role of family and social context. *Infant and Child Development, 21*(1), 107–133.

Milevsky, A. (2011). *Sibling relationships in childhood and adolescence: Predictors and outcomes.* New York: Columbia University Press.

Mills, M., & Blossfeld, H. P. (2013). The second demographic transition meets globalization: A comprehensive theory to understand changes in family formation in an era of rising uncertainty. In A. Evans & J. Baxter (Eds.) *Negotiating the life course* (pp. 9–33). Netherlands: Springer.

Ogburn, W. F. (1932). The family and its functions. In W. F. Ogburn (Ed.), *Recent social trends* (pp. 661–708). New York: McGraw-Hill.

Oliva, A., & Arranz, E. (2005). Sibling relationships during adolescence. *European Journal of Developmental Psychology, 2*(3), 253–270.

Parke, R. D. (2004). Development in the family. *Annual Review of Psychology, 55*, 365–399.

Parke, R. D., & Buriel, R. (2006). Socialization in the family: Ethnic and ecological perspectives. In N. Eisenberg (Ed.), *Handbook of child psychology: Vol. 3. Social, emotional, and personality development* (6th ed., pp. 429–504). Hoboken, NJ: Wiley.

Parsons, T. (1944). The social structure of the family. In R. N. Anshen (Ed.), *The family: Its function and destiny* (pp. 173–201). New York: Harper & Row.

Petermann, F., Niebank, K., & Scheithauer, H. (2004). *Entwicklungswissenschaft. Entwicklungspsychologie – Genetik – Neuropsychologie* [Developmental science. Developmental psychology – Genetics – Neuropsychology]. Heidelberg: Springer.

Petersen, A. C. (1988). Adolescent development. In M. R. Rosenzweig (Ed.), *Annual review of psychology* (pp. 583–607). Palo Alto, CA: Annual Reviews.

Pike, A. (2012). The importance of behavioural genetics for developmental science. *International Journal of Developmental Science, 6*(1–2), 13–15.

Plomin, R., & Daniels, D. (1987). Why are children in the same family so different from one another? *Behavior & Brain Sciences, 10*, 1–60.

Popenoe, D. (1993). American family decline, 1960–1990: A review and appraisal. *Journal of Marriage and the Family, 55*, 527–555.

Reis, H. T., Collins, W. A., & Berscheid, E. (2000). The relationship context of human behavior and development. *Psychological Bulletin, 126*(6), 844–872.

Ripoll-Núñez, K., & Carrillo, S. (2014). Sibling relationships and children's social well-being. In A. Ben-Arieh, F. Casas, I. Frønes, & J. E. Korbin (Eds.), *Handbook of child well-being* (pp. 1817–1842). Dordrecht, Netherlands: Springer.

Sameroff, A. E. (2009). *The transactional model of development: How children and contexts shape each other.* Washington, DC: American Psychological Association.

Sameroff, A. J., & MacKenzie, M. J. (2003). Research strategies for capturing transactional models of development: The limits of the possible. *Development and Psychopathology, 15*, 613–640.

Scheithauer, H., Niebank, K., & Gottlieb, G. (2007). To see an elephant: Developmental science. *European Journal of Developmental Science, 1*, 6–22.

Scheithauer, H., Niebank, K., & Ittel, A. (2009). Developmental science: Integrating knowledge about dynamic processes in human development. In J. Valsiner, P. Molenaar, M. Lycra, & N. Chaudhary (Eds.), *Dynamic process methodology in the social and developmental sciences* (pp. 595–617). New York: Springer.

Schermerhorn, A. C., Chow, S. M., & Cummings, E. M. (2010). Developmental family processes and interparental conflict: Patterns of microlevel influences. *Developmental Psychology, 46*(4), 869–885.

Schermerhorn, A. C., & Cummings, M. E. (2008). Transactional family dynamics: A new framework for conceptualizing family influence processes. *Advances in Child Development and Behavior, 36*, 187–250.

Schlegel, A. (2000). The global spread of adolescent culture. *Negotiating adolescence in times of social change* (pp. 71–88). Cambridge: Cambridge University Press.

Siddiqui, A., & Ross, H. S. (2004). Mediation as a method of parent intervention in children's disputes. *Journal of Family Psychology, 18*, 147–159.

Smith, J., & Ross, H. (2007). Training parents to mediate sibling disputes affects children's negotiation and conflict understanding. *Child Development, 78*, 790–805.

Solmeyer, A. R., McHale, S. M., & Crouter, A. C. (2013). Longitudinal associations between sibling relationship qualities and risky behavior across adolescence. *Developmental Psychology, 50*(2), 600–610. doi:10.1037/a0033207

Stacey, J. (1996). *In the name of the family: Rethinking family values in the postmodern age.* Boston, MA: Beacon Press.

Steinberg, L. (1990). Autonomy, conflict, and harmony in the family relationship. In S. Feldman & G. Elliot (Eds.), *At the threshold: The developing adolescent* (pp. 255–276). Cambridge, MA: Harvard University Press.

Stevenson, H. W., & Zusho, A. (2002). Adolescence in China and Japan: Adapting to a changing environment. In B. B. Brown, R. Larson, & T. S. Saraswathi (Eds.), *The world's youth: Adolescence in eight regions of the Globe* (pp. 141–170). New York: Cambridge University Press.

Thelen, E., & Smith, L. B. (1994). *A dynamic systems approach to the development of cognition and action.* Cambridge, MA: Bradford/MIT Press.

Todd, Z., Nerlich, B., McKeown, S., & Clarke, D. D. (Eds.). (2004). *Mixing methods in psychology: The integration of qualitative and quantitative methods in theory and practice.* Abingdon, Oxon.: Psychology Press.

Turkheimer, E., & Waldron, M. (2000). Nonshared environment: A theoretical, methodological, and quantitative review. *Psychological Bulletin, 126*, 78–108.

Weisfeld, G. (1979). An ethological view of human adolescence. *Journal of Nervous and Mental Disease, 167*(1), 38–55.

Whiteman, S. D., McHale, S. M., & Soli, A. (2011). Theoretical perspectives on sibling relationships. *Journal of Family Theory & Review, 3*(2), 124–139.

Witherington, D. C. (2007). The dynamic systems approach as metatheory for developmental psychology. *Human Development, 50*(2–3), 127–153.

APPENDIX

Contents

Selected international sibling projects

We now offer an overview of ongoing sibling research around the globe. We identify thematic and methodological trends and profile a selection of contemporary studies. Researchers with publications and conference presentations on sibling relationships were contacted and asked to provide information on their recent projects. Those who agreed then completed a short survey regarding the duration, sample, methodology, and research questions that led to their current work. The search was not territorially confined, though, as with the majority of research on adolescence and siblings, most of the studies were conducted within the United States of America and Western Europe. Studies included in this overview examined siblings within the age range of 10 through 21 years. Despite the numerous replies, the following compendium by no means claims to provide an exhaustive summary of current sibling investigations, and this section predominantly focuses on the work of researchers with who we were in direct contact. For full researcher contact information, please refer to the catalogue at the end of the chapter.

Trends in sibling research

Sibling relationship quality, individual development, and adjustment

One of the main interests in sibling research relates to the quality of the relationship and the impact on one another's development. Particular relational characteristics such as warmth and conflict have been linked to psychosocial and behavioural adjustment (Bullock & Dishion, 2002), emotional well-being (Cole & Kerns, 2001), and scholastic support (Tucker, McHale, & Crouter, 2001), among others. However, as expressed earlier, sibling relationships are not only studied as antecedents of various individual developmental processes – relationship quality between adolescent siblings itself has been treated as the outcome of several factors.

Alfredo Oliva and his research team from the University of Seville, Spain, for instance, concentrate their research on sibling relationship quality perception from adolescence through emerging adulthood (for a thorough definition of this recently conceptualized life stage, see Arnett, 2000). Within their 10-year longitudinal study '*From Adolescence to Emerging Adulthood: A Longitudinal Study on Life Trajectories*', these researchers emphasize the role of siblings on an individual's adjustment throughout adolescence. Initial reports found support for the hypothesis that sibling relationship quality is affected by and affects the quality of other familial and peer relationships. In addition, structural characteristics such as age, gender composition, as well as birth order impact these perceptions.

Although working with a methodologically different approach, Corinna Jenkins Tucker from the University of New Hampshire, USA, follows similar interests. Her key areas of investigation encompass adolescents' socio-cognitive development, their relationships with siblings and parents, family relationship experiences, as well as differences in these experiences within the same family. Jenkins Tucker collaborates with other faculty and fellows as part of the Carsey Center for Rural Youth and currently occupies the position of co-investigator for the Panel Study of Coös County Youth, analyzing data from Add Health. In a prior cross-sectional study '*UNH Study on Adolescence*' teenaged sibling pairs were asked to report the frequency and content of their daily conversations using a daily diary. At the end of each day, adolescents also responded to a series of qualitative and quantitative questions about their interactions and activities with the target sibling. Here, Tucker examines how the frequency and content of siblings' daily conversations are linked to adolescents' psychosocial well-being.

Miriam Walser further appraised the role of siblings in adolescent adjustment, more specifically psychosocial well-being, within the small-scale research project '*The Role of Attachment in the Experience, Consequences and Coping of and with*

Traumata' at the University of Innsbruck, Austria. Walser assessed the extent to which sibling relationships serve as protective agents, that is, buffers in adverse conditions during development. Her sample included 64 children and 53 foster mothers from a SOS Children's Village. SOS Children's Villages focus on family-based, long-term care of children who, for various reasons, could not remain in their families of origin. Walser recruited her child–mother control group from 50 intact families. Results supported the assumption that the presence of at least one sibling is positively connected to children's behaviour: children who did not have biological siblings in the same Children's Village family showed more social problems and aggressive behaviour than those who did. Interestingly, the importance of siblings was also discovered for children in the control group. More precisely, Walser found that the more siblings children have, the lower their exhibition of aggressive behaviour or social problems.

Maike Watzlawik from the University of Braunschweig, Germany, examined social interactions between siblings and how they relate to the development of individual and dyadic identity in adolescents (*'Who am I and Who Are We? How Sibling Relationships Influence Identity Development During Adolescence'*). Watzlawik and colleagues inspected differences in identity development processes in twins and non-twin sibling dyads by following 200 sibling pairs (twins and non-twins) over a period of 3 years using home interviews and video recording to collect data. The project also examined whether girl-dyads differ from boy-dyads and mixed dyads and whether identity development influences sibling relationship quality, in particular the emotional attachment of siblings.

Siblings in their families

A second theme in the literature concerns the multifaceted nature of family dynamics and parental involvement and how they relate to sibling relationships. The sibling dyad is incorporated into family structures that affect sibling relationship quality and are reciprocally affected, in turn. Various aspects of family life such as parenting styles, differential treatment of siblings, and parental sibling conflict intervention styles are points of interest for the following research initiatives.

Avidan Milevsky and his research team from Kutztown University, USA, focus on longitudinal effects of social support in relation to stress that often accompanies the transition into late adolescence and early adulthood (*'SEA – The Siblings of Early Adolescents and Emerging Adults Project'*). Students in 9th (14 years) and 11th grade (16 years) as well as first year college students between the ages of 17 and 22 completed questionnaires in order to shed light on parenting style characteristics and parental sibling-conflict-involvement styles associated with close and supportive sibling relationships. Furthermore, Milevsky and colleagues explore psychological and academic outcomes that are hypothesized to be linked to sibling support. Some of this particular research group's empirical findings are highlighted in Milevsky's subsequent book, *Sibling Relationships: Childhood and Adolescent Predictors,* which proves particularly useful for those interested in the positive buffering effects of siblinghood.

Aside from research on parental involvement as a correlate of sibling relationship quality, other explorations adopt a systemic approach to siblings and their relationship patterns and how they affect family dynamics. The research team spearheaded by Susan McHale and Ann C. Crouter at Pennsylvania State University, USA, organized two longitudinal sibling projects under the *Penn State Family Relationships Project (Gender Socialization in Middle Childhood and Adolescence; Gender Socialization in Mexican American Families (Juntos)* along with Arizona State University) to approach this topic. Both projects generated in-depth knowledge about adolescents' experiences of parental differential treatment and the role of gender in the family, and the same sample is being now being restudied after a 7- to 10-year break. The study '*Gender Socialization in Middle Childhood and Adolescence*' includes two ethnically dissimilar samples (Caucasian, African American families). Data were collected using two procedures: first, four family members – both parents and two adolescent siblings – were interviewed annually in their homes; second, families participated in a series of seven telephone interviews to gain information about daily activities and relationship experiences. The data collection design is identical in the '*Gender Socialization in Mexican American Families*' project. Moreover, the ethnically homogeneous design of each investigation allows researchers to critically examine how culture specifically impacts family dynamics.

Lew Bank and colleagues from the Oregon Social Learning Center, USA, pursued a similar avenue of exploration of the role of parental involvement as a correlate of sibling relationship quality, but concentrated on intervention and prevention research. The researchers enlisted a prevention–intervention framework in order to identify the particular role of siblings in the project '*Preventing Adjustment Problems in Young Siblings*' that addressed family life and sibling relationships during middle childhood. The project explored longitudinally the effectiveness of intervention with siblings in reducing family conflict and boosting the social and academic development of older target children and a younger brother or sister. The project investigated the contribution of siblings in the development of adult antisocial lifestyles, sibling conflict and unskilled parenting as determinants of adolescent behaviour and peer relationships, sibling relationship contributions to individual and family well-being, older siblings' benefit from family-based preventive intervention of at-risk preschoolers, as well as the consequences of an older brother's antisocial behaviour for younger brothers and sisters.

Alison Pike, Judy Dunn, Tina Kretschmer, and co-researchers at the University of Sussex, UK, used behavioural genetic means among others to explore sibling relationships within and outside of their families. Their study, '*SiBS: The Sisters and Brothers Study*' seeks to depict 'ordinary' family relationships through the longitudinal investigation of 173 families with two children. As the study adopted a family systems approach, perspectives from each family member were assessed to explore relationship dynamics, children's well-being, important socio-ecological influences, as well as structural differences between single-mother and dual-parent households. The next project for Pike along with Bonamy Oliver will look at twins and their families from across the nited ingdomUK although this study draws from children born in 2009/2010. '*Twins, Families, and Behaviour (TFaB)*' will explore children's behaviour and family relationships via behavioural genetics and is currently in its recruitment phase.

Siblings and health and risk behaviour

A further area of interest among sibling researchers is how delinquency and substance misuse are linked to sibling interaction and whether these aspects of problem behaviour are linked in turn to sibling relationship quality. Longitudinal studies can often shed light on questions as to whether these sibling effects extend to early adulthood. Additionally, some of these investigations focus not only on social interaction that might promote delinquent behaviour but also include genetic influences. As described in Chapter 4, comparing monozygotic twins, full- and half-siblings, as well as adoptive siblings helps to identify genetic and environmental effects on various kinds of health and risk behaviour.

Richard Rende and colleagues from Brown University, USA, studied sibling influences on substance use. The project '*Sibling Influences on Smoking in Everyday Settings*' attempts to investigate sibling effects on smoking using real-time settings. Applying the Ecological Momentary Assessment (EMA), intensive daily diaries of sibling interaction and interaction with others, as well as affect, social context, stress, and urge for the use of nicotine are recorded. The issues of which social contexts facilitate sibling effects on smoking and whether there are links between siblings, mutual friends, and risk-taking behaviours are of predominant interest in this study. In a second thematically linked study, Rende and colleagues applied behavioural genetic models to the observed connection between sibling relationship quality and risk for smoking (*Sibling Contagion for Smoking: Social and Genetic Influences in Early Adulthood*). The sample used in this study consists of sibling pairs (twins and non-twins) drawn from the National Longitudinal Study of Adolescent Health (also known as Add Health study). Further research interests include longitudinal sibling effects on smoking as well as interactions between sibling relationship quality and genetic sensitivity to nicotine.

Cheryl Slomkowski from Brown University, USA, similarly investigated genetic processes and sibling relationships. The longitudinal study '*Siblings and Deviancy: Social and Genetic Processes*' examined twin and non-twin siblings from the Nonshared Environment on Adolescent Development (NEAD) project. Applying micro-social coding to videotaped sibling interactions, Slomkowski and colleagues explored whether social reinforcement behaviour between siblings moderate shared environmental influences on delinquency and substance use. Furthermore, the research team employed univariate and multivariate behavioural genetic methods to shed light on potential interactions with underlying genetic propensity for delinquency and substance use.

Within the scope of her doctoral research, Zeena Harakeh from Utrecht University, Netherlands, explored substance use among siblings. Harakeh's longitudinal study '*Adolescents as Chameleons? Social-environmental Factors Involved in the Development of Smoking*' was part of the larger project Family & Health that consisted of 428 intact Dutch families. Harakeh examined whether smoking-specific parenting practices (smoking versus non-smoking parents) prevent or discourage their adolescent offspring from smoking. In this context, Harakeh and her research team explored if parents and their adolescents were able to provide accurate reports of each other's smoking behaviour and whether these proxy reports were stable over a 1-year period. Furthermore, the research examined how best friends and/or siblings affect adolescent smoking and how the adolescents' personality is associated with lifetime smoking and/or smoking onset. In addition, birth order of siblings was tested as a potential moderator on the association between personality traits and adolescent smoking. Currently, Harakeh continues to do work on adolescents and smoking, focusing on peer-pressure and parent-related factors.

Katherine J. Conger from University of California, USA, also focuses on social interaction among adolescent siblings, among other aspects. Conger further studies sibling relationship course and quality, sibling influences on maladjustment and competence, social processes within families, particularly the interaction between familial conflict and adolescent adjustment. Some of Conger's work on families draws from '*The Iowa Youth and Families Project (IYFP)*' (1989–1993) and '*Critical Transitions in Rural Families at Risk*' headed by Rand Conger and Glenn Elder, which are grouped under the Family Research Group at UC Davis, USA. This group of four interconnected projects focuses upon the manner in which children, adolescents, emerging adults, and their families develop and change across time in relation to their socio-economic contexts. The IYFP is an extensive longitudinal panel study of 451 families from 1989 until the present and focuses on economic hardship, family relationships, and individual health and well-being; the sample included two-parent families with an adolescent in 7th grade at high school and a sibling within 4 years of age, and in 1991, single-mother families were added. For the '*Critical Transitions in Rural Families at Risk*' study, sibling pairs were matched in age on the target child (all 9th graders in 1991). This cohort has been followed up to the present.

Conger's study is characterized by a mixed-methods approach, including self-report questionnaire data obtained from each parent and adolescent as well as observer ratings of videotaped interaction tasks. The overall aim of this study was to investigate the social and behavioural interaction patterns of siblings in the context of parent–child and family conditions that are expected to promote competent behaviours (mastery and self-control) or contribute to the development of problem behaviours (delinquency and substance use) during the adolescent years. Currently, Conger examines the influences of siblings on delinquency in adolescence, with a focus on girls as well as the development, maintenance, and consequences of social support between siblings from adolescence through early adulthood. This three-generation study allows the exploring of the involvement of siblings in one another's lives once both siblings leave the family of origin and the implications for health and well-being in adulthood.

Summing up

As we have seen, contemporary sibling research is characterized by an impressive variety of themes, enriched from multiple fields such as behavioural genetics and sociological family analysis. The thematic abundance explored by researchers and the diversity of applied methods and procedures to collect data are noteworthy. While many studies are based on a cross-sectional design, only longitudinal data allow for an in-depth look into developmental processes between siblings and their socio-environmental contexts. Interpretations about the directions of effects between the variables in question, for instance, sibling relationship quality and individual adjustment, are only possible when multiple time points are examined. Nevertheless, 'snapshot' studies often provide us with important specific examples that help add to the growing body of international research.

References

Arnett, J. J. (2000). Emerging adulthood: A theory of development from the late teens through the twenties. *American Psychologist, 55*(5), 469–480.

Bullock, B. M., & Dishion, T. J. (2002). Sibling collusion and problem behaviour in early adolescence: Toward a process model for family mutuality. *Journal of Abnormal Child Psychology, 30*(2), 143–153.

Cole, A., & Kerns, K. A. (2001). Perceptions of sibling qualities and activities of early adolescents. *Journal of Early Adolescence, 21*(2), 204–227.

Tucker, C. J., McHale, S. M., & Crouter, A. C. (2001). Conditions of sibling support in adolescence. *Journal of Family Psychology, 15*(2), 254–271.

Annex

Register of sibling projects in alphabetic order by authors' last name

Lew Bank: Preventing Adjustment Problems in Young Siblings. Oregon Social Learning Center. Sponsor/Grant: Child and Adolescent Treatment and Preventive intervention Research Branch, DSIR, NIMH, U.S. PHS. Contact: lewb@oslc.org

Katherine J. Conger: (1) The Iowa Youth and Families Project (IYFP). (2) Critical Transitions in Rural Families at Risk. University of California. Sponsor/Grant: National Institute of Child Health and Human Development, National Institute on Drug Abuse, National Institute of Mental Health, Bureau of Maternal and Child Health, McArthur Foundation Research Network on Successful Adolescent Development Among Youth in High-Risk Settings, Iowa State University, University of California Agricultural Experiment Station. Contact: kjconger@ucdavis.edu

Zeena Harakeh: Adolescents as Chameleons? Social-environmental Factors Involved in the Development of Smoking. Utrecht University. Sponsor/Grant: Dutch Organization for Scientific Research (NWO). Contact: Z.Harakeh@uu.nl

Susan McHale/Ann C. Crouter: (1) Gender Socialization in Middle Childhood and Adolescence. (2) Gender Socialization in Mexican American Families. Penn State University. Sponsor/Grant: National Institute for Child Health and Human Development. Contact: x2u@psu.edu, ac1@psu.edu. www.ssri.psu.edu/

Avidan Milevsky: The Siblings of Early Adolescents and Emerging Adults Project (The SEA Project). Kutztown University. Sponsor/Grant: Pennsylvania State System of Higher Education, Faculty Professional Development. Contact: Milevsky@Kutztown.edu

Alfredo Oliva: From Adolescence to Emerging Adulthood. A longitudinal Study on Life Trajectories. University of Seville. Sponsor/Grant: Spanish Ministry of Education. Contact: oliva@us.es

Alison Pike/Judy Dunn/Tina Kretschmer: (1) SiBS: The Sisters and Brothers Study. (2) Twins, Families, and Behaviour (TFaB). University of Sussex. Sponsor/Grant: (1) Joseph Rowntree Foundation and the Institute of Psychiatry. Contact: alisonp@sussex.ac.uk; bonamy.oliver@sussex.ac.uk

Richard Rende: (1) Sibling Influences on Smoking in Every Day Settings. (2) Sibling Contagion for Smoking: Social and Genetic Influences in Early Adulthood. Brown University. Sponsor/Grant: National Institute of Drug Abuse. Contact: Richard_Rende@Brown.EDU

Cheryl Slomkowski: Siblings and Deviancy: Social and Genetic Processes. Brown University. Sponsor/Grant: National Institute of Mental Health. Contact: Cheryl_Slomkowski@Brown.EDU

Corinna Jenkins Tucker: UNH Study on Adolescence. University of New Hampshire. Sponsor/Grant: University of New Hampshire, Vice President of Research Discretionary Fund. Contact: c.j.tucker@unh.edu

Miriam Walser: The Role of Attachment in Reference to the Experience of Traumata, Outcomes and Coping. University of Innsbruck. Sponsor/Grant: SOS Children's Village. Contact: Miriam.Walser@student.uibk.ac.at

Meike Watzlawik: Who am I and who are we? How sibling relationships influence identity development during adolescence. University of Braunschweig. Sponsor/Grant: German Research Foundation. Contact: m.watzlawik@tu-bs.de

INDEX

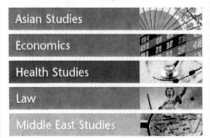